Instant Electric Pressure Cooking

Quick & Easy Delicious Instant Recipes For Smart People
Author: Rachael Martin

Table of Content

Introduction

At first, congratulations for choosing *Instant Electric Pressure Cooker Recipes* and welcome to the talented chefs who are looking for simple and easy recipes, which can be made without much difficulty. Coming to the facts, there are so many different types of benefits of the safe ways to cook in an electric pressure cooker, but due to lack of awareness, people are missing to learn an easy way of cooking.

This book has around 200 tasty and friendly recipes with proper directions and nutritional information based on a 2000 calorie diet plan. There are a number of ways to make delicious and nutritious recipes in less time without much effort than simply adding bunches of ingredients willy-nilly. So, to avoid this, in the following chapters will explain each and every step of preparation method including health benefits and nutritional information.

Before you get started, make sure that you will learn different types of helpful tricks and tips to ensure that you can do safely and as quickly and easily as possible. This recipe ensures that you will definitely make delicious recipes in less time period without difficulty.

A pressure cooker recipe creates independence and freedom to complete tasks on your own. It allows you to learn new things and expands your palate.

The key to successfully starting cooking is learning everything that you can do within your power with a strong mind and dedication tasty recipes without the help of parents by following our book.

Why Electric Pressure Cooker

Buying a pressure cooker is an investment in both money and time that will quickly be repaid for the body by providing healthy long life including money savings. Pressure cookers have changed quite a bit in the last few years and there are many more different options and types to consider before purchasing. Here's our guide to help you choose the right pressure cooker for your needs.
These are the things that make electric pressure cookers special.

Fast
Cuts cooking time to 1/3 (or more) less . Normally, a roast that would ordinarily take 2-3 hours is ready in 20-40 minutes, soaked chickpeas only need 13 minutes only.

Healthy
Retains 50% more nutrients. Research studies have shown that pressure cooking retains more vitamins and minerals than steaming without pressure and even microwaving.

Savings
Uses 70% less gas, electricity, and water. Pressure cookers are more efficient at using the energy, their efficiency is comparable to the energy savings of switching to energy-saving light bulbs. So if you've changed the lightbulbs in your house to save energy, it's time to change the cookware too.

Simple & Easy
Just add water and monitor. Electric pressure cooking is just like regular cooking except it always needs a little bit of water takes less time, once you learn the workings of your electric pressure cooker it just needs minimum monitoring when it's coming up to pressure (no supervision needed at all for electrics).

Clean
No more splatters and spurts. Cooking in a sealed vessel means no need to clean spills from the stovetop or oven. Plus, most electric pressure cooker bases are dishwasher safe.

Safe
Multiple safety mechanisms. Today's electric pressure cookers have fool-proof safety features with back-ups (just in case).

Tips and Tricks to Control Kitchen

Before starting to make any recipe, make sure that you read the direction of recipes twice and decide that you can make it or not. It is not important to have high fancy pressure cooking equipment to get started with cooking. Some of the essential things we should know before you start are:

Safety
Safety is one of the important things to remember before you start cooking, it is fun to work in the kitchen, but is not without hazards. You should be careful with sharp objects, stove, can opener, microwave, back oven and blender that can cause injuries if you are not careful with them.

Cleanliness
Before you start working in the kitchen, always wash your hands with warm and soapy water to keep bacteria away from the food you cook and eat.

Washing
Always gentle wash fruits, vegetables, and meat before you start cooking with water; washing will remove some traces of bacteria from soil and packing. If you are handling meat, be sure that you wash it twice before and after cutting into pieces.

Pre-prepare your ingredients
You can prepare or gather all required ingredients in advance before you start cooking to avoid last movement confusions.

Read Twice
Be sure that you read the entire recipe twice before you begin cooking. After reading the recipe, make sure that you have all ingredients listed in it and how long a recipe takes to prepare.

Apron
It is important to wear a cooking apron while cooking and cutting, to avoid marks on the dress and also tie back hair in case if you having hair.

Pot Holders & Hot Pads
In the kitchen, these things are your friends, which help to avoid serious burns. So, make sure that you use these things while handling hot items.

Cutting Board
The cutting board is one of the essential tools for making any recipe. After using it, make sure that you clean it thoroughly to avoid fungus.

Peeler
It is also one of the essential tools for the grating skin of the vegetables. Be careful while peeling and keep your fingers away from the sharp holes.

Knife's
While beginning you should know about three types of knife's, the first one "serrated knife", used to cut baked goods such as bread and cakes. Second knife "french knife", used to cut meat products and the third knife is "parking knife", used to cut vegetables and fruits.

Great way to learn
Teaches you to boost your self-confidence, which helps to manage and handle things yourself and improve your social, physical and educational life.

Highly portable
Recipes can be prepared in required time period and make your dream come true, which can be stored for a long time in a cool place.

Self-confidence
Cooking is the one way to boost self-confidence, which helps to manage and handle things yourself and improve your social, physical and educational life.

History of the Instant Electric Pressure Cooker

Before the Instant Electric Pressure Cooker took its first step in the earth, there were a lot of simple pressure cooking devices doing simple cooking. Actually, first pressure cooker developed in 1679 by Denis Papin, the main intention is to save fuel and time while cooking food items.

Since the first patent was filed on January 9th, 1991. Based on the cooking control capability, we can classify electric pressure cookers into four generations.

1st Generation: Mechanical Timer

The 1st Generation electric pressure cookers already have the essential pressure and temperature sensors. Both sensors act as a threshold moderator. When either the threshold of pressure or that of temperature is reached, the power to the heating element is cut. The only user-accessible control is via the mechanical cooking time controller. This mechanical controller offers estimated control on cooking duration. There is no delayed cooking capability.

Basic safety mechanisms, such as locking the lid under pressure and excess pressure protection, have been implemented in the 1st Generation cookers.

2nd Generation: Digital Controller

The 2nd Generation electric pressure cooker builds on top of the capability of the 1st Generation with a digital controller. Delayed cooking becomes possible. The pressure sensor is also electronically connected to the controller so that a count-down timer can be shown when working pressure is reached.

Safety is also improved with additional sensors. Most notably, if the lid is not fully locked, pressure cooking would not start. This avoids the potential risk of blowing up the lid under pressure cooking.

3rd Generation: Smart Programming

With the advance in pressure and temperature sensor accuracy, the 3rd Generation electric pressure cookers implement sophisticate control with digital technology. Two most remarkable features are Smart Programming and Enhanced Safety. These features greatly improve the cooking result, maintain consistency and enhance safety.

Each 3rd Generation cooker is fitted with a microprocessor. With the accurate readings from pressure and temperature sensors, the microprocessor can be programmed to perform complex cooking tasks. The Smart Programs are tailor-made for the specific cooking purpose of varying heating intensity, temperature, pressure and cooking duration, to achieve an optimized cooking result and maintain consistency. A typical example is a multigrain cooking program where the grains are soaked at ~60C/86F for a period to soften the grains before cooking starts. Please see our Smart Programming article for more details.

With the microprocessor programs, more sophisticated safety mechanisms become possible. For instance, one common mistake is misplacing the stream release at the open position while starting cooking. With the steam release open, pressure never builds up in the cooking pot. Earlier generation cookers would continue heating. If the situation is not corrected on time, all liquid in the cooking pot would evaporate and the food would be spoiled. The 3rd Generation cooker implements a mechanism called, Leaky Lid Protection, where the microprocessor detects the excess long pre-heating period and stops the heating with an alarm. More on the safety features here. All Instant Pot models are 3rd Generation electric pressure cookers.

4th Generation: Multi-Functional Programming

The latest 4th generation model programmable electric pressure cooker unit that features 8-in-1 multi-functions including rice, eggs, beans, yogurt, pressure, warmer, steamer, Sauté and slow cooking. It comes pre-programmed with 16 built-in Smart Programs and 12 cooking options with their own preset times as well as the option to use a manual time setter. The delay timer gives you the option to have food cooked and ready for a designated time. It comes with a stainless steel steam rack and basket, a rice scooper and a measuring cup.

How Electric Pressure Cooker Works

An electric pressure cooker consists of three parts, the **lid**, **inner pot**, and **housing**. See the diagram for an idea. The most important essential things to know about electric pressure cookers are the safety valves and smart control box.

Steam release
Float valve
Cover handle
Exhaust valve
Cover
Steam release handle

Gasket
Gasket support
Cover insider
Grommet
Anti-block shield

Inner pot

External cover
Exterior pot
Control box
Pot handle
Control panel
Housing
Base & Heating unit
Electricity plug

Scoop shelf

The Inner Pot

The inner pot is a removable cooking pot. It is generally made from aluminum or stainless steel. The aluminum inner pots may be stamped and buffed or anodized, but this metal is unsuitable for the dishwasher. Higher quality stainless steel inner pot is made with the sturdy, three-ply, or copper-clad bottom for uniformed heating.

The size of the inner pot determines the size of the housing, and to some degree the price of the cooker. The inner pot capacity typically ranges from 3 quarts) to 10 quarts.

Lid Lock

The lid has a gasket or sealing ring. When the lid is played on the cooker in the sealed position, the lid and the inner pot form an air-tight chamber. The pressure inside this chamber increases when heat is applied to the inner pot. There would be an unsafe operating condition if the lid is not in the locked position when a significant amount of pressure is generated inside the chamber. Some electric cookers have the pin lock mechanism to prevent the lid from being accidentally opened while there is a significant amount of pressure inside. The pin is essentially a float valve. If there is enough pressure inside the inner pot, the float valve is pushed up by the pressure. Once pushed up, the pin of the float valve serves as latch lock and prevents the lid from the turning movement, even under force.

Electric pressure cooker also extends such safety assurance with a safety power switch. If the lid is not in the desired fully closed position, the electronic control system of Electric pressure cookers can detect the situation and will not switch on the power for heating.

Safety Valves

Similar to the conventional pressure cooker, the pin of the float valve can be self-destroyed by excessive temperature or pressure. The float valve without the pin becomes a pressure escape hole, and the pressure inside the chamber has released this hole. Although in such a case the float valve is permanently damaged and possible a lid replacement may be required, this is an effective last line of defense from the safety perspective. The modern electric pressure cookers also use other safety assurance measures before this last line defense kicks in. Innovative push-down pressure release mechanism to release excessive pressure, even in the unlikely case where the pin of the float valve cannot destroy. Electric pressure cooker provides a multi-level in-depth defense system to offer unprecedented safety assurance to the consumers.

Normally, the only way the pressure can escape is through a pressure release regulator valve on the lid. The pressure release valve has anti-block shield inside the lid. The pressure release regulator valve is made not to release the pressure under normal operating pressure range when in the seal position. If the pressure increases beyond the safe operating range, the pressure release regular valve will be pushed up, similar to that on the conventional pressure cooker, to release excessive pressure built up inside the chamber.

Housing

The housing unit contains a heating element, pressure and temperature sensors and a control box. The functional diagram of the housing unit is shown on the right.

The control box is the heart of the intelligence of the electric pressure cooker. It monitors the temperature and pressure of inner pot with the sensors. It is equipped with a microprocessor to control the timing, heating, and complex cooking cycles. This is how a positive feedback system is formed to achieve precise cooking conditions. If an unsafe operating condition is detected, it will sound an audible alarm or cut off the power supply to the heating element. The control panel, being the user

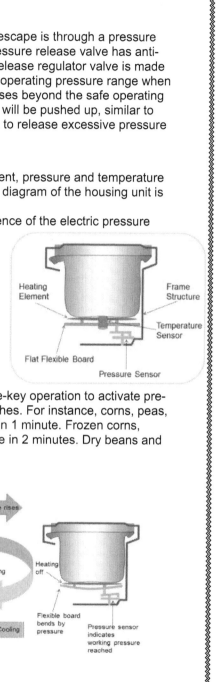

interface of the control box, allows the one-key operation to activate pre-programmed cooking cycle for various dishes. For instance, corns, peas, cauliflower, and broccoli can be steamed in 1 minute. Frozen corns, peas, cauliflower, and broccoli will be done in 2 minutes. Dry beans and bones will take only 30~40 minutes.

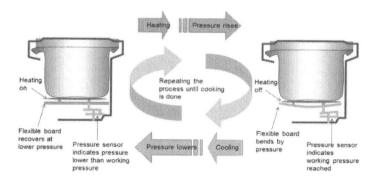

Operation Method

Electric pressure cookers normally operate at a pressure range of 70-80 kilopascal (kPa) or 10.15~11.6 psi (pound-force per square inch). This translates to the temperature of 115°C~118°C or 239°F~244°F. Initially, pressure may reach 105kPa/15.2 psi, due to the heat dissipation delay from the heating element. This is comparable to stove-top pressure cooker reaching 15 psi and then heat being turned down.

Some electric pressure cooker has intelligent cooking capabilities to achieve the best result, such as,

- Automatically altering the cooking time and pressure based on the chosen food type; for example rice, soup, meat, vegetable, etc.
- Adjusting cooking cycle based on the amount of food in the cooker, by measuring pre-heating duration.

Basic Accessories

Silicone Pinch Mitts: Getting under the lip of the insert and lifting it out of the cooker can be quite a challenge. These pinch-mitts are thin enough to fit under the lip and give you a good secure grip to pull the insert out of the pressure cooker without fear of it slipping back down and splattering dinner everywhere.

Silicone Steamer Basket: For all electric pressure cookers with non-stick liner, a silicone steamer basket is an essential accessory to be able to expand the cooking capabilities. Now, with the steamer basket, the cook can steam and roast without worry of scratching the insert. The wider the steamer basket, the more vegetables you can fit in it. Do not get one with a center "stem" that way it can be used as a trivet in the pressure cooker as well! Also, works with oval pressure cookers.

Silicone Tipped Utensils: Nothing is more delicate on the non-stick insert of your electric pressure cooker than utensils specifically designed not to damage the coating on non-stick cookware.

Benefits of the Instant Electric Pressure Cooker

Electric pressure cookers are best for:

- Those who are nervous about fiddling with heat settings; the electric pressure cooker will do it automatically, just set it and forget it, Everything it will take care without any problem.
- The electric pressure cooker can replace other appliances like a slow cooker, rice cooker, yogurt maker, etc.
- Busy parents who need to schedule dinner to be ready when they walk in the door will appreciate the cooking delay timer available in some models which start dinner before anyone is home.
- College students with limited kitchens: the electric pressure cooker is a complete cooking tool it browns/Sautés, pressure cooks and keeps the food warm-some do even more.
- Elderly or otherwise abled persons-no need to remember if the gas is on, plus the cooker can be placed at any height.
- Expert cooks who already moved all of their cooking to pressure and often have more than one cooker running an electric is a great addition to the ensemble.

How To Use The Electric Pressure Cooker

If you're just getting started with your new electric pressure cooker, don't be intimidated by the word electric and pressure, the new electric pressure cookers are super safe and easy to use. Before you start cooking, there are three basic tests, you need to do.

Water Test

First thing, get to know how your pressure cooker comes to pressure by pressure cooking with just water. Often called a water test, all you do is:

- Add a cup of water to the pressure cooking pot, you always use the inner pot lock the lid in place
- Make sure the valve is in the sealing/pressure cooking position
- Select a pressure cooking button with a short cook time. The Fish button on the Power Pressure Cooker or Manual and 5 minutes on the electric pressure cooker for example
- Watch while the pressure cooker does all the work. It will take about 5 minutes for the water to heat up and build pressure when pressure is reached the time will start counting down

Pressure Release

You need to know is, how to release the pressure once it's done pressure cooking. The easiest way is to do nothing and let the pressure release all by itself. When you're cooking something that cooks quickly, you'll want to release the pressure quickly so it doesn't overcook. There are two types of methods to release pressure, "*Quick Pressure Release*" and "*Natural Pressure Cooker Release*".

Quick Pressure Release

After the pressure cooking time has finished. You can release the pressure two ways. A quick pressure release is when you open the valve and allow the steam to release quickly.

Keep your face and hands away from the steam as it's released. Don't release pressure under hanging cabinets, which can be damaged by the steam. I just turn my pressure cooker so the steam is released away from the cabinets.

Using a quick pressure release stops the pressure cooking quickly. Use a quick pressure release when you are cooking ingredients, like vegetables, that you want to avoid overcooking. It should take about 1 to 2 minutes.

Natural Pressure Release

A natural pressure release is when the cooking time is over and you leave the valve closed and allow the pressure to decrease without doing anything.

Electric pressure cookers automatically switch to the Keep Warm setting. As soon as it switches to the Keep Warm Setting the pressure begins to drop. The time it takes for the pressure to release will vary depending on the ingredients and amount of liquid in the pressure cooker.

A natural pressure release can take from 5 to 30 minutes in the electric pressure cooker. When the pressure is fully released, the float valve will drop and the lid will unlock and open. There is no beep or signal when the pressure is released. Sometimes you can hear the float valve drop if you're close by. So, use a natural pressure release when making steel cut oats or a large pot of soup or pasta.

High, Medium, Low Pressure

Depending on what you're cooking, you will want to use high, medium, or low pressure. Not all electric pressure cookers have a medium pressure option. The manual that came with your electric pressure cooker should indicate which type of pressure to use for which type of food.

Buttons

All the buttons can be confusing. You don't have to worry about which button to use, almost all the electric pressure cooking buttons cook exactly the same way, they just have different times programmed for different ingredients. Let's see most common buttons and it's functionalities.

Sauté Function

Use the Sauté button to Sauté in the pressure cooking pot with the lid off. You can also press Sauté and the adjust button once (more) for browning. Press Sauté and the Adjust button twice (less) to simmer.

Keep Warm/Cancel Button

Use this button to cancel a function or turn off your pressure cooker. On the Smart, you can use the Adjust button to reduce or increase the keep the warm temperature from 145° (normal) to 133° (less) and 167° (more).

Manual Button
This button is an all-purpose button. Use the manual button if a recipe says to pressure cook on high pressure for a specific number of minutes. Use the "+" and "-" buttons to increase or decrease the cooking time.

Soup
High pressure 30 minute cook time. Press soup and the Adjust button once (more) to cook for 40 minutes. Press soup and the Adjust button twice (less) to cook for 20.

Meat/Stew
High pressure 35 minute cook time. Adjusted to more – 45 minute cook time, adjusted to less – 20 minute cook time.

Bean/Chili
High pressure 30 minute cook time. Adjusted to more – 40 minute cook time; adjusted to less – 25 minute cook time.

Poultry
High pressure 15 minute cook time. Adjusted to more – 30 minute cook time; adjusted to less – 5 minute cook time.

Rice
Cooks on low pressure and is the only fully automatic program. It's for cooking white rice and will adjust the cooking time depending on the amount of water and rice in the cooking pot. (You can also prefer to cook rice for a shorter time on high pressure.)

Multi Grain
High pressure 40 minute cook time. Adjusted to less – 20 minutes cook time. Adjusted to more – 45 minutes warm water soaking time and 60 minutes pressure cooking time.

Porridge
High pressure 20 minute cook time. Adjusted to more – 30 minute cook time, adjusted to less 15 – a minute cook time.

Steam
High pressure 10 minute cook time. Adjusted to more – 15 minute cook time and adjusted to less – 3 minute cook time. Use this function with a rack or steamer basket because it heats at full power continuously while it's coming to pressure and you don't want food in direct contact with the bottom of the electric pressure cooking pot. Once it reaches pressure, the steam button regulates pressure by cycling on and off similar to the other pressure buttons.

Slow Cooker
Defaults to a 4 hour slow cook time. Use the adjust button to slow cook on low (190-201°F), normal (194-205°F) or high (199-210°F). Use the "+" and "-" buttons to increase or decrease the cooking time.

Yogurt
This button used for making yogurt in the pot or in individual jars.

Timer
This is for delayed cooking. You need to select a cooking function first, make any adjustments, then press the timer button and adjust with the "+" and "-" buttons.

Important While Cooking

Timing
This is where your cooking intuition generally goes out the window. Don't let that freak you out. Cooking time will vary depending on the PSI (pounds per square inch) of your low and high-pressure setting of your electric pressure cooker. If something is underdone, it's easy to fix: just add a couple more minutes and bring your cooker back to pressure.

Liquid
Your electric pressure cooker will require a minimum amount of liquid to work, as well as a maximum amount of food and liquid that it can hold. This should be clearly marked in your manual. Generally, you shouldn't fill your electric pressure cooker more than 2/3 full.

Don't Open
Most modern electric pressure cookers make it impossible for someone to open the cooker while internal pressure exceeds outside pressure. But regardless – just don't attempt to open it while in use. Turn off your pressure cooker if you need to, and release pressure before opening.

Electric Pressure Cooker Cooking Times

Required CookingTime for Dry and Soaked Legume:

Legume	Dry (minutes)	Soaked (minutes)	Pressure	Method
Adzuki or Azuki, red and green	20	9	High	Natural
Anasazi	22	7	High	Natural
Black Beans	24	6	High	Natural
Black-eyed Peas	7	5	High	Natural
Borlotti	25	10	High	Natural
Cannellini	30	8	High	Natural
Chickpeas	40	15	High	Natural
Chole	40	15	High	Natural
Corona	30	10	High	Natural
Cranberry	25	10	High	Natural
Fava, dried	30	12	High	Natural
Fava, fresh	8	-	High	Both
Flageolet	20	8	High	Natural
Garbanzo	40	15	High	Natural
Giant White Beans	30	10	High	Natural
Great Northern Beans	30	8	High	Natural
Green Beans (see VEGETABLES)				
Harticots	30	8	High	Natural
Kidney Bean, white	30	8	High	Natural
Lentils, Black Beluga	8		High	Natural
Lentils, French Green, green, or mini	10	5	High	Natural
Lentils, Split - Red, Orange, or Yellow	1	-	High	Natural
Lentils, regular	12	-	High	Natural
Lima, baby or large	15	7	High	Natural
Lobia	7	5	High	Natural
Masoor	5	-	High	Natural
Mung	20	9	High	Natural
Navy	20	8	High	Natural
Peanuts, Fresh		50	High	Natural
Peas, whole green	18	10	High	Natural
Peas, split, green	5	-	High	Natural
Peas, split, yellow or orange	10	5	High	Natural
Pinto	25	10	High	Natural
Rajma	24	8	High	Natural
Red Kidney	24	8	High	Natural
Scarlet runner	20	8	High	Natural
Soy, yellow	40	22	High	Natural
Soy, red	22	7	High	Natural
White Beans	30	8	High	Natural

Required Cooking Time for Seafood:

Seafood	Minutes	Pressure	Method
Calamari	20	High	Normal

Carp	6	High	Normal
Clams, canned/jarred	add after pressure cooking		Normal
Clams, fresh	6	High	Normal
Cod	3	Low	Normal
Crab	3	Low	Normal
Eel	10	High	Normal
Fish fillet	3	Low	Normal
Fish soup or stock	6	High	Normal
Fish steak	4	High	Normal
Fish, mixed pieces (for fish soup)	8	Low	Normal
Fish, whole, gutted	6	Low	Normal
Fish, in packet	15	High	Normal
Frog's Legs	8	High	Normal
Haddock	7	Low	Normal
Halibut	7	Low	Normal
Lobster	12	Low	Normal
Lobster, 2 lb (1k)	3	Low	Normal
Mussels	1	Low	Normal
Ocean Perch	7	Low	Normal
Octopus	20	High	Both
Oysters	6	Low	Normal
Perch	6	Low	Normal
Prawns	2	Low	Normal
Salmon	6	Low	Normal
Scallop	1	High	Normal
Scampi	2	Low	Normal
Shrimp	2	Low	Normal
Squid	4	High	Both
Trout	12	Low	Normal

Required Cooking Time for Fruits:

Fruits	Minutes	Pressure	Method
Apricot (fresh)	4	High	Natural
Apricot (dried	4	High	Natural
Blackberries	8	High	Natural
Blueberries	6	High	Natural
Cherries	2	High	Natural
Chestnuts (fresh)	20	High	Natural
Chestnuts (dried)	40	High	Natural
Coconut Milk	1	High	Normal, Natural
Cranberries (fresh)	8	High	Natural
Cranberries (dried)	3	High	Natural
Figs (Fresh)	3	Low/High	Natural
Figs (Dried)	8	Low/High	Natural
Grapes	2	High	Normal, Natural
Kumquat, slices	13	High	Natural
Lemon, wedges	15	High	Natural
Mango	7	High	Natural
Orange, wedges	15	High	Natural
Peaches	4	High	Natural
Pears, sliced	4	High	Normal, Natural
Pears, whole	5	High	Natural
Raisins	7	High	Normal, Natural
Plums	5	High	Natural
Prunes	10	High	Natural
Quince	10	High	Natural
Raspberries	1	High	Natural
Strawberries	1	High	Natural

Required Cooking Time for Eggs:

Eggs	Minutes	Pressure	Method
Egg, Hardboiled	5	Low	Normal
Egg, Medium-boiled	4	Low	Normal
Egg, Soft-boiled	3	Low	Normal

Required Cooking Time and Liquid Ratio for Rice:

Rice Type	Liquid per 1 cup Rice	Minutes	Pressure	Method
Arborio Rice (risotto)	2 cups (500 ml)	5	High or Low	Slow Normal
Basmati Rice	1 1/2 cups (375 ml)	3	High or Low	10-Min. Natural
Basmati Rice (rinsed)	1 1/4 cups (315 ml)	1	High or Low	10-Min. Natural
Basmati Rice (soaked)	1 cup (250 ml)	1	High or Low	10-Min. Natural
Black Rice	1 1/4 cups (315 ml)	20	High	10-Min. Natural
Brown Rice	1 1/4 cups (315 ml)	20	High	10-Min. Natural
Cargo Rice)	1 1/4 cups (315 ml)	20	High	10-Min. Natural
Carnaroli Rice	2 cups (500 ml)	5	High or Low	Slow Normal
Forbidden Rice	1 1/4 cups (315 ml)	20	High	10-Min. Natural
Jasmine Rice (rinsed)	1 cup (250 ml)	1	High or Low	10-Min. Natural
Jasmine Rice (un-rinsed)	1 1/4 cup (312 ml)	1	High or Low	10-Min. Natural
Parboiled Rice (Uncle Ben's)	1 1/2 cups (375 ml)	5	High or Low	Slow Normal
Red Rice	1 1/4 cups (315 ml)	20	High	10-Min. Natural
Risotto	2 cups (500 ml)	5	High or Low	Slow Normal
Romano Rice	2 1/4 (560 ml)	5	High or Low	10-Min. Natural
Sushi Rice (rinsed)	1 1/2 (375 ml)	7	High or Low	5-Min. Natural
White long-grain Rice	1 1/2 cups (375 ml)	3	High or Low	10-Min. Natural
White short-grain Rice	1 1/2 cups (375 ml)	8	High or Low	Slow Normal
Wild Rice	3 cups (750 ml)	25	High	Natural

Required Cooking Time and Liquid Ratio for Oats:

Type	Single Serving	Liquid per 1 cup Rice	Minutes	Pressure	Method
Oat Bran	1/3 cup bran & 1 cup liquid	3 cups (750 ml)	1	High	Natural
Oat Groat	1/3 cup groats & 1/3 cup liquid	1 cup (250 ml)	20	High	Natural
Rolled Oats	1/3 cup oats & 2/3 cup liquid	2 cups (500 ml)	10	High	Natural
Steel-cut Oats (quick)	1/4 cup oats & 3/4 cup liquid	3 cups (750 ml)	3	High	Natural
Steel-cut Oats	1/4 cup oats & 3/4 cup liquid	3 cups (750 ml)	15	High	Natural
Porridge Oats	1/3 cup oats & 2/3 cup liquid	2 cups (500ml)	1	High	Natural
Quick Oats	1/3 cup oats & 2/3 cup liquid	2 cups (500ml)	1	High	Natural
Quick Oats (creamy)	1/4 cup oats & 3/4 cup liquid	3 cups (750ml)	1	High	Natural
Scottish Oats	1/4 cup oats & 3/4 cup liquid	3 cups (750 ml)	5	High	Natural
Stone-ground Oats	1/4 cup oats & 3/4 cup liquid	3 cups (750 ml)	5	High	Natural

Required Cooking Time and Liquid Ratio for Meat Items:

Meat, Poultry, Dairy	Minutes	Frozen	Pressure	Method
Beef, brisket	70	no	High	Natural
Beef, flank steak	15	+ 10	High	Normal, Natural
Beef, ground	6	+4	High	Natural
Beef, Osso buco	25	+ 10-15	High	Natural
Beef, ox tail	45	+15	High	Natural
Beef, ribs	60	+10	High	Natural
Beef, roast	75	no	High	Natural
Beef, round	60	no	High	Natural
Beef, stew (cubed)	12	+5		Normal, Natural
Beef, stock (bones, ect.)	60	+15	High	Natural
Beef, tongue	50	no	High	Natural
Boar, roast	45	no	High	Natural
Boar, stew (cubed)	20	+10	High	Normal, Natural
Chicken, breast boneless & skinless (boil, steam)	1, 6	+4	High	Natural
Chicken, ground	5	+4	High	Natural
Chicken, liver	3	+4	High	Normal
Chicken, bone-in pieces (leg, thigh, breast, wings)	10	+ 5-7	High	Natural
Chicken, stock (bones, ect.)	35	+10	High	Natural
Chicken, strips	1	+4	High	Natural
Chicken, whole (up to 4lbs/2k)	20-25	+10	High	Natural
Cornish Hen, whole	10	+10	High	Natural
Deer, Saddle	20	no	High	Natural
Deer, roast	30	no	High	Natural
Duck, pieces	8	+ 5-7	High	Natural
Duck, whole	30	+10	High	Natural
Eggs, poached	2	-	Low	Normal
Elk, roast	30	no	High	Natural
Elk, stew (cubed)	20	+10	High	Normal
Gammon (see Pork, leg)				
Goat	20	+ 10-15	High	Natural
Goose, pieces	20	+ 5-7	High	Natural
Ham (see Pork, Leg)				
Hare	35	+10	High	Natural
Lamb, Chops	7	+5	High	Normal
Lamb, Ground	12	+5	High	Normal
Lamb, leg/shank	35	+ 10-15	High	Natural
Lamb, roast	20	no	High	Natural
Lamb, shoulder	25	no	High	Natural
Lamb, stew (cubed)	15	+10	High	Normal
Ox, tail	45	+15	High	Natural
Pheasant	20	+10	High	Natural
Pigeon	25	+10	High	Natural
Pork, Belly	40	no	High	Natural
Pork, Chops or Steaks	8	+4	High	Normal
Pork, foot/ham hock	40	+ 20-30	High	Natural
Pork, ground	5	+5	High	Natural
Pork, leg/shank	35	no	High	Natural

Pork, loin	12	no	High	Natural
Pork, roast	30	no	High	Natural
Pork , stew (cubed)	8	+5	High	Normal
Pork Sausage	8	+5	High	Normal
Pork, ribs	20	+ 10-15	High	Natural
Pork, shoulder	50	no	High	Natural
Pork, stock (bones, ect.)	60	+10	High	Natural
Quail	9	+7	High	Natural
Rabbit	18	+ 10-15	High	Natural
Roast beef, medium	8 to 10	no	High	Natural
Roast beef, rare	6 to 8	no	High	Natural
Roast beef, well done	10 to 12	no	High	Natural
Squab	25	+10	High	Natural
Tripe	15	+10	High	Natural
Turkey, breast (stuffed/rolled)	20	no	High	Natural
Turkey, breast sliced	9	+4	High	Normal
Turkey, legs	35	+ 15-20	High	Natural
Turkey, wings	20	+10	High	Natural
Veal, Chop or Steak	8	+ 4-6	High	Normal
Veal, ground	6	+4	High	Natural
Veal, Osso buco	20	+10	High	Natural
Veal, Roast	20	no	High	Natural
Veal, stock (bones, ect.)	60	+10	High	Natural
Veal, Tounge	40	no	High	Natural
Venison	45	no	High	Natural

Required Cooking Time for Vegetables:

Vegetables	Minutes	Pressure	Method
Artichoke, hearts	3	High or Low	Normal
Artichoke, pieces or baby	4	High or Low	Normal
Artichoke, whole (small, med, large)	5, 8, 11	High or Low	Normal
Asparagus	1	High or Low	Normal
Beet, Cubed	4	High or Low	
Beet, Greens	2		Normal
Beet, Whole (small, med, large)	10, 15, 20	High	Normal
Bok Choy, baby	1	High or Low	Normal
Bok Choy	5 to 7	High or Low	Normal
Broccoli	3 to 5	High or Low	Normal
Brussels Sprouts	4	High or Low	Normal
Cabbage, Red, Green, Savoy	3	High or Low	Normal
Capsicums	3 to 4	High or Low	Normal
Carrots, sliced	1 to 2	High or Low	Normal
Carrots, whole	3 to 4	High or Low	Normal
Cauliflower, florets	2 to 3	High or Low	Normal
Cauliflower, whole	10	High or Low	Normal
Celeriac	3 to 4	High or Low	Normal
Celery, sliced	2 to 3	High or Low	Normal
Chard, swiss	2	High or Low	Normal
Chicory	5 to 7	High or Low	Normal
Chinese Cabbage	5 to 7	High or Low	Normal
Collards	3 to 4	High or Low	Normal
Corn, kernels	1	High or Low	Normal
Corn, on the cob	2	High or Low	Normal
Corn, in husk	12	High or Low	Natural
Eggplant	2 to 3	High or Low	Normal
Endive	1 to 2	High or Low	Normal
Escarole	1 to 2	High or Low	Normal
Fennel	2 to 3	High or Low	Normal
Garlic	5 to 6	High or Low	Normal
Green Beans, fresh or frozen	2 to 3	High or Low	Normal
Greens, chopped	2 to 3	High or Low	Normal
Kale	1	High or Low	Normal
Kohlrabi, pieces	2 to 3	High or Low	Normal
Leeks	3	High or Low	Normal
Mushrooms, dry	10	High	Normal
Mushrooms, fresh	5	High or Low	Normal
Mustard greens	5 to 7	High or Low	Normal
Okra	2 to 3	High or Low	Normal
Onions	3	High or Low	Normal
Onions, baby	2 to 3	High or Low	Normal
Parsnips	2 to 3	High or Low	Normal
Peas, fresh or frozen	2 to 3	High or Low	Normal
Peppers, bell	3 to 4	High or Low	Normal
Peppers, small	1	High or Low	Normal
Potatoes, baby or fingerling	5 to 6	High or Low	Normal
Potatoes, quartered	5	High or Low	Normal, Natural
Potatoes, small, new, or red	5	High or Low	Normal, Natural

Potatoes, Sweet whole	15	High	Natural
Potatoes, whole (small, med, large)	5, 8, 10	High	Natural
Pumpkin, sliced	3	High	Normal, Natural
Rutabagas	1	High or Low	Normal
Spinach, fresh or frozen	1	High or Low	Normal
Squash, Acorn, halved	8	High	Normal, Natural
Squash, Banana, cubed	3 to 4	High or Low	Normal, Natural
Squash, Butternut, halves	6	High or Low	Normal, Natural
Squash, Butternut, large chunks	4	High or Low	Normal, Natural
Squash, Spaghetti, Halved	3 to 4	High or Low	Normal, Natural
Squash, Summer	2 to 3	High or Low	Normal
Tomato, sauce	6	High or Low	Normal
Tomato, slices	3	High or Low	Normal
Turnips, sliced	3	High or Low	Normal
Turnips, whole	5	High or Low	Normal
Yams	15	High	Natural
Zucchini	2 to 3	High or Low	Normal

Required Cooking Time and Liquid Ratio for Grains:

Grain Type	Liquid per 1 cup Grain	Minutes	Pressure	Method
Amaranth	2 cups (500 ml)	8	High	Natural
Barley, flakes	4 1/2 cups (1125 ml)	9	High	Natural
Barley, pearl	2 cups (500 ml)	20	High	10-Min. Natural
Barley, whole	2 1/4 cups (130 ml)	35	High	10-Min. Natural
Bread	see instructions		High	Normal
Buckwheat	2 cups (500 ml)	3	High	10-Min. Natural
Bulgur	3 cups (750 ml)	10	High	10-Min. Natural
Corn Meal	6 cups (1.5l)	240 (4 hours)	High	Natural
Farro (semi-perlated)	2 1/2 cups (625 ml)	10	High	Normal
Hominy (dry un-soaked)	6 cups (1.5l)	240 (4 hours)	High	Natural
Hominy (soaked)	4 cups (1l)	25	High	Natural
Kamut, whole	3 cups (750ml)	35	High	Natural
Kamut, whole (soaked)	2 cups (500 ml)	18	High	Natural
Millet	1 1/2 cups (375 ml)	1	High	10-Min. Natural
Pasta	see instructions		Low	Normal
Polenta, Coarse	4 cups (1l)	8	High	Normal
Polenta, Fine (not instant)	3 cups (750 ml)	5	High	Slow Normal
Quinoa	1 1/2 cups (375 ml)	1	High	Natural
Semolina	3 cups (750 ml)	6	Low	Slow Normal
Spelt berries (see Farro)	2 1/2 cups (625 ml)	10	High	Normal
Wheat berries	3 cups (750 ml)	40	High	Natural

Measurements:

Dry Volume

Standards	Metric
1/8 teaspoon	.5 ml
1/4 teaspoon	1 ml
1/2 teaspoon	2 ml
3/4 teaspoon	4 ml
1 teaspoon	5 ml
1 tablespoon	15 ml
1/4 cup	59 ml
1/3 cup	79 ml
1/2 cup	118 ml
2/3 cup	158 ml
3/4 cup	177 ml
1 cup	225 ml
2 cups or 1 pint	450 ml
3 cups	675 ml
4 cups or 1 quart	1 liter
1/2 gallon	2 liters
1 gallon	4 liters

Mass Weights

Standards (Ounces)	Metric (Grams)
1/2 ounce	15 grams
1 ounce	30 grams
3 ounces	85 grams
3.75 ounces	100 grams
4 ounces	115 grams
8 ounces	225 grams
12 ounces	340 grams
16 ounces or 1 pound	450 grams

Oven Temperatures

Standards	Metric
250° F	130° C
300° F	150° C
350° F	180° C
400° F	200° C
450° F	230° C

Liquid Volume

Standards (Cups & Quarts)	Standards (Ounces)	Metric (Milliliters & Liters)
2 tbsp	1 fl. oz.	30 ml
1/4 cup	2 fl. oz.	60 ml
1/2 cup	4 fl. oz.	125 ml
1 cup	8 fl. oz.	250 ml
1 1/2 cups	12 fl. oz.	375 ml
2 cups or 1 pint	16 fl. oz.	500 ml
4 cups or 1 quart	32 fl. oz.	1000 ml or 1 liter
1 gallon	128 fl. oz.	4 liters

Dry Measure Equivalents

3 teaspoons	1 tablespoon	1/2 ounce	14.3 grams
2 tablespoons	1/8 cup	1 ounce	28.3 grams
4 tablespoons	1/4 cup	2 ounces	56.7 grams
5 1/3 tablespoons	1/3 cup	2.6 ounces	75.6 grams
8 tablespoons	1/2 cup	4 ounces	113.4 grams
12 tablespoons	3/4 cup	6 ounces	.375 pound
32 tablespoons	2 cups	16 ounces	1 pound

Safe Ways To Clean Your Electric Pressure Cooker

For cleaning of any specific part, you should refer your electric pressure cooker manual. Clean your electric pressure cooker regularly to ensure that your cooker will operate at optimal performance for a longer time.

Before Cleaning

Unplug the electric pressure cooker from the electric outlet and allow it to cool if it is hot after use. Remove the lid and cooking pot from the main body of the electric pressure cooker.

Main Body Cleaning

Take a clean damp cloth and then gently wipe the main body. You can use warm soapy water for dampening the cloth if the food residue does not get cleaned with water. Do not submerge the main body in the sink full of water or in a dishwasher. Some electric pressure cookers have small units or reservoirs for collecting the excess condensation. You can remove this unit and wash in warm soapy water. Do remember to dry it thoroughly before attaching it back to the main body.

Cooking Pot Cleaning

Usually, Cooking Pots can be washed in a dishwasher. Read your manual to confirm. If you are cleaning the cooking pot by hand then use warm soapy water. The inner side of the cooking pot is usually non-stick coated. So use soft cloth or sponge while cleaning the interior of the cooking pot. Completely dry the cooking pot before putting it back into the main body.

Lid Cleaning

Use warm water or warm soapy water to clean the lid. Take care in cleaning the various values, knobs and pressure regulator on the lid. Clean and dry them thoroughly. Some electric pressure cooker lids have a rubber gasket. To clean the rubber gasket, remove it from the lid and rinse it in warm soapy water. Dry it completely before attaching it back to the lid. Pay special attention to the rubber gasket's shape. If it is distorted or hardened then replace it with a new one.

Drying

Completely dry each and every part before attaching them back. You can use a soft cloth for drying the parts. Not cleaning your electric pressure cooker properly or avoiding it all together can cause it to malfunction or cause the formation of stale odors inside it. And in extreme cases, it can even spoil the food being prepared.

Additional Information For Vegetarians And Vegans

When it comes to the vegetarian and vegan lifestyle, everyone will have misconceptions regarding protein deficiency because protein is one of the main sources to build, maintain and replace the tissues in the body but it is a false conception. We can get the required protein in our body by eating plant-based food products also.

Protein Requirement

A recent study says and recommends that the protein requirement for a healthy person is 0.5 grams per pound of body weight. For example: if your weight is 100 pounds, you can multiply 100 x 0.5 = 50 grams of protein for your daily healthy body needs.

Great Source of Protein

We have known that amino acids play a key role in building blocks of protein in our body because the body cannot produce by itself. There are 22 types of amino acids, among them 9 are essential. Let's see, what are the nine essential amino acids, its functionalities and from which plant source we can get them.

Leucine

Leucine is for stimulating growth and strength of muscle and helps to regulate your blood sugar by controlling insulin in the body, even help to prevent and treat depression. Some of the food items that you can find leucine are apple, pumpkin, peas, sesame seeds, watercress, turnip greens, fig, soy, sunflower seeds, kidney beans, avocados, raisins, dates, blueberries, olives, and banana.

Isoleucine

Isoleucine is to produce hemoglobin and energy to the body and also helps in growth of nitrogen within the muscle cells in children. Some of the food items that you can find are cashews, almonds, oats, lentils, beans, brown rice, cabbage, hemp seeds, chia seeds, spinach, cranberries, quinoa, apples, and kiwis.

Lysine

Lysine helps in absorption of calcium to strengthen the bones and collagen production. Deficiency of this amino acid leads to nausea, depression, fatigue and muscle depletion. Some of the food items that you can find are watercress, spirulina, parsley hemp seeds, chia seeds, avocados, soy protein, almonds, and cashews.

Methionine
Methionine helps to form cartilage with help of sulfur, deficiency of methionine leads to damage of tissues, arthritis pain, and poor healing and also helps in the formation of creatine. Some of the food items that you can find are onions, cacao, sunflower seeds, sunflower seed butter, hemp seeds, chia seeds, oats, wheat, brazil nuts, figs, whole grain rice, legumes, beans, and raisins.

Phenylalanine
Phenylalanine helps to form brain chemicals and thyroid hormones, deficiency of this leads to brain fog, lack of energy, lack of appetite, depression and memory problems. Some of the food items that you can find phenylalanine are rice, avocado, pumpkin, beans, almonds, peanuts, figs, leafy greens, berries, and olives.

Threonine
Threonine is one of the essential amino acids supports a healthy immune system, central nervous system, liver and heart and also helps to produce *glycine* and *serine* in the body (responsible for healthy hair, bones, skin and nails). The food items with the highest percentage of this threonine are watercress, spirulina, soybeans, sprouted grains, sesame seeds, hemp seeds, chia seeds, leafy greens, and wheat.

Tryptophan
Tryptophan helps in the functionality of neurotransmitter, it is also known as relaxing amino acid, it creates a happy feeling tied to depression and stress. There are tons of plant-based sources of this amino acid, there are oats bran, oats, spinach, sweet potatoes, beets, asparagus, mushrooms, all lettuces, oranges, celery, pepper, winter squash, carrots, onions, and peas.

Valine
Valine is needed for optimal growth and repair of muscles. Some the food items that have valine are legumes, broccoli, sesame seeds, beans, peanuts, sprouted grains, blueberries, cranberries, and apricots.

Histidine
These amino acids act as messengers to the brain; muscle cells and also helps in detoxifying the red and white blood cells. Deficiency of this amino acid causes sexual dysfunction, arthritis and even makes the body more susceptible to the AIDS virus. Some of the food items that have histidine are rice, wheat, rye, legumes, cantaloupe, buckwheat, potatoes, cauliflower, and corn.

Recipe 1: Baked Sweet Potatoes

Tips to cook properly
- Make small scratch over sweet potatoes before cooking

Ingredients
- 2-3 large sweet potatoes
- 1/2 cup water
- Tad of extra virgin olive oil

Preparation Method
- Scrub potatoes, coat very lightly with olive oil, wrap in aluminum foil. Pour 1/2 cup of water in pressure cooker pot, add potatoes on top.
- Press the steam button and set time to 15 minutes. Remove foil, cut a slit in the top of sweet potatoes and enjoy.
- Topping, add a little of one or two of your favorites: walnuts, ground flax seeds, Greek yogurt, low-fat cream cheese, etc.
- If a kid is eating, 3-4 miniature marshmallows on warm sweet potatoes go over big.

Nutritional Information
- Preparation Time: 20 minutes
- Total Servings: 2
- Amount per Serving: 1
- Calories: 180
- Calories from Fat: 65
- Total Fat: 0.4g
- Saturated Fat: 0g
- Cholesterol: 0mg
- Sodium: 72mg
- Potassium: 800mg
- Total Carbohydrates: 42g
- Fiber: 3.3g
- Sugar: 6g
- Protein: 4g

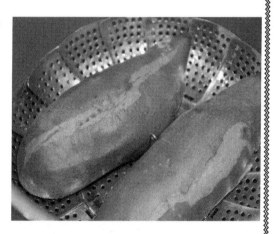

Recipe 2: Creamy Rice Pudding

Tips to cook properly
- Sprinkle cinnamon on top for better taste and flavor

Ingredients
- Rice 1½ cup
- Sugar 150g
- Salt ½ teaspoon
- Milk 5 cups
- Vanilla extract 2 teaspoons
- Raisins 1 cup

Preparation Method
- In pressure cooker pot, combine rice, sugar, salt, and milk. Select Sauté and bring to a boil, stirring constantly to dissolve sugar.
- Select low pressure and set timer for 16 minutes
- While rice is cooking, whisk eggs and vanilla
- When beeps sound, turn off pressure cooker, wait 10 minutes
- Stir the egg mixture into the pot. Select Sauté and cook uncovered until mixture just starts to boil. Turn off the pressure cooker.
- Stir in raisins and serve

Nutritional Information
- Preparation Time: 15 minutes
- Total Servings: 8
- Amount per Serving: 1
- Calories: 366
- Calories from Fat: 62
- Total Fat: 6.9g
- Saturated Fat: 3.8g
- Cholesterol: 64mg
- Sodium: 237mg
- Potassium: 325mg
- Total Carbohydrates: 67.6g
- Fiber: 0.9g
- Sugar: 22.6g
- Protein: 8.8g

Recipe 3: Apple Butter

Tips to cook properly
- After cooling, you should use blender

Ingredients
- 2 Apples
- 1 cup water
- 1 teaspoon cinnamon
- Sugar (as needed)
- 1 teaspoon nutmeg
- 1 teaspoon pumpkin pie spice

Preparation Method
- Fill your pressure cooker to the line with apples. Add 1 cup water.
- Set pressure cooker to steam setting. Adjust time to 4 minutes.
- When you hear the beeps indicating it's done, just leave it. Let the pressure return to normal on its own.
- Open the lid and using an immersion blender, blend until it reaches apple butter consistency.
- Put in cinnamon, sugar (use Splenda) to taste. You can also add a pinch of nutmeg and pumpkin pie spice.
- Put into containers or into canning jars with new lids, and into a water bath for 25 minutes.
- This is a great breakfast treat on fresh baked bread, or over pancakes and waffles.

Nutritional Information
- Preparation Time: 45 minutes
- Total Servings: 2
- Amount per Serving: 1
- Calories: 34
- Calories from Fat: 0g
- Total Fat: 0g
- Saturated Fat: 0g
- Cholesterol: 0g
- Sodium: 5mg
- Potassium: 21mg
- Total Carbohydrates: 9g
- Fiber: 0.5g
- Sugar: 8.3g
- Protein: 1g

Recipe 4: Blueberry Oats

Tips to cook properly
- Add fresh blueberries on top for better taste

Ingredients
- 1 tablespoon butter
- 1 cup steel cut oats
- 3 cups water
- 1/2 cup half and half
- 2 tablespoons sugar
- 1 tablespoon lemon zest
- 1/4 teaspoon salt
- 1 cup fresh or frozen blueberries
- 1/4 cup chia seeds

Preparation Method
- Add butter to electric pressure cooking pot, select Sauté. When butter is melted add the oats and toast, stirring constantly, until they smell nutty, about 3 minutes.
- Add water, half and half, sugar, zest, and salt. Select 10 minutes cook time.
- When beep sounds, turn off pressure cooker and stir oats, blueberries and chia seeds.
- Cover and let sit five minutes until oats are desired thickness. Top with additional blueberries, honey or agave, sliced almonds, and a splash of milk.

Nutritional Information
- Preparation Time: 15 minutes
- Total Servings: 2
- Amount per Serving: 1
- Calories: 210
- Calories from Fat: 50g
- Total Fat: 5.6g
- Saturated Fat: 1.3g
- Cholesterol: 5mg
- Sodium: 36mg
- Potassium: 271mg
- Total Carbohydrates: 33.3g
- Fiber: 5.4g
- Sugar: 11.9g
- Protein: 6.9g

Recipe 5: Vanilla Latte Oats

Tips to cook properly
- Wait until pressure releases naturally

Ingredients
- 2 1/2 cups water
- 1 cup milk
- 1 cup oats
- 2 tablespoons sugar
- 1 teaspoon espresso powder
- 1/4 teaspoon salt
- 2 teaspoon vanilla extract
- Freshly whipped cream
- Finely grated chocolate

Preparation Method
- Add water, milk, oats, sugar, espresso powder, and salt to electric pressure cooking pot. Stir to dissolve espresso powder. Lock the lid in place. Select 10 minutes cook time.
- When beep sounds, turn off pressure cooker and stir vanilla extract and additional sugar to taste. Cover and let sit five minutes until oats are desired thickness. Serve topped with whipped cream and grated chocolate.

Nutritional Information
- Preparation Time: 15 minutes
- Total Servings: 4
- Amount per Serving: 1
- Calories: 200
- Calories from Fat: 20g
- Total Fat: 3.5g
- Saturated Fat: 2g
- Cholesterol: 15mg
- Sodium: 130mg
- Potassium: 205mg
- Total Carbohydrates: 38.1g
- Fiber: 4.6g
- Sugar: 13.2g
- Protein: 15g

Recipe 6: Corn Cob

Tips to cook properly
- Make sure that, corn never touches the water

Ingredients
- 6 ears of corn

Preparation Method
- Lay inside the electric pressure cooker, use the rack that comes with it. Break some corn ears in half. Stagger them to allow steam to pass through.
- Add 1 cup of water. Press the manual button for 8 minutes.

Nutritional Information
- Preparation Time: 10 minutes
- Total Servings: 6
- Amount per Serving: 1
- Calories: 94
- Calories from Fat: 10g
- Total Fat: 1.1g
- Saturated Fat: 0.2g
- Cholesterol: 0mg
- Sodium: 14mg
- Potassium: 246mg
- Total Carbohydrates: 21.5g
- Fiber: 2.4g
- Sugar: 7.1g
- Protein: 2.9g

Recipe 7: Pumpkin Smash

Tips to cook properly
- Before cooking, wash and remove skin

Ingredients
- 1 large sugar pumpkin

Preparation Method
- Place 1/2 cup water in the bottom of the electric pressure cooker. Place the pumpkin on the rack and cook high pressure 13 to 15 minutes. Quick release and set aside to cool.
- Scoop flesh out into a bowl and puree in a blender or with an immersion blender and serve with herb sauce.

Nutritional Information
- Preparation Time: 20 minutes
- Total Servings: 5
- Amount per Serving: 1
- Calories: 189
- Calories from Fat: 7g
- Total Fat: 0.7g
- Saturated Fat: 0.4g
- Cholesterol: 0mg
- Sodium: 7mg
- Potassium: 247mg
- Total Carbohydrates: 47.2g
- Fiber: 3.6g
- Sugar: 9.9g
- Protein: 7.3g

Recipe 8: Vegan Creamy Peaches Oats

Tips to cook properly
- Properly add water to pot to avoid over cooking

Ingredients
- Diced peaches 2
- Oats 2 cups
- Coconut or almond milk 1 cup
- Water 1-2 cup
- Vanilla extract ½ tablespoon

Preparation Method
- Add everything to the inner pot of your electric cooker
- Set for 5 minutes at pressure (Adjust to 3)
- Cool it down for 10 minutes
- Optional: Sweetener as needed

Nutritional Information
- Preparation Time: 15 minutes
- Total Servings: 2
- Amount per Serving: 165g
- Calories: 106.6
- Calories from Fat: 12g
- Total Fat: 1.3g
- Saturated Fat: 0.2g
- Cholesterol: 0mg
- Sodium: 6.2mg
- Potassium: 360mg
- Total Carbohydrates: 21.3g
- Fiber: 3g
- Sugar: 6.7g
- Protein: 3.1g

Recipe 9: Mango Rice Pudding

Tips to cook properly
- Try to add fresh shredded coconut as a topping

Ingredients
- 3/4 cup Arborio Rice
- 1 1/2 cups water
- 1 can coconut milk
- 1 teaspoon salt
- 1/3 cup brown sugar
- 1 teaspoon vanilla
- 1 mango, peeled and cubed
- 1/4 cup shredded coconut
- 1/4 cup almonds

Preparation Method
- Add rice, water, coconut milk, sugar, and salt to the pressure cooker.
- Use the manual setting and set the time to 7 minutes at High pressure.
- Let the cooker to cool down naturally. Unlock the lid and uncover rice. Add vanilla, and chopped mango. Stir together. Serve in small bowls with toasted coconut and almonds over top.

Nutritional Information
- Preparation Time: 12 minutes
- Total Servings: 2
- Amount per Serving: 1
- Calories: 630
- Calories from Fat: 240
- Total Fat: 24g
- Saturated Fat: 21g
- Cholesterol: 10g
- Sodium: 170mg
- Potassium: 200mg
- Total Carbohydrates: 96g
- Fiber: 5g
- Sugar: 9g
- Protein: 10g

Recipe 10: Cranberry Sauce

Tips to cook properly
- Cranberry sauce is great as a jam-like spread, topping for desserts, filling for pastries, glaze for meat
- Add water on medium heat to adjust the cranberry sauce's thickness
- White Sugar Substitution: Sweeteners such as maple syrup or honey

Ingredients
- Cranberries 340g
- Orange zest 12g
- Fresh orange juice 65ml
- Honey 30ml
- Salt 0.36g
- White sugar 150g

Preparation Method
- Rinse cranberries under cold running water. Discard the soft, discolored & wrinkly ones
- In pressure cooker, add all ingredients except salt and cook on high heat for 1 minute + 7 minutes
- Click Sauté button, stir and break the cranberries with a wooden spoon
- Stir and the heat will instantly melt the sugar to form a thick cranberry sauce
- Add a pinch of salt. Taste and add more sugar if desired
- Serve cold or warm with your favorite dish

Nutritional Information
- Preparation Time: 20 minutes
- Total Servings: 1 cup
- Amount per Serving: 1
- Calories: 95
- Calories from Fat: 0.5g
- Total Fat: 0.1g
- Saturated Fat: 0g
- Cholesterol: 0g
- Sodium:10mg
- Potassium: 71mg
- Total Carbohydrates: 24.2g
- Fiber: 1.5g
- Sugar: 21.3g
- Protein: 0.4g

Recipe 11: Vegetable Breakfast

Tips to cook properly
- This dish tastes better after it has been cooled and refrigerated

Ingredients
- White wheat berries 2 cups
- Butter 1 tablespoon
- Salt 1 teaspoon
- Sliced medium potatoes 2
- Sliced carrots 2
- Sliced onions 2
- Sliced celery stalks 5
- Poultry seasoning 1 teaspoon
- Thyme ¼ teaspoon

Preparation Method
- Soak 2 cups white wheat berries overnight in lots of water
- Use multi-grain setting and cook wheat, potatoes, and carrots
- Garnish with flat leaf parsley and serve as is or with plain yogurt

Nutritional Information
- Preparation Time: 15 minutes
- Total Servings: 4
- Calories: 115
- Calories from Fat: 28g
- Total Fat: 4.6g
- Saturated Fat: 0.8g
- Cholesterol: 4mg
- Sodium: 298mg
- Potassium: 180mg
- Total Carbohydrates: 24.1g
- Fiber: 4.9g
- Sugar: 2.3g
- Protein: 5.12g

Recipe 12: Breakfast Quinoa

Tips to cook properly
- Try to use fresh berries for better taste

Ingredients
- 1 1/2 cups uncooked quinoa
- 2 1/4 cups water
- 2 tablespoons maple syrup
- 1/2 teaspoon vanilla
- 1/4 teaspoon ground cinnamon
- Pinch of salt
- Toppings: milk, fresh berries, sliced almonds

Preparation Method
- Add quinoa, water, maple syrup, vanilla, cinnamon, and salt to the electric pressure cooking pot.
- Select 1 minute cook time. When beep sounds turn pressure cooker off, wait 10 minutes and carefully remove the lid.
- Fluff the quinoa and serve hot with milk, berries, and sliced almonds.

Nutritional Information
- Preparation Time: 15 minutes
- Total Servings: 6
- Amount per Serving: 1
- Calories: 538
- Calories from Fat: 66
- Total Fat: 7.3g
- Saturated Fat: 0.9g
- Cholesterol: 5mg
- Sodium: 112mg
- Potassium: 1013mg
- Total Carbohydrates: 98.7g
- Fiber: 8.9g
- Sugar: 37.4g
- Protein: 21.5

Recipe 13: Almond Oats

Tips to cook properly
- Make sure that almonds are roasted well in purified butter for better taste

Ingredients
- 1 tablespoon butter
- 1 cup steel cut oats
- 3 1/2 cups almond coconut milk
- 1/4 teaspoon salt
- 1/4 cup toasted shredded coconut
- 1/4 cup mini chocolate chips
- 1/4 cup sliced almonds

Preparation Method
- Add butter to electric pressure cooking pot, select Sauté. When butter is melted add the oats and toast, stirring constantly, until they smell nutty, about 3 minutes.
- Add milk and salt. Select 10 minutes cook time. When beep sounds, turn off pressure cooker and stir oats.
- Cover and let sit five minutes until oats are desired thickness. Top with shredded coconut, chocolate chips, sliced almonds, and a splash of milk.

Nutritional Information
- Preparation Time: 15 minutes
- Total Servings: 4
- Amount per Serving: 1
- Calories: 278
- Calories from Fat: 44
- Total Fat: 4.9g
- Saturated Fat: 0.6g
- Cholesterol: 0.90mg
- Sodium: 206mg
- Potassium: 157mg
- Total Carbohydrates: 58.1g
- Fiber: 5.8g
- Sugar: 14.7g
- Protein: 8.6g

Recipe 14: Scotch Eggs

Tips to cook properly
- Make sure that boiled egg stays in water for at least 1minutes before removing shells

Ingredients
- 4 large eggs
- 450g country style ground sausage
- 1 tablespoon vegetable oil

Preparation Method
- Put a steamer basket in the electric pressure cooker pot. Add 1 cup water and the eggs. Select 6 minutes cooking time
- When the timer beeps, do a quick pressure release. When the pressure is released, carefully remove the lid. Remove the steamer basket from the pressure cooking pot. Put eggs into ice cold water to cool.
- When the eggs are cool remove the shells. Divide the sausage into four equal pieces. Flatten each piece into a flat round. Place the hard-boiled egg in the center and gently wrap the sausage around the egg.
- Heat the electric pressure cooking pot on Sauté or browning. When the pot is hot, add oil and brown the Scotch eggs on four sides.
- Remove the Scotch Eggs from the pressure cooker and add 1 cup water. Put a rack in the pressure cooking pot and place the Scotch Eggs on the rack.
- Cook on high pressure for 6 minutes. When the pressure is released, carefully remove and enjoy the taste.

Nutritional Information
- Preparation Time: 30 minutes
- Total Servings: 4
- Amount per Serving: 1
- Calories: 659
- Calories from Fat: 485
- Total Fat: 53.9g
- Saturated Fat: 13.5g
- Cholesterol: 323mg
- Sodium: 1324mg
- Potassium: 423mg
- Total Carbohydrates: 16.6g
- Fiber: 0.9g
- Sugar: 2.1g
- Protein:25.9g

Recipe 15: Pumpkin Oats with Pecan Pie

Tips to cook properly
- Maple syrup can be substituted for brown sugar

Ingredients
- 1 tablespoon butter
- 1 cup oats
- 3 cups water
- 1 cup pumpkin puree
- 1/4 cup maple syrup
- 2 teaspoons cinnamon
- 1 teaspoon pumpkin pie spice
- 1/4 teaspoon salt

Preparation Method
- Add butter to electric pressure cooking pot, select Sauté. When butter is melted add the oats and toast, stirring constantly, until they smell nutty, about 3 minutes.
- Add water, pumpkin puree, maple syrup, cinnamon, pumpkin pie spice, and salt. Select high pressure and 10 minutes cook time.
- When beep sounds, turn off the pressure cooker, stir oats. Remove cooking pot from the pressure cooker and let oats rest in the cooking pot uncovered for 5 - 10 minutes until oats thicken to desired consistency.
- Serve warm with pecan pie granola, milk, and maple syrup if desired.

Nutritional Information
- Preparation Time: 30 minutes
- Total Servings: 6
- Amount per Serving: 1
- Calories: 219
- Calories from Fat: 36
- Total Fat: 4g
- Saturated Fat: 1.4g
- Cholesterol: 5mg
- Sodium: 18.1mg
- Potassium: 232
- Total Carbohydrates: 38.7g
- Fiber: 5.9g
- Sugar: 9.4g
- Protein: 8.0g

Recipe 16: Morning Fresh Fruit Yogurt

Tips to cook properly
- Make sure that, lids on loosely place into the pressure cooker

Ingredients
- 5 2/3 cups of organic milk
- 4 tablespoons sugar
- 4 tablespoons milk powder
- 2 cups of chopped fresh fruits
- 4 jars

Preparation Method
- Add 1 1/2 cup of water to the bottom of the pressure cooker. Put 1 1/3 Cup of Milk in each Jar place lids on loosely place into the pressure cooker.
- Adjust timer to 2 minutes, after that remove jar using jar lifter. Add your yogurt culture safely to the milk. Add 1 tablespoons of Sugar to each jar.
- Add 1 tablespoon of milk powder to each jar and mix well.
- Add 1/2 cup of fresh fruit to each jar. Carefully not to overfill the jars.
- Close and place jars back into the pressure cooker. Make sure it still has the 1 1/2 cup of water in the bottom the pressure cooker.
- Press the Yogurt cycle on the pressure cooker then increase the time from 8 hours to 12 hours.
- After the cycle is complete place them into the refrigerator cooling it down stops the cooking process by reducing the temperature.

Nutritional Information
- Preparation Time: 9-12 Hours
- Total Servings: 3
- Amount per Serving: 1
- Calories: 208
- Calories from Fat: 48
- Total Fat: 9g
- Saturated Fat: 6g
- Cholesterol: 21mg
- Sodium: 125mg
- Potassium: 88mg
- Total Carbohydrates: 26g
- Fiber: 2g
- Sugar: 26g
- Protein: 5g

Recipe 17: Mushroom Oatmeal

Tips to cook properly
- Make sure that, you add mushrooms in the end

Ingredients
- 2 tablespoons butter
- 1/2 medium onion
- 2 cloves garlic
- 1 cup oats
- 400g chicken broth
- 1/2 cup water
- 3 sprigs fresh thyme
- 1/4 teaspoon salt
- 2 tablespoons olive oil
- 225g mushrooms
- 1/2 cup smoked gouda
- Salt and freshly ground pepper

Preparation Method
- Add butter to electric pressure cooking pot, select Sauté. When butter is melted, Add the onions and cook, stirring frequently, until softened about 3 minutes.
- Add the garlic and cook for 1 minute. Add oats and Sauté 1 minute. Add broth, water, thyme, and salt. Select 10 minute cooking time.
- While oats are cooking, heat a large Sauté pan over medium heat until hot. Add olive oil and mushrooms and cook until golden brown on both sides, then do a quick pressure release.
- Stir oats. Stir in gouda until melted. Stir in mushrooms. Season with additional salt and fresh ground pepper to taste. Serve garnished with thyme leaves.

Nutritional Information
- Preparation Time: 20 minutes
- Total Servings: 4
- Amount per Serving: 1
- Calories: 443.3
- Calories from Fat: 170
- Total Fat: 18.9g
- Saturated Fat: 2.8g
- Cholesterol: 0mg
- Sodium: 9.8mg
- Potassium: 264mg
- Total Carbohydrates: 58.1g
- Fiber: 9g
- Sugar: 1.9g
- Protein: 12.2g

Recipe 18: Cinnamon Roll Oats

Tips to cook properly
- Add more milk to make an icing that will swirl

Ingredients
- 1 tablespoon butter
- 1 cup steel cut oats
- 3 1/2 cups water
- 1/4 teaspoon salt
- 3/4 cup raisins

Brown Sugar Topping:
- 1/4 cup brown sugar
- 1 teaspoon cinnamon

Cream Cheese Topping:
- 56g cream cheese
- 2 tablespoons powdered sugar
- 1 teaspoon milk

Preparation Method
- Add butter to electric pressure cooking pot, select Sauté. When butter is melted add the oats and toast, stirring constantly, until they start to darken and smell nutty about 3 minutes.
- Add water and salt to pressure cooking pot. Select high pressure and set 10 minutes cook time.
- When valve drops carefully remove and stir oats, stir in raisins. Cover and let sit five or 10 minutes until oats are desired thickness.
- Prepare brown sugar topping: In a small bowl, mix together brown sugar and cinnamon.
- Prepare cream cheese topping: In a small bowl, whisk together cream cheese, powder sugar, and milk. Add more milk or powdered sugar as necessary to make an icing that will swirl.
- Serve in individual bowls topped with brown sugar topping and a swirl of cream cheese topping.

Nutritional Information
- Preparation Time: 30 minutes
- Total Servings: 2
- Amount per Serving: 1
- Calories: 169
- Calories from Fat: 28
- Total Fat: 2.8g
- Saturated Fat: 0.8g
- Cholesterol: 5mg
- Sodium: 240mg
- Potassium: 135mg
- Total Carbohydrates: 39g
- Fiber: 4g
- Sugar: 10g
- Protein: 7g

Recipe 19: Strawberries Cream Oats

Tips to cook properly
- It will be good with little vanilla extract and plain milk before you serve

Ingredients
- 1 tablespoon butter
- 1 cup steel cut oats
- 4 cups water
- 1/4 cup cream
- 3 tablespoons light brown sugar
- 1/4 teaspoon salt
- 1/4 cup chia seeds
- 1 1/2 cups sliced strawberries

Preparation Method
- Add butter to electric pressure cooking pot, select Sauté. When butter is melted add the oats and toast, stirring constantly, until they smell nutty, about 3 minutes.
- Add water, cream, brown sugar and salt. Select 10 minutes cook time.
- When beep sounds, turn off pressure cooker and stir oats, strawberries and chia seeds. Cover and let sit five or 10 minutes until oats are desired thickness.
- Top with additional sliced strawberries, brown sugar, sliced almonds, and a splash of cream.

Nutritional Information
- Preparation Time: 24 minutes
- Total Servings: 2
- Amount per Serving: 1
- Calories: 334.7
- Calories from Fat: 105
- Total Fat: 11.7g
- Saturated Fat: 6g
- Cholesterol: 34.2mg
- Sodium: 121.9mg
- Potassium: 198mg
- Total Carbohydrates: 44g
- Fiber: 5.4g
- Sugar: 3.9g
- Protein: 15g

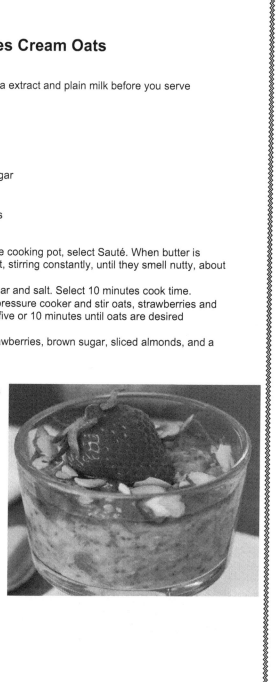

Recipe 20: Apple with Cherries

Tips to cook properly
- Instead of using brown sugar, use Splenda to avoid sugar intake

Ingredients
- 2 tablespoons butter
- 1 1/2 cups arborio rice
- 2 large apples
- 1 1/2 teaspoons cinnamon
- 1/4 teaspoon salt
- 1/3 cup brown sugar
- 1 cup apple juice
- 3 cups milk
- 1/2 cup dried cherries

Preparation Method
- Heat the butter in the electric pressure cooker pot for 2 to 3 minutes. Stir in the rice and cook, stirring frequently, until rice becomes opaque, about 3 to 4 minutes.
- Add the apples, spices, and brown sugar. Stir in the juice and milk. Select 6 minutes cook time. After 6 minutes, turn off pressure cooker and stir dried cherries.
- Serve topped with additional brown sugar, sliced almonds and a splash of milk.

Nutritional Information
- Preparation Time: 15 minutes
- Total Servings: 2
- Amount per Serving: 1
- Calories: 363
- Calories from Fat: 57
- Total Fat: 6.4g
- Saturated Fat: 3.2g
- Cholesterol: 69mg
- Sodium: 282mg
- Potassium: 491mg
- Total Carbohydrates: 69.2g
- Fiber: 2.1g
- Sugar: 32.9g
- Protein: 9.2g

Recipe 21: Pumpkin Chocolate Cake

Tips to cook properly
- You can use little yellow cake mix also and use Splenda to avoid sugar intake

Ingredients
- 1 1/2 cups all-purpose flour
- 1/2 teaspoon pumpkin pie spice
- 1 teaspoon ground cinnamon
- 1/4 teaspoon salt
- 1/2 teaspoon baking soda
- 1/2 teaspoon baking powder
- 1/2 cup butter
- 1 cup granulated sugar
- 2 large eggs
- 1 cup pumpkin puree
- 3/4 cup mini chocolate chips

Preparation Method
- In a medium bowl, mix the flour, spices, salt, baking soda, and baking powder and set aside.
- In the bowl of a stand mixer cream the butter and the sugar until fluffy, about two minutes. Add eggs one at a time mixing well after each addition. Add the pumpkin and mix until combine well.
- Add the dry ingredients mixing until just combined. Stir in chocolate chips.
- Spoon batter into half sized bundt pan sprayed with non-stick spray. Cover with foil.
- Pour 1 1/2 cups of water into the pressure cooker and place the trivet in the bottom. Close and set the timer for 25 minutes. When beep sounds, turn off pressure cooker and use a natural pressure release for 10 minutes.
- Carefully remove the bundt pan to a wire rack to cool uncovered for 10 minutes. After 10 minutes, remove from pan and cool on a wire rack.

Nutritional Information
- Preparation Time: 50 minutes
- Total Servings: 8
- Amount per Serving: 1
- Calories: 236
- Calories from Fat: 111
- Total Fat: 12.4g
- Saturated Fat: 2.4g
- Cholesterol: 46mg
- Sodium: 241mg
- Potassium: 107mg
- Total Carbohydrates: 30.5g
- Fiber: 1.4g
- Sugar: 20.4g
- Protein: 3.5g

Recipe 22: Egg Muffins

Tips to cook properly
- Make sure that, you fill muffin cups to about ¾ full

Ingredients
- 4 eggs
- 1/4 teaspoon lemon pepper
- 4 tablespoons shredded cheddar cheese
- 1 green onion
- 4 slices cooked bacon

Preparation Method
- Put the steamer basket in the electric pressure cooker pot and add 1 1/2 cups water.
- Break eggs into a large measuring bowl with pour spout, add lemon pepper, and beat well.
- Divide the cheese, bacon and green onion evenly between the four silicone muffin cups. Pour the beaten eggs into each muffin cup and stir with a fork to combine.
- Place muffin cups in a steamer basket and steamer basket in a pressure cooker. Select 8 minutes cook time. When the timer beeps, turn off, wait two minutes and lift out the steamer basket, and remove muffin cups.
- Serve immediately or muffins will keep more than a week in the refrigerator. Microwave on high about 30 seconds to reheat.

Nutritional Information
- Preparation Time: 10 minutes
- Total Servings: 5
- Amount per Serving: 2
- Calories: 147
- Calories from Fat: 52
- Total Fat: 3.8g
- Saturated Fat: 1.1g
- Cholesterol: 157mg
- Sodium: 612 mg
- Potassium: 432mg
- Total Carbohydrates: 5g
- Fiber: 1.3g
- Sugar: 2.9g
- Protein: 15.6g

Recipe 23: Cinnamon Raisin Bread Pudding

Tips to cook properly
- Aluminum foil helps keep food moist, ensures it cooks evenly, keeps leftovers fresh, and makes clean-up easy.

Ingredients
- 4 tablespoons butter
- 1/2 cup brown sugar
- 3 cups whole milk
- 3 eggs
- 1 teaspoon vanilla extract
- 1/2 teaspoon ground cinnamon
- 1/4 teaspoon salt
- 7 (3/4 inch) thick slices cinnamon bread
- 1/2 cup raisins

Caramel Pecan Sauce:
- 3/4 cup brown sugar
- 1/4 cup corn syrup
- 2 tablespoons heavy cream
- 2 tablespoons butter
- 1/2 teaspoon salt
- 1 teaspoon vanilla extract
- 1/2 cup pecans

Preparation Method
- In a large bowl, whisk together melted butter, brown sugar, milk, beaten eggs, vanilla, cinnamon, and salt. Mix in cubed bread and raisins. Let rest 20 minutes until the bread absorbs the milk, stirring occasionally.
- Pour bread pudding into a buttered 1 1/2-quart glass or metal baking dish (be sure it fits in your electric pressure cooking pot). Cover dish with foil. Prepare a foil sling for lifting the dish out of the pressure cooking pot by taking an 18" strip of foil and folding it lengthwise twice.
- Pour 1 1/2 cups water into the electric pressure cooking pot and place the trivet in the bottom. Center the dish on the foil strip and lower it into the pressure cooker.
- Select and set the timer for 20 minutes. When beep sounds, turn off the pressure cooker, remove the dish from pressure cooking pot. If desired, put the dish in preheated 350° oven for 5 - 10 minutes to crisp up the top.

Prepare Caramel Pecan Sauce:
- In a small saucepan, combine brown sugar, corn syrup, heavy cream, butter, and salt. Cook over medium heat, stirring constantly until sauce comes to a boil. Reduce heat and simmer until sugar is dissolved and sauce is smooth. Stir in vanilla and chopped pecans.

Nutritional Information
- Preparation Time: 50 minutes
- Total Servings: 6
- Amount per Serving: 1

- Calories: 540
- Calories from Fat: 250
- Total Fat: 27.8g
- Saturated Fat: 15.7g
- Cholesterol: 103mg
- Sodium: 329mg
- Potassium: 196mg
- Total Carbohydrates: 68.2g
- Fiber: 1.2g
- Sugar: 50.3g
- Protein: 7.8g

Recipe 24: Crustless Meat Quiche

Tips to cook properly
- Make sure that cheese and broil melted to light brown color

Ingredients
- 6 large eggs
- 1/2 cup milk
- 1/4 teaspoon salt
- 1/8 teaspoon ground black pepper
- 4 slices bacon (cooked and crumbled)
- 1 cup cooked ground sausage
- 1/2 cup diced ham
- 2 large green onions
- 1 cup shredded cheese

Preparation Method
- Put a metal trivet in the bottom of the electric pressure cooker pot and add 1 1/2 cups water.
- In a large bowl whisk together the eggs, milk, salt, and pepper. Add bacon, sausage, ham, green onions, and cheese to a 1-quart souffle dish and mix well. Pour egg mixture over to the top of the meat and stir to combine.
- Loosely cover the souffle dish with aluminum foil. Use an aluminum foil sling to place the dish on the trivet in the electric pressure cooking pot.
- Select 30 minutes cook time. When timer beeps, turn off, wait 10 minutes, then use a quick pressure release.
- Carefully lift out the dish and remove the foil. If desired, sprinkle the top of the quiche with additional cheese and broil until melted and lightly browned. Serve immediately.

Nutritional Information
- Preparation Time: 50 minutes
- Total Servings: 4
- Amount per Serving: 1
- Calories: 291
- Calories from Fat: 169
- Total Fat: 18.8g
- Saturated Fat: 9.3g
- Cholesterol: 170mg
- Sodium: 804mg
- Potassium: 243mg
- Total Carbohydrates: 12.9g
- Fiber: 0.4g
- Sugar: 3.7g
- Protein: 17g

Recipe 25: Cranberry Baked French Toast

Tips to cook properly
- Make sure that, you select high pressure while cooking

Ingredients

Cranberry Orange Sauce:
- 2 cups fresh cranberries
- 1/4 cup fresh orange juice
- 1/2 cup granulated sugar
- 1/4 teaspoon ground cinnamon
- 1/4 teaspoon salt

French Toast:
- 4 tablespoons butter
- 1/2 cup sugar
- 2 cups whole milk
- 3 eggs
- 1 orange zest
- 1 teaspoon vanilla extract
- 1/4 teaspoon salt
- 1 loaf challah bread

Preparation Method
- Bring cranberries, orange juice, 1/2 cup sugar, 1/4 teaspoon cinnamon, and 1/4 teaspoon salt to a boil in a saucepan over medium-high heat.
- Cook until the berries have popped and thickened slightly about 5 minutes. Remove from heat. Pour into a buttered 7x3" cake pan, or similar glass or metal baking dish. (Be sure it fits in your electric pressure cooking)
- In a large bowl, whisk together melted butter and 1/2 cup sugar. Add milk, beaten eggs, orange zest, vanilla, and salt. Mix in cubed bread. Let rest until the bread absorbs the milk, stirring occasionally.
- Spread bread mixture on top of cranberry sauce in the pan. Prepare a foil sling for lifting the dish out of the electric pressure cooking pot by taking an 18" strip of foil and folding it lengthwise twice.
- Pour 1 cup water into the electric pressure cooking pot and place the trivet in the bottom. Center the pan on the foil strip and lower it into the pressure cooker.
- Select High Pressure and set the timer for 25 minutes. Remove dish from pressure cooking pot. If desired, put the dish under the broiler to brown up the top.

Nutritional Information
- Preparation Time: 35 minutes
- Total Servings: 6-8
- Amount per Serving: 1
- Calories: 332
- Calories from Fat: 128
- Total Fat: 14.3g

- Saturated Fat: 4.7g
- Cholesterol: 138mg
- Sodium: 454mg
- Potassium: 237mg
- Total Carbohydrates: 38.9g
- Fiber: 2.6g
- Sugar: 7.3g
- Protein: 13.3g

Recipe 26: Tomato Spinach Quiche

Tips to cook properly
- Be careful while lifting the dish from cooking

Ingredients
- 12 large eggs
- 1/2 cup milk
- 1/2 teaspoon salt
- 1/4 teaspoon fresh ground black pepper
- 3 cups fresh baby spinach
- 1 cup diced seeded tomato
- 3 large green onions
- 4 tomato slices for topping the quiche
- 1/4 cup shredded Parmesan cheese

Preparation Method
- Put a trivet in the bottom of the electric pressure cooker pot and add 1 1/2 cups water.
- In a large bowl whisk together the eggs, milk, salt, and pepper. Add chopped spinach, tomato, and green onions to a 1 1/2 quart baking dish and mix well.
- Pour egg mixture over the veggies and stir to combine. Gently place sliced tomatoes on top and sprinkle with Parmesan cheese.
- Use a sling to place the dish on the trivet in the electric pressure cooking pot. Select 20 minutes cook time. When timer beeps, turn off, wait 10 minutes.
- Carefully open the lid, lift out the dish and if desired, broil until lightly browned.

Nutritional Information
- Preparation Time: 40 minutes
- Total Servings: 6
- Amount per Serving: 1
- Calories: 274
- Calories from Fat: 5.2
- Total Fat: 17.1g
- Saturated Fat: 5.2g
- Cholesterol: 136mg
- Sodium: 442mg
- Potassium: 195mg
- Total Carbohydrates: 19
- Fiber: 2g
- Sugar: 1.2g
- Protein: 11.4g

Recipe 27: Breakfast Berry Cake

Tips to cook properly
- Make sure that when you are adding batter, swirl in with a knife

Ingredients

Breakfast Cake:
- 5 eggs
- 1/4 cup sugar
- 2 tablespoons butter
- 3/4 cup ricotta cheese
- 3/4 cup vanilla yogurt
- 2 teaspoons vanilla extract
- 1 cup wheat flour
- 1/2 teaspoon salt
- 2 teaspoons baking powder
- 1/2 cup Berry Compote
- Sweet Yogurt Glaze
- Berry Compote

Sweet Yogurt Glaze:
- 1/4 cup yogurt
- 1/2 teaspoon vanilla extract
- 1 teaspoon milk
- 2 tablespoons powdered sugar

Preparation Method
- Prepare the Berry Compote beforehand so it is cold and thick. If used warm, it has a tendency to sink to the bottom of the pan. For the Breakfast Cake, generously grease a 6 cup bundt pan with nonstick cooking spray.
- Beat together the eggs and sugar until smooth. Add the butter, ricotta cheese, yogurt, and vanilla and mix until smooth.
- In a separate bowl, whisk together the flour, salt, and baking powder. Combine with the egg mixture. Pour into the prepared bundt pan.
- Using 1/2 cup of Berry Compote, drop by tablespoons on top of the batter and swirl in with a knife.
- Add 1 cup of water to the electric pressure cooker pot and place a trivet inside. Carefully place the bundt pan on the trivet. Cook at high pressure for 25 minutes.
- While the cake is cooking, make the Sweet Yogurt Glaze by whisking together the yogurt, vanilla, milk, and powdered sugar, set aside.
- When electric pressure cooking is done, remove the pan from the electric pressure cooker. Let cool slightly. Loosen the sides of the cake from the pan and gently turn over onto a plate. Drizzle with Sweet Yogurt Glaze and serve warm.

Nutritional Information
- Preparation Time: 35 minutes
- Total Servings: 6

- Amount per Serving: 1
- Calories: 440
- Calories from Fat: 148
- Total Fat: 17.5g
- Saturated Fat: 4.9g
- Cholesterol: 54mg
- Sodium: 457mg
- Potassium: 82mg
- Total Carbohydrates: 67.6g
- Fiber: 1.4g
- Sugar: 36.3g
- Protein: 4.5g

Recipe 28: Bread Pudding

Tips to cook properly
- Use a casserole dish that is sloped up to 8 inches in diameter and 3 inches high and wait an additional 15 minutes before removing

Ingredients
- Coconut oil 1 teaspoon
- Coconut milk 1 cup
- Whole milk 1 cup
- Beaten eggs 3
- Stale bread 4 cups
- Cranraisins ½ cup
- Cinnamon 1 teaspoon
- Salt ¼ teaspoon
- Vanilla extract ½ teaspoon

Preparation Method
- Put 2 cups of water in the electric pressure cooker inner pot
- Use a casserole small enough to fit into the pot, but large enough to hold the bread and liquids
- Cut bread in cubes and mix the rest of the ingredients in a bowl to combine. Put in the cubed bread crumbs. Mix well
- Set cooker to steam and adjust time to 15 minutes

Nutritional Information
- Preparation Time: 30 minutes
- Total Servings: 4
- Amount per Serving: 1
- Calories: 450
- Calories from Fat: 199
- Total Fat: 22.7g
- Saturated Fat: 5.1g
- Cholesterol: 141mg
- Sodium: 392mg
- Potassium: 303mg
- Total Carbohydrates: 50.3g
- Fiber: 2.8g
- Sugar: 22.9g
- Protein: 13.7g

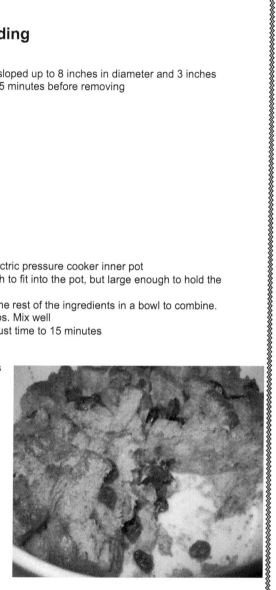

Recipe 29: Beef Sandwich

Tips to cook properly
- Make sure that bread is steamed with butter or purified butter

Ingredients
- 900g Beef
- 2 cups Water
- 4 cups shredded cabbage
- 1/2 cup barbecue sauce
- 1 cup ketchup
- 1/3 cup Worcestershire Sauce
- 1 tablespoon horseradish
- 1 tablespoon mustard

Preparation Method
- Add and stir in ingredients to your pressure cooker and set it on the "Meat" setting (approximately 35 minutes).
- Pull out the Beef and fork shred it. Return it to the sauce and simmer until it cooks down. Do this on the "Sauté" setting.
- I make a steamed bread and put pulled barbecue beef on top of bread along with Swiss or Cheddar Cheeses and grilled caramelized Sweet Vidalia Onions or fried Onion Ring.

Nutritional Information
- Preparation Time: 40 minutes
- Total Servings: 4-5
- Amount per Serving: 1
- Calories: 452
- Calories from Fat: 284
- Total Fat: 31.6g
- Saturated Fat: 10.5g
- Cholesterol: 70mg
- Sodium: 2011mg
- Potassium: 247mg
- Total Carbohydrates: 22g
- Fiber: 0.8g
- Sugar: 16.3g
- Protein: 18.1g

Recipe 30: Carrot Cake Oatmeal

Tips to cook properly
- Top with additional nuts and maple for better taste

Ingredients
- 1 tablespoon butter
- 1 cup steel cut oats
- 4 cups water
- 1 cup grated carrots
- 3 tablespoons maple syrup
- 2 teaspoons cinnamon
- 1 teaspoon pumpkin pie spice
- 1/4 teaspoon salt
- 3/4 cup raisins
- 1/4 cup chia seeds

Preparation Method
- Add butter to electric pressure cooking pot, select Sauté. When butter is melted add the oats and toast, stirring constantly, until they smell nutty, about 3 minutes.
- Add water, carrots, maple syrup, cinnamon, pumpkin pie spice, and salt. Select 10 minutes cook time.
- When beep sounds, carefully remove the lid and stir oats, raisins and chia seeds. Cover and let sit five or 10 minutes until oats are desired thickness. Top with additional raisins, maple syrup, chopped nuts, and milk.

Nutritional Information
- Preparation Time: 18 minutes
- Total Servings: 6
- Amount per Serving: 1
- Calories: 160
- Calories from Fat: 16
- Total Fat: 3.4
- Saturated Fat: 0.5g
- Cholesterol: 10mg
- Sodium: 164mg
- Potassium: 180mg
- Total Carbohydrates: 30.8g
- Fiber: 4.1g
- Sugar: 14.4g
- Protein: 4.6g

Recipe 1: Pineapple and Cauliflower Rice

Tips to cook properly
- If you desire, add chopped cashews and peanuts

Ingredients
- 2 cups of rice
- 1/2 minced pineapple
- 1 minced cauliflower
- 2 teaspoons oil
- 1 teaspoon salt

Preparation Method
- Put all ingredients into the electric pressure cooker and then press the rice button. Then that is it, simple, fast, delicious, retaining flavor and nutrition, consistent results all the time.

Nutritional Information
- Preparation Time: 30 minutes
- Total Servings: 6
- Calories: 257
- Calories from Fat: 57
- Total Fat: 4.1g
- Saturated Fat: 1.1g
- Cholesterol: 0mg
- Sodium:598mg
- Potassium: 456mg
- Total Carbohydrates: 43.2g
- Fiber: 4.2g
- Sugar: 3.3g
- Protein:5g

Recipe 2: Bavarian Red Cabbage

Tips to cook properly
- It should not be blended more and it is a traditional favorite for a german feast

Ingredients
- 1000g red cabbage
- 2 tablespoons unsalted butter
- 1 large onion, small dice
- 2 large granny smith apple
- 1/4 cup red wine vinegar
- 1 cup dry red wine
- 3 bay leaves
- 1 cup beef broth
- 2 teaspoons salt
- 1/2 teaspoon ground cloves
- 1 cinnamon stick
- 3 tablespoons brown sugar
- 2 tablespoons all-purpose flour

Preparation Method
- Put cabbage in a food processor fitted with a slicing disk. Set aside.
- Set pressure cooker to Sauté and add butter and let melt. Add the onion and apple and Sauté until very soft, about 10 minutes. Hit Cancel button. Add the cabbage.
- Add the red wine vinegar, red wine, beef broth, bay leaves, salt, cinnamon stick, ground cloves and brown sugar. Sprinkle flour over top of cabbage and gently stir, just until you don't see any lumps.
- Select manual and adjust the time to 10 minutes. Do a quick release 10 minutes after the end of cooking cycle. Hit Cancel. Press Sauté and adjust to More. Bring to a boil and add corn starch slurry. Stir and let boil for about 5 minutes until thickened.

Nutritional Information
- Preparation Time: 30 minutes
- Total Servings: 6-8
- Amount per Serving: 150g
- Calories: 120
- Calories from Fat: 33
- Total Fat: 3.7g
- Saturated Fat: 0.5g
- Cholesterol: 0mg
- Sodium: 170mg
- Potassium: 180mg
- Total Carbohydrates: 22.4g
- Fiber: 3.2g
- Sugar: 15.5g
- Protein: 1.8g

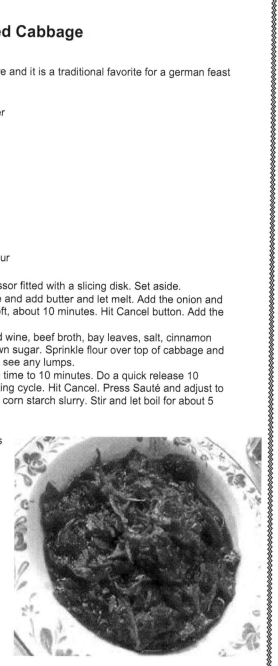

Recipe 3: Red Borscht Soup

Tips to cook properly

- Don't forget to add sour cream and parsley as a topping

Ingredients

- 3 large beets
- 3 carrots
- 3 red potatoes
- 1 tablespoon vegetable oil
- 1 medium onion chopped
- Fresh dill (for taste)
- Water with beef bouillon powder
- 2 cups of sauerkraut
- ½ fresh shredded cabbage
- ½ sauerkraut
- 2 cups fresh tomatoes
- 3 cloves garlic
- Salt and pepper
- 1 tablespoon Red wine vinegar
- 1 tablespoon sugar
- Topping: 1/4 cup sour cream
- Garnish: fresh parsley

Preparation Method

- Place your beets on steaming rack into the pressure cooker. Put in a cup and a half water into the pressure cooker and pressure cook beets for about 30 minutes.
- Dice the beets and cut fresh beet tops into one-inch pieces.
- Clean pressure cooker pot and add oil and put on Sauté. When the oil is hot, Sauté the onions, parsley, pepper, salt and dill until onions translucent.
- Now add sliced beets, carrots, potatoes, sauerkraut, tomatoes, garlic to pot. Add water to make as thin or thick a soup as you like.
- Add wine vinegar, sugar, and ketchup and stir. Taste it to see if right sweet/sour consistency for you pressure cook for 10 minutes.
- Let pressure release naturally. Scoop the wonderful vegetables into a bowl, top with sour cream and fresh parsley.

Nutritional Information

- Preparation Time: 45 minutes
- Total Servings: 6
- Calories: 299
- Calories from Fat: 148
- Total Fat: 12.5g
- Saturated Fat: 4.8g
- Sodium: 762mg
- Potassium: 921mg
- Total Carbohydrates: 28.2g
- Fiber: 5.5g
- Sugar: 9.8g
- Protein: 14.1g

Recipe 4: Mashed Potatoes with Greek Yogurt

Tips to cook properly

- Add grated cheese when potatoes are hot in serving bowl

Ingredients

- 680g peeled baking potatoes
- 1/2 cup water
- 1/2 tablespoon butter
- 1/2 cup skim milk
- 1/2 cup whole milk Greek yogurt
- 1/2 teaspoon minced garlic
- 1/2 teaspoon salt
- 1/2 teaspoon pepper
- Garnish: cheddar cheese

Preparation Method

- Pour 1/2 cup water in the pressure cooker, add the trivet that came with the pot, set the potatoes on top of the trivet.
- Press the steam button, and set the time to 35 minutes, do a quick release of the pressure. Insert a fork in the largest potato to confirm that it is soft in the middle.
- Turn the cooker off. With the potatoes still piping hot and still in the pot, add the butter, half of the skim milk, yogurt and garlic.
- Insert a potato masher and mash the potatoes and add a little more of the skim milk until you reach the consistency.
- Add salt and pepper to taste. Transfer the mashed potatoes to a serving bowl and garnish with grated cheese.

Nutritional Information

- Preparation Time: 40 minutes
- Total Servings: 6
- Calories: 115
- Calories from Fat: 2
- Total Fat: 0.2g
- Saturated Fat: 0g
- Cholesterol: 2mg
- Sodium: 154mg
- Potassium: 575mg
- Total Carbohydrates: 25.1g
- Fiber: 3g
- Sugar: 1.2g
- Protein: 5.8g

Recipe 5: Pressure Cooker Pork Carrot Soup

Tips to cook properly
- Add sea salt in final stage of cooking

Ingredients
- 680 grams carrots
- 800 grams green radish
- 680 grams pork shank
- 4 liters water
- 1 ginger
- 2 dried jujubes
- 1 small piece of chenpi
- Sea salt (as needed)

Preparation Method
- Clean the Pork Shank; bring 2 liters of water to a boil. Then, boil the pork shank for 3 minutes to clean and remove the excess fat. Remove the pork shank and rinse it in cold tap water. We take this step whenever we make Chinese soups with pork shank or any other bones and meat.
- Prepare the ingredients; soak 1 small piece of chenpi in cold water for 20 minutes. Wash the dried jujubes with cold running tap water. Prepare the rest of the ingredients as listed.
- Pressure cooker soup; place all the ingredients into the pressure cooker. Pour 2 liters of cold running tap water into the pot. Do not add any salt. Keep pressure cooks at high pressure for 30 minutes.
- Heat up the pressure cooker to bring the soup back to a full boil. Add sea salt to taste. Serve hot.

Nutritional Information
- Preparation Time: 60 minutes
- Total Servings: 6-8
- Calories: 115
- Calories from Fat: 46
- Total Fat: 12.1g
- Saturated Fat: 1.6g
- Cholesterol: 2mg
- Sodium: 516mg
- Potassium: 297mg
- Total Carbohydrates: 13.7g
- Fiber: 2.9g
- Sugar: 6.9g
- Protein: 5g

Recipe 6: Pressure Cooker Cassoulet

Tips to cook properly
- Try to use a liner in your cooker for easier cleanup

Ingredients
- 2 tablespoons olive oil
- 900g boneless pork ribs (cut into 1-inch)
- 2 cups great northern beans
- 1 cup beef broth
- 1 carrot, diced
- 1 celery stalk, diced
- ½ white onion, diced
- 2 tablespoons dried rosemary
- 4 cloves garlic, minced
- 2 cups herbed croutons
- Optional: 1 cup goat cheese

Preparation Method
- Heat olive oil over medium-high heat in a large skillet. Sprinkle pork ribs with salt and pepper, then brown in the skillet on all sides.
- Add the pork to the electric pressure cooker, and then add the beans, broth, carrot, celery, onion, rosemary and garlic. Cook on the stew setting for 35 minutes.
- Dish cassoulet into 4-6 large soup bowls, then top with equal amounts of croutons and goat cheese. Serve.

Nutritional Information
- Preparation Time: 45 minutes
- Total Servings: 4-6
- Calories: 521
- Calories from Fat: 190
- Total Fat: 20.8g
- Saturated Fat: 6.1g
- Cholesterol: 104mg
- Sodium: 521mg
- Potassium: 998mg
- Total Carbohydrates: 40.2
- Fiber: 12.3g
- Sugar: 3.4g
- Protein: 21.7g

Recipe 7: Kale Soup

Tips to cook properly
- Don't Sauté kale more and try to avoid more grated cheese

Ingredients
- 1 small chopped onion
- 100g kale
- 2 tablespoons coconut or almond milk
- 1 teaspoon ground garlic
- 100g ground sausage
- 50g potatoes
- 1 tablespoon thyme
- 120ml chicken stock
- red pepper and salt (as needed)
- Topping: parmesan cheese

Preparation Method
- Put onion, garlic and ground sausage and press Sauté button.
- Add potatoes and seasoning (thyme, salt, a little crushed red pepper) and chicken stock, stir well.
- Hit soup button and set timer for 25 minutes, add chopped kale and a generous coconut/almond milk, continue to heat on "Sauté" if needed.
- Serve topped with a little Parmesan. It tastes great next day also.

Nutritional Information
- Preparation Time: 30 minutes
- Total Servings: 3
- Calories: 266
- Calories from Fat: 155
- Total Fat: 17g
- Saturated Fat: 8.1g
- Cholesterol: 45mg
- Sodium: 389mg
- Potassium: 466mg
- Total Carbohydrates: 16.1g
- Fiber: 1.5g
- Sugar: 3.1g
- Protein: 10.6g

Recipe 8: Salsa Shredded Chicken

Tips to cook properly
- Try to put salsa only on top on chicken pieces

Ingredients
- 450g chicken breast
- 1/2 teaspoon kosher salt
- 3/4 teaspoon cumin
- Pinch black pepper
- Pinch oregano
- 1 cup chunky salsa

Preparation Method
- Season chicken on both sides with spices.
- Place into the electric pressure cooker and cover with salsa.
- over and press the "poultry" button then add 5 minutes to cook the chicken for a total of 20 minutes.
- Once the cooker releases the pressure, put the chicken onto a plate and use two forks to shred.
- Makes 2 1/2 cups chicken.

Nutritional Information
- Preparation Time: 25 minutes
- Total Servings: 5
- Calories: 125
- Calories from Fat: 68
- Total Fat: 6g
- Saturated Fat: 2.2g
- Cholesterol: 66mg
- Sodium: 379mg
- Potassium:
- Total Carbohydrates: 3g
- Fiber: 1g
- Sugar: 0g
- Protein: 22g

Recipe 9: Sweet Pineapple and Ginger Risotto

Tips to cook properly
- Before serving, try to add little extra coconut on top for delicious taste

Ingredients
- 4 cups non-dairy milk
- 1 3/4 cups risotto rice
- 1/2 cup unsweetened coconut
- 560g pineapple
- 1/4 cup candied ginger
- Garnish: Cilantro, lime

Preparation Method
- Place all of the above items into the pressure cooker.
- Press the "Manual" button and adjust the time to 12 minutes.
- Serve immediately and enjoy

Nutritional Information
- Preparation Time: 15 minutes
- Total Servings: 3
- Calories: 266
- Calories from Fat: 51
- Total Fat: 5.6g
- Saturated Fat: 1.1g
- Cholesterol: 46
- Sodium: 374mg
- Potassium: 256mg
- Total Carbohydrates: 39.6g
- Fiber: 1.7g
- Sugar: 5.5g
- Protein: 7.8g

Recipe 10: Cooked Vegetable Duck

Tips to cook properly
- Before serving sprinkle little pepper on top

Ingredients
- 1 medium size duck
- 1 cucumber cut into pieces
- 2 carrots cut into pieces
- 1 tablespoon cooking wine
- 2 cups water
- 1 small piece of ginger cut into pieces
- 2 teaspoons salt

Preparation Method
- Put all ingredients into the electric pressure cooker and then press the meat/stew button. Then that is it, simple, fast, delicious, retaining flavor and nutrition, consistent results all the time.

Nutritional Information
- Preparation Time: 40 minutes
- Total Servings: 6
- Calories: 199
- Calories from Fat: 64
- Total Fat: 2.9g
- Saturated Fat: 0.9g
- Cholesterol: 55mg
- Sodium: 567mg
- Potassium: 289mg
- Total Carbohydrates: 29.3g
- Fiber: 4.1g
- Sugar: 2.7g
- Protein: 19.3g

Recipe 11: Basmati Rice with Veggies

Tips to cook properly
- Before serving, try to add grated cheese

Ingredients
- 1/2 onion
- 1/2 teaspoon cumin
- 1 cup basmati rice
- 3 cup water
- 3/4 teaspoon salt
- 1/2 garam masala
- 1 tablespoon olive oil
- Optional: 1 1/2 cup frozen mixed vegetables

Preparation Method
- Turn pressure cooker to Sauté option, heat oil and add cumin,garam masala and stir to temper the spices. Then add onions and Sauté until they turn translucent.
- Add rice to the pan and pour in water. Stir in salt and switch pressure cooker over to rice until done. Stir and serve.
- Add frozen veggies to the top of the rice before closing lid. Once the rice has completed cooking, stir to incorporate the vegetables.

Nutritional Information
- Preparation Time: 30 minutes
- Total Servings: 4
- Calories: 366
- Calories from Fat: 182
- Total Fat: 20.3g
- Saturated Fat: 10g
- Cholesterol: 45mg
- Sodium: 1098mg
- Potassium: 227mg
- Total Carbohydrates: 31.8g
- Fiber: 3.8g
- Sugar: 0.6g
- Protein: 15.6g

Recipe 12: Balsamic Chicken Thighs

Tips to cook properly
- Before serving sprinkle with dry basil leaves and dry oregano

Ingredients
- 1800g chicken thighs
- 1/2 cup white vinegar
- 1/2 cup soy sauce
- 4 cloves garlic
- 1 teaspoon black peppercorns
- 3 bay leaves

Preparation Method
- Set your Pot to the Poultry setting and add the chicken and all ingredients. You do not have to Sauté anything.
- Close the lid, and cook for 15 minutes. Serve with white Jasmine rice.

Nutritional Information
- Preparation Time: 20 minutes
- Total Servings: 4-5
- Calories: 544
- Calories from Fat: 272
- Total Fat: 30.2g
- Saturated Fat: 6.7g
- Cholesterol: 142mg
- Sodium: 1852mg
- Potassium: 445mg
- Total Carbohydrates: 26.6g
- Fiber: 0.8g
- Sugar: 22g
- Protein: 38.9g

Recipe 13: Lime Chicken

Tips to cook properly
- Before serving, try to add fresh chopped basil leaves

Ingredients
- 900g boneless skinless chicken thighs
- 1 cup lime juice
- 1/2 cup fish sauce
- 1/4 cup olive oil
- 2 tablespoons coconut milk
- 1 tablespoon grated fresh ginger
- 1 tablespoon chopped fresh mint
- 2 tablespoon chopped fresh cilantro

Preparation Method
- Rinse chicken breasts and trim excess fat. Place in bottom of the instant pot.
- Combine all remaining ingredients in a mason jar and shake well. Pour over chicken.
- Select "poultry" Instant Pot setting and reduce time to 10 minutes.
- Use quick release lid setting when done. Drain excess liquid and enjoy.

Nutritional Information
- Preparation Time: 20 minutes
- Total Servings: 4
- Calories: 220
- Calories from Fat:96
- Total Fat:10.7g
- Saturated Fat: 4.5g
- Cholesterol: 84mg
- Sodium: 555mg
- Potassium: 341mg
- Total Carbohydrates: 2.6g
- Fiber: 0.3g
- Sugar: 0.6g
- Protein: 27.7g

Recipe 14: Chicken Stew with Corn

Tips to cook properly
- If you like you can add 1 more extra tablespoon of chopped cilantro

Ingredients
- 800g skinless chicken drumsticks
- 1/2 teaspoon kosher salt
- 1/2 teaspoon garlic powder
- 1 teaspoon olive oil
- 1/2 medium onion, chopped
- 3 scallions, chopped
- 1 plum tomato, diced
- 1 garlic, crushed
- 1/4 cup chopped cilantro
- 225g tomato sauce
- 2 cups water
- 1/2 teaspoon cumin
- 2 corn on the cobb
- Garnish: 1 tablespoon cilantro

Preparation Method
- Season chicken with salt and garlic powder.
- Sauté the onions, scallions, tomato and garlic in olive oil until soft, 2 to 3 minutes. Add 1/4 cup cilantro and stir 1 minute. Add tomato sauce, water, cumin, and stir.
- Place the chicken in the sauce. Top with corn, cover and cook on high pressure 20 minutes. Let pressure release and top with remaining cilantro.

Nutritional Information
- Preparation Time: 30 minutes
- Total Servings: 4
- Calories: 315
- Calories from Fat: 134
- Total Fat: 10g
- Saturated Fat: 0g
- Cholesterol: 177mg
- Sodium: 434mg
- Potassium: 948mg
- Total Carbohydrates: 18g
- Fiber: 3g
- Sugar: 4.5g
- Protein: 42g

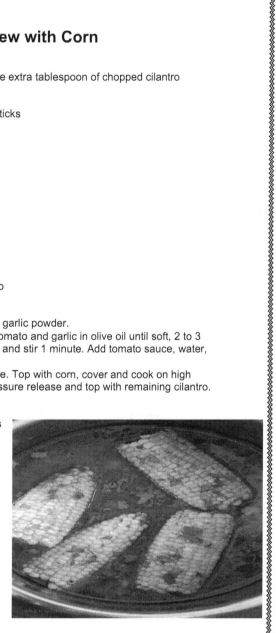

Recipe 15: Barbeque Pork

Tips to cook properly
- Aluminum foil can be used to keep food moist, cook it evenly, and make clean-up easier.

Ingredients
- Pork butt roast 3628g
- Garlic powder 1 teaspoon
- Salt and Pepper (as needed)
- Barbecue sauce 340g

Preparation Method
- Season the pork with garlic powder, salt, and pepper
- Place into a 4 to 6-quart pressure cooker, fill with enough water to cover
- Close the lid and cook for 1 hour. Release the pressure and drain off juices, reserving about 2 cups
- Shred the pork and mix with barbecue sauce, adding reserved liquid if needed to reach your desired consistency

Nutritional Information
- Preparation Time: 65 minutes
- Total Servings: 16
- Amount per Serving: 1 (220g)
- Calories: 353
- Calories from Fat: 192
- Total Fat: 21.3
- Saturated Fat: 7.8
- Cholesterol: 89
- Sodium: 537
- Potassium: 416
- Total Carbohydrates: 15.4
- Fiber: 0.3
- Sugar: 11
- Protein: 23.1

Recipe 16: Barbeque Chicken

Tips to cook properly
- The amount of chicken can be increased to up to 3 pounds in this recipe
- Make sure to cook the chicken long enough if not means sauce will be too watery

Ingredients
- Chicken thighs 900g
- Ground paprika 1 teaspoon
- Salt and pepper (as needed)
- Minced onion 1
- Water ½ cup
- Chile or hot sauce ½ cup
- Vinegar 2 tablespoons

Preparation Method
- Heat pressure cooker over medium heat and cook chicken until browned approximately 10 minutes. Sprinkle paprika, salt, and pepper onto chicken
- Combine onion, Chile sauce, water, and vinegar in a bowl; pour over chicken
- Close cooker over medium heat and cook according to manufacturer's instructions, approximately 15 minutes.
- Remove from heat and release pressure through natural release method and open pressure cooker carefully

Nutritional Information
- Preparation Time: 25 minutes
- Total Servings: 8
- Calories: 218
- Calories from Fat: 107
- Total Fat: 11.9
- Saturated Fat: 3.3
- Cholesterol: 71
- Sodium: 313
- Potassium: 280
- Total Carbohydrates: 7
- Fiber: 0.8
- Sugar: 3.1
- Protein: 19.8

Recipe 17: Braised Turkey Thighs

Tips to cook properly
- If you want dry, increase the cooking time or if you more gravy decrease the cooking time

Ingredients
- 2 turkey thighs
- 1 cup chicken broth
- 1 tablespoon red-wine vinegar
- 1 cup thinly sliced onions
- 1 cup sliced portobello mushrooms
- 2 teaspoons minced garlic
- ½ teaspoon each dried rosemary, sage, thyme, salt and pepper

Preparation Method
- Set pressure cooker to Sauté and brown the turkey thighs. Add the rest of the ingredients and set cooker to poultry setting and cook turkey for 1 hour
- After 1 hour, place a towel or pot holder over the pressure valve and do a quick pressure release, check for done-ness, if meat is not forked tender add 15 minutes and resume cooking on Poultry setting
- When meat is done, remove turkey thighs to cutting board and cover loosely with foil
- Making gravy, in a small bowl, whisk flour and water until well blended. Whisk flour mixture into liquid, onions, and mushrooms in cooker, mixing well
- Turn cooker to Keep warm and simmer the gravy for 15 minutes or until thickened.

Nutritional Information
- Preparation Time: 35 minutes
- Total Servings: 4
- Calories: 506
- Calories from Fat: 156
- Total Fat: 17.4g
- Saturated Fat: 4.8g
- Cholesterol: 178mg
- Sodium: 693mg
- Potassium: 847mg
- Total Carbohydrates: 9.6g
- Fiber: 1.8g
- Sugar: 3.6g
- Protein: 18.7g

Recipe 18: Honey Drumstick

Tips to cook properly

- Add roasted sesame seeds as a topping

Ingredients

- 1/4 cup soy sauce
- 3 tablespoons rice wine
- 2 tablespoons honey
- 2 cloves garlic
- 1 teaspoon fresh grated ginger
- 1 teaspoon sriracha sauce
- 8 chicken drumsticks
- 1 tablespoon sesame seeds (900g)
- Chopped scallions

Preparation Method

- Use Sauté button, when hot add soy sauce, rice wine, honey, garlic, ginger and sriracha and cook 2 minutes.
- Add the chicken. Cook on high pressure 15 to 20 minutes until the chicken is tender. When pressure releases, finish with scallions and sesame seeds.

Nutritional Information

- Preparation Time: 55 minutes
- Total Servings: 4
- Calories: 309
- Calories from Fat: 177
- Total Fat: 7.5g
- Saturated Fat: 1.1g
- Cholesterol: 152mg
- Sodium: 994mg
- Potassium:
- Total Carbohydrates: 22g
- Fiber: 0.5g
- Sugar: 18.5g
- Protein: 34.5g

Recipe 19: French Lentil Cassoulet with Pancetta

Tips to cook properly
- Add tablespoon of chopped fresh basil with cilantro and also lemon juice

Ingredients
- 5 tablespoons extra-virgin olive oil
- 110g pancetta (cut into 1/2-inch)
- 1 medium onion (cut into 1/2-inch)
- 450g french green lentils
- 4 fresh thyme sprigs
- 2 quarts water
- 1-quart chicken broth
- 1 large garlic clove
- Kosher salt (as needed)
- 8 pieces of chicken
- 3/4 pound garlic salami, sliced crosswise 1/2 inch thick
- 340g lean slab bacon (cut into 1-inch cubes)
- 4 tablespoons chopped parsley

Preparation Method
- In the cooker, use Sauté function to heat 3 tablespoons of the olive oil. Add the pancetta and onion and cook until the fat has been rendered about 5 minutes.
- Add the lentils, thyme, water, chicken broth, garlic, chicken, salami, and bacon.
- Use manual mode to cook for 15 minutes and let it cool for 10 minutes.
- Discard thyme, garlic clove and add salt to taste. Run the Sauté function to thicken the sauce. Stir in parsley and serve.

Nutritional Information
- Preparation Time: 30 minutes
- Total Servings: 8
- Calories: 439
- Calories from Fat: 211
- Total Fat: 14g
- Saturated Fat: 4g
- Cholesterol: 2.3mg
- Sodium: 324mg
- Potassium: 434mg
- Total Carbohydrates: 34g
- Fiber: 12g
- Sugar: g
- Protein: 21g

Recipe 20: Quinoa Soup with Beef

Tips to cook properly
- Add salt and pepper before serving

Ingredients
- 2 teaspoons olive oil
- 6-7 chopped scallions
- 2 cloves garlic
- 1 tomato
- 1 teaspoon cumin
- 1/2 teaspoon homemade seasonings
- 225g beef, cubed into small pieces
- 5 cups water
- Beef bullion
- 1 carrot
- 2 tablespoons yellow bell pepper
- 2 medium potatoes
- 1 cup cooked quinoa
- 6 tablespoons fresh chopped cilantro
- Salt and pepper (to taste)

Preparation Method
- Sauté oil in a pressure cooker; add scallions and garlic and Sauté until soft over medium heat, about 3 minutes. Add tomato, cumin, season with achiote, 1/4 cup cilantro and cook another 2 minutes.
- Add beef, water, bullion, carrot, bell pepper, salt and bring to a boil. cook on low about 45 minutes, until meat is tender.
- Add potato and cooked quinoa and cook an additional 10 minutes. Add remaining chopped cilantro and serve.

Nutritional Information
- Preparation Time: 60 minutes
- Total Servings: 4
- Calories: 307.9
- Calories from Fat: 152
- Total Fat: 13.8g
- Saturated Fat: 1.5g
- Cholesterol: 66mg
- Sodium: 379mg
- Potassium: 444mg
- Total Carbohydrates: 31.3g
- Fiber: 4.6g
- Sugar: 0g
- Protein: 15.7g

Recipe 21: Smoked Turkey mixed Bean Soup

Tips to cook properly
- Wait for natural release

Ingredients
- 1/2 tablespoons extra virgin light olive oil
- 1 large onion, chopped
- 1 carrot, chopped
- 1 celery stalk, chopped
- 1/2 cup chopped parsley
- 3 garlic cloves, through garlic press
- 6 cups water
- 1 smoked turkey drumstick
- 2 bay leaves
- 2 cups dried black beans
- 1 1/4 teaspoons kosher coarse salt
- 1/4 teaspoon fresh ground black pepper

Preparation Method
- Place the olive oil and onions, carrots, celery and parsley in an electric pressure cooker over medium-high heat and cook until fragrant, about 8 to 10 minutes.
- Add the garlic and cook 1 minute. Add water, bay leaves, beans, turkey leg, and black pepper and bring to boil. Cook for 45 minutes. Discard bay leaves and set turkey legs aside.
- Discard skin from the turkey leg and cut the meat off the bone into bite-size pieces.
- Using an immersion or traditional blender, puree the beans leaving the soup chunky, or to your desired consistency.
- If you use the immersion blender you can puree the beans right in the pressure cooker. If you use a traditional blender, blend in batches and return the beans to the pot after beans are pureed. Add the salt and return the turkey to the soup.

Nutritional Information
- Preparation Time: 55 minutes
- Total Servings: 8
- Calories: 133
- Calories from Fat:66
- Total Fat: 2g
- Saturated Fat: 0.8g
- Cholesterol: 21mg
- Sodium: 476mg
- Potassium: 345mg
- Total Carbohydrates: 26g
- Fiber: 16g
- Sugar: 1g
- Protein: 19g

Recipe 22: Sweet Glazed Meatloaf

Tips to cook properly
- You can add extra ketchup before serving

Ingredients

Meatloaf:
- 450g ground beef
- 2/3 cup bread crumbs
- 1 egg white
- 1 small onion diced
- 6 black olives
- 2 fresh basil leaves
- 1/2 teaspoon salt
- 1/2 teaspoon black pepper
- 2 tablespoons ketchup
- 1 teaspoon minced garlic
- 1 tablespoon ground flaxseed

Glaze:
- 1 tablespoon brown sugar
- 1 tablespoon spicy brown mustard
- 1/4 cup ketchup

Preparation Method
- Mix all ingredients except the glaze ingredients together by hand and then form a loaf in the Pyrex dish.
- Stir the glaze ingredients together, and then spread the glaze on top of the meatloaf. Cover the Pyrex bowl tightly with foil.
- Pour one cup of water into the pressure cooker, add the provided trivet, and then place your meatloaf on top of the trivet. Press the Meat/Stew button, and set the time for 45 minutes and walk away.
- When the cooker beeps that it is finished, do a quick pressure release.

Nutritional Information
- Preparation Time: 50 minutes
- Total Servings: 4
- Calories: 270
- Calories from Fat:181
- Total Fat: 20.1g
- Saturated Fat: 7.9g
- Cholesterol: 112mg
- Sodium: 763mg
- Potassium: 375mg
- Total Carbohydrates: 24.1g
- Fiber: 0.4g
- Sugar: 11.4g
- Protein: 18.4g

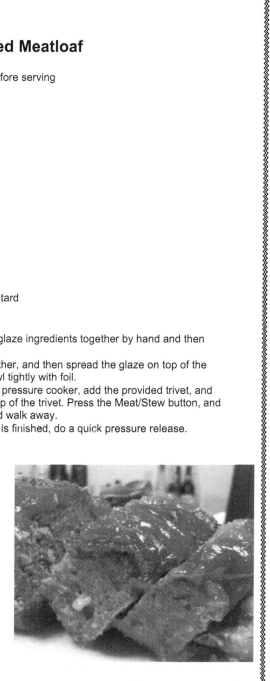

Recipe 23: Pressure Cooker Pasta Meal

Tips to cook properly
- Before serving add chopped basil and grated cheese

Ingredients
- 1 tablespoon olive oil
- 100g bacon
- 500g sausage meat
- 1 chopped onion
- 2 cloves garlic
- 2 cups tomato puree
- 500g pasta (tortellini)
- Water to cover the pasta
- 1 tablespoon chopped basil
- 1/4 cup parmesan cheese

Preparation Method
- Set the pressure cooker on Sauté. Once it says hot, add the olive oil. Render the bacon about 3-4 minutes. Remove the bacon onto a plate and brown sausage meat until cooked through.
- Add the onion and garlic and Sauté them for a few minutes, scraping the up the brown bits from the bottom of the pot as you go.
- Cancel the Sauté mode. Pour in the tomato puree and salt to taste. Add dry pasta and stir to coat, then flatten until level. Add water to just cover the pasta.
- Choose manual, low pressure for 5-8 minutes. Once the cooking is done, release the pressure by the quick pressure release. Stir in chopped basil and parmesan cheese.

Nutritional Information
- Preparation Time: 20 minutes
- Total Servings: 4
- Calories: 293
- Calories from Fat: 91
- Total Fat: 10.1g
- Saturated Fat: 2.9g
- Cholesterol: 24mg
- Sodium: 1159mg
- Potassium: 634mg
- Total Carbohydrates: 35.5g
- Fiber: 6.7g
- Sugar: 2.4g
- Protein: 15.4g

Recipe 24: Barbacoa Beef

Tips to cook properly
- Garnish with chopped red onions, cilantro, lime pieces before serving

Ingredients
- 5 cloves garlic
- 1/2 medium onion
- 1 lime juice
- 4 tablespoons chipotles in adobo sauce
- 1 tablespoon ground cumin
- 1 tablespoon ground oregano
- 1/2 teaspoon ground cloves
- 1 cup water
- 1350g beef eye of round or bottom round roast
- 2 1/2 teaspoons kosher salt
- black pepper
- 1 teaspoon oil
- 3 bay leaves

Preparation Method
- Place garlic, onion, lime juice, cumin, oregano, chipotles, cloves and water in a blender and puree until smooth.
- Trim all the fat off meat, cut into 3-inch pieces. Season with 2 teaspoons salt and black pepper. Heat the pressure cooker on high (use Sauté button on the cooker), when hot add the oil and brown the meat, in batches on all side, about 5 minutes.
- Add the sauce from the blender and bay leaves, cover and cook on the high pressure until the meat is tender and easily shreds with 2 forks, about 65 minutes.
- Once cooked and the meat is tender, remove the meat and place in a dish. Shred with two forks, and reserve the liquid for later (discard the bay leaf).
- Return the shredded meat to the pot, add 1/2 teaspoon salt or to taste, 1/2 tsp cumin and 1 1/2 cups of the reserved liquid.

Nutritional Information
- Preparation Time: 80 minutes
- Total Servings: 9
- Calories: 153
- Calories from Fat: 65
- Total Fat: 4.5g
- Saturated Fat: 2.3g
- Cholesterol: 44mg
- Sodium: 334.5mg
- Potassium: 656mg
- Total Carbohydrates: 2g
- Fiber: 0g
- Sugar: 0g
- Protein: 24g

Recipe 25: Buffalo Chicken Macaroni Cheese

Tips to cook properly
- Top the macaroni and feta with another layer of celery before serving, if desired.

Ingredients
- 450g frozen chicken tenders
- 3 cups rigatoni Pasta (uncooked)
- 3 cups chicken stock
- 1 small onion chopped
- 3 ribs celery chopped
- 4 large chopped carrots
- 2/3 cup hot wing sauce
- 1 tablespoon ranch seasoning
- ½ cups light whipped cream cheese
- 1 cup shredded sharp cheddar
- 1 cup shredded macaroni
- 1/2 cup feta cheese

Preparation Method
- Place the tenders, pasta, stock, celery, onions, carrots, wing sauce and ranch seasoning into the electric pressure cooker.
- Stir and press the rice function and set the timer for 15 minutes. When cook time is complete, open and stir in the cream cheese till dissolved.
- Add the cheddar, mozzarella, and feta and again stir till dissolved.

Nutritional Information
- Preparation Time: 20 minutes
- Total Servings: 6
- Calories: 304
- Calories from Fat: 137
- Total Fat: 15.2g
- Saturated Fat: 3.8g
- Cholesterol: 37mg
- Sodium: 608mg
- Potassium: 281mg
- Total Carbohydrates: 24.3
- Fiber: 0.9g
- Sugar: 4.4g
- Protein:17g

Recipe 26: Spaghetti Squash with Meat Sauce

Tips to cook properly
- It will taste better if you add grounded cheese on top before serving

Ingredients
- 450g ground beef
- 1 small chopped onion
- 3 cloves crushed garlic
- 1 teaspoon kosher salt
- black pepper, to taste
- 800g crushed tomatoes
- bay leaf
- pecorino romano cheese
- 1800g spaghetti squash
- Topping: grated cheese

Preparation Method
- Sauté the beef with onion, garlic, salt, pepper. Added crushed tomatoes, bay leaf and cheese rind, stir. Pierce the spaghetti squash all over with a knife and place over the sauce.
- Cook high pressure 15 minutes, or until the skin of squash easily gives when pressed with a spoon. Let the pressure release, discard bay leaf and rind and transfer the squash to a bowl to let cool.
- When cool enough to handle, cut in half with a large knife, discard the seeds and scoop the strands out with a fork. Place in a colander to drain well (I use paper towels as well to soak up any excess moisture) then serve sauce over squash with grated cheese if desired.

Nutritional Information
- Preparation Time: 30 minutes
- Total Servings: 6
- Amount per Serving: 1 cup
- Calories: 210
- Calories from Fat: 89
- Total Fat: 6g
- Saturated Fat: 0g
- Cholesterol: 47mg
- Sodium: 266mg
- Potassium: 549mg
- Total Carbohydrates: 21g
- Fiber: 5g
- Sugar: 8.5g
- Protein: 19.5g

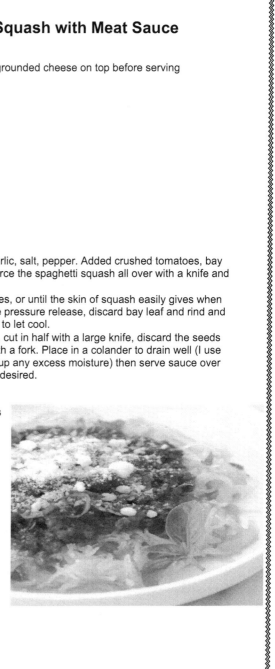

Recipe 27: Chicken Sauce with Rice

Tips to cook properly
- Before serving add freshly chopped cilantro

Ingredients
- 6 chicken thighs
- 4 garlic cloves
- 1 very thin slice ginger
- 1 ½ tablespoon cornstarch mixed with 2 tablespoons water
Sauce:
- 60ml soy sauce
- 60ml Rice wine
- 1.25 ml sesame oil
- 28g white sugar
Rice:
- 250ml water
- 230g normal rice

Preparation Method
- Marinade the chicken thighs with the sauce for 20 minutes.
- Pour the marinade into the pressure cooker and add 4 crushed garlic cloves and 1 very thin slice of ginger into the pressure cooker. Let the sauce mixture come to a boil and let it boil for 30 seconds to allow the alcohol in sake to evaporate.
- Add the chicken thighs into the pressure cooker with the skin side up. Place a steamer rack into the pressure cooker and carefully place a bowl with 1 cup of normal rice (230 g) onto the rack. Pour 1 cup of water (250 ml) into the bowl of rice. Make sure all the rice are soaked with water. Immediately close the lid and cook at High Pressure for 6 minutes.
- Fluff the rice and set aside. Set aside the chicken thighs. Remove the ginger slice and garlic cloves. Press Sauté button and taste the seasoning one more time. Add more soy sauce or sugar if desired.
- Mix the cornstarch with water and mix it into the sauce one-third at a time until desired thickness.Serve immediately with rice and other side dishes.

Nutritional Information
- Preparation Time: 55 minutes
- Total Servings: 2-4
- Calories: 564
- Calories from Fat: 253
- Total Fat: 28.1g
- Saturated Fat: 7.8g
- Cholesterol: 160mg
- Sodium: 1941mg
- Potassium: 431mg
- Total Carbohydrates: 29.6g
- Fiber: 0.5g
- Sugar: 12.2g
- Protein: 41g

Recipe 28: Chicken Cola Wings

Tips to cook properly
- Serve with basmati rice

Ingredients
- 1 ½ pound chicken wings
- 4 garlic cloves
- 1 stalk green onion, cut 2 inches long
- 1 tablespoon sliced ginger
- 200ml regular coca cola
- 2 tablespoons light soy sauce
- 1 tablespoon dark soy sauce
- 1 tablespoon rice wine
- 1 tablespoon peanut oil

Preparation Method
- Heat up the pressure cooker (Sauté button). Make sure your pot is as hot as it can be when you place the ingredients into the pot.
- Sauté the Garlic, Ginger, and Green Onion, pour in 1 tablespoon of peanut oil into the cooker. Ensure to coat the oil over the whole bottom of the pot. Add the crushed garlic, sliced ginger, and green onions into the pot, then stir for roughly a minute until fragrant.
- Sauté the Chicken Wings by Add the chicken wings into the pot and stir fry them together with the garlic, ginger slices, and green onions for roughly one to two minutes.
- Deglaze the Pot, When the edges of the chicken skin start to brown, pour in the coca cola and fully deglaze the bottom of the pot with a wooden spoon. Add 2 tablespoons of light soy sauce, 1 tablespoon of dark soy sauce, and 1 tablespoon of rice wine. Mix well. Keep pressure cook at High Pressure for 5 minutes. Turn off the heat and fully natural release (roughly 10 minutes).
- open the lid carefully and taste one of the chicken wings and the cola sauce (It shouldn't taste like coca cola). Reduce and season the sauce with more salt if desired. Serve immediately with rice or other side dishes.

Nutritional Information
- Preparation Time: 30 minutes
- Total Servings: 2-4
- Calories: 280
- Calories from Fat: 115
- Total Fat: 14.1g
- Saturated Fat: 3.1g
- Cholesterol: 78mg
- Sodium: 267mg
- Potassium: 199mg
- Total Carbohydrates: 14.2g
- Fiber: 0g
- Sugar: 12.8g
- Protein: 19g

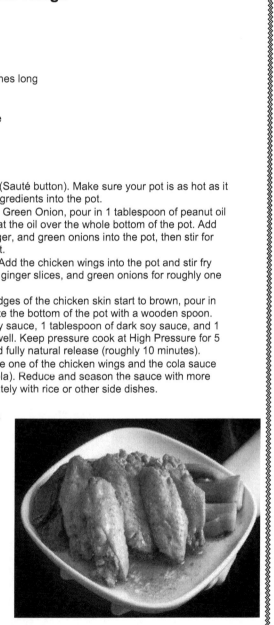

Recipe 29: Pork Loin Chop with Onion Sauce

Tips to cook properly

- If desired, you can add 1 tablespoon of honey with onion sauce

Ingredients

- 4 boneless pork loin chops (1.25 inches thick)
- 1 small onion
- 1 tablespoon olive oil
- 1 tablespoon balsamic vinegar
- 1 tablespoon Worcestershire sauce
- 1 tablespoon light soy sauce
- 1 teaspoon sugar
- 180 ml unsalted homemade chicken stock
- 1 ½ tablespoon cornstarch mixed with 2 tablespoons water
- kosher salt

Marinade:

- 1 tablespoon light soy sauce
- 1 tablespoon Shaoxing wine
- ¼ teaspoon salt
- ½ teaspoon sugar
- ¼ teaspoon ground white pepper
- ¼ teaspoon sesame oil

Preparation Method

- Cut pork loin to tenderize the meat.
- Marinate the tenderized pork loin chops for 20 minutes with a ½ teaspoon of sugar, ¼ teaspoon of salt, ¼ teaspoon of sesame oil, ¼ teaspoon ground white pepper, 1 tablespoon of light soy sauce, and 1 tablespoon of Shaoxing wine.
- Heat up your pressure cooker and press Sauté. Make sure your pot is as hot as it can be when you place the pork loin chops into the pot. This will prevent the pork loin chops from sticking to the pot.
- Add 1 tablespoon of olive oil into the pot. Ensure to coat the oil over the whole bottom of the pot. Add the marinated pork loin chops into the pot, then let it brown for roughly 1 minutes on each side. Remove and set aside.
- Add in the sliced onions. Add a pinch of kosher salt and ground black pepper to season if you like. Cook the onions for roughly 1 minute until soften.
- Deglaze: Add 1 tablespoon of balsamic vinegar and partially deglaze the bottom of the pot with a wooden spoon.
- Onion sauce: Add in 180 ml of unsalted chicken stock, 1 tablespoon of Worcestershire sauce, 1 tablespoon of light soy sauce, 1 teaspoon of sugar. Mix well and fully deglaze. Taste the seasoning and adjust with kosher salt if necessary.
- Pressure Cook: Place the pork loin chops with all the meat juice into the pot. Pressure cook at High Pressure for 1 minute.
- Remove the pork loin chops and set aside. Turn heat to medium (press Sauté button). Taste the seasoning and add more salt if desired. Mix the cornstarch with water and mix it into the onion sauce.

- Serve: Drizzle the onion sauce over the pork loin chops and serve immediately.

Nutritional Information
- Preparation Time: 30 minutes
- Total Servings: 2-4
- Calories: 345
- Calories from Fat: 69
- Total Fat: 7.7g
- Saturated Fat: 2.4g
- Cholesterol: 69mg
- Sodium: 1008mg
- Potassium: 864mg
- Total Carbohydrates: 39g
- Fiber: 3.7g
- Sugar: 7.9g
- Protein: 22.1g

Recipe 30: Italian Chicken Soup

Tips to cook properly
- Don't cook spinach more

Ingredients
- Olive oil 2 teaspoons
- Turkey sausage 4
- Diced onion 1
- Minced garlic cloves 3
- Pearl barley ½ cup
- Green lentils 1 cup
- Chicken breast 1 piece
- Fresh parsley ½ cup
- Chicken stock 3 cups
- Garbanzo beans 420g
- Fresh spinach 450g
- Mild salsa 1 cup

Preparation Method
- Heat 1 teaspoon olive oil in a pressure cooker over medium heat. Add sausage meat, and cook until browned, breaking it into crumbles
- Remove sausage to a plate and drain oil. Add another 1 teaspoon of olive oil to pressure cooker, cook onion, and garlic until onion is transparent
- Add barley and stir 1 minute. Return sausage to pressure cooker. Add lentils, chicken, parsley, and chicken stock to cooker, adding enough stock to completely cover chicken
- Close cover securely places pressure regulator on vent pipe. Bring pressure cooker to full pressure over high heat (this may take 15 minutes)
- Reduce heat to medium high, cook for 9 minutes. Pressure regulator should maintain a slow steady rocking motion; adjust heat if necessary.
- Remove pressure cooker from heat, use quick-release following manufacturer's instructions or allow pressure to drop on its own
- Open cooker and remove chicken, shred meat and return to soup. Add garbanzo beans, spinach, and salsa. Stir to blend and heat through before serving

Nutritional Information
- Preparation Time: 50 minutes
- Total Servings: 8
- Amount per Serving: 1
- Calories: 245
- Calories from Fat: 29
- Total Fat: 3.3
- Saturated Fat: 0.6
- Cholesterol: 16
- Sodium: 527
- Potassium: 755

- Total Carbohydrates: 37.3
- Fiber: 12.5
- Sugar: 2.7
- Protein: 17.4

Recipe 1: Popcorn

Tips to cook properly
- You can switch off pressure cooker, in case you stop hearing pops after 1-2 minutes
- If desire, garnish with melted caramel

Ingredients
- 1-2 tablespoons coconut oil
- ½ cup popcorn kernels

Preparation Method
- Add the coconut oil to your electric pressure cooker pot. Press Sauté and adjust to high.
- When oil begins to sizzle, add in a few kernels and wait until they pop. Add the remaining popcorn kernels and stir well.
- Set timer for 3 minutes and quick release.

Nutritional Information
- Preparation Time: 5 minutes
- Total Servings: 3
- Calories: 137
- Calories from Fat: 28
- Total Fat: 3.1g
- Saturated Fat: 0.4g
- Cholesterol: 0g
- Sodium:389mg
- Potassium: 97mg
- Total Carbohydrates: 24.6g
- Fiber: 4.9g
- Sugar: 0.4g
- Protein: 4.1g

Recipe 2: Kale Chips

Tips to cook properly
- You can add different seasonings, or just use your favorite seasoned salt with pepper

Ingredients
- 1 Large Bunch Kale
- 2 tablespoon Olive Oil
- 1 tablespoon Seasoned Salt

Preparation Method
- Remove your bindings on your bunch of kale. Separate the leaves from the stems of your kale. You want to try to get as little stem as possible.
- Rinse your kale with cold water. Add it to your vegetable spinner and remove as much water as possible. Add your kale to a kitchen towel and remove excess water drops.
- Put your kale into a Ziploc bag and add olive oil. Mix it well so that it coats every single leaf.
- Add oil to electric pressure cooker and press Sauté button. When oil is hot add slowly kale and wait until it becomes crispy.
- After removing, put on a paper towel, it helps to remove excess oil from kale.
- Add your salt to the finished kale and serve. You can add different seasonings, or just use your favorite seasoned salt.

Nutritional Information
- Preparation Time: 20 minutes
- Total Servings: 4
- Calories: 77
- Calories from Fat: 21
- Total Fat: 7.3g
- Saturated Fat: 0.2g
- Cholesterol: 11mg
- Sodium: 188mg
- Potassium: 325mg
- Total Carbohydrates: 2.3g
- Fiber: 0.3g
- Sugar: 0.1g
- Protein: 1.5g

Recipe 3: Pumpkin Pot Cakes

Tips to cook properly
- If desire, serve with raw honey, it gives delicious taste

Ingredients
- 1 cup Almond Meal
- 2 large Eggs
- 1/4 cup Pumpkin Puree
- 1/4 cup Sour Cream
- 2 tbsp. Butter
- 1 teaspoon Pumpkin Pie Spice
- 1 teaspoon Baking powder
- 1/4 teaspoon Salt

Preparation Method
- Mix the eggs, pumpkin puree, sour cream, and butter together. Mix the almond meal, pumpkin pie spice, baking powder, and salt together.
- Slowly add wet ingredients to dry ingredients to get a smooth consistency.
- Keep your pressure cooker in Sauté mode and add 1 tablespoon of butter, when butter is hot, pour 1/4 cup of batter.
- Cook until bubbles are visible on top, then flip the pancake over and cook until the other side is golden brown and serve warm.

Nutritional Information
- Preparation Time:15 minutes
- Total Servings: 8
- Calories: 151
- Calories from Fat: 64
- Total Fat: 12.8g
- Saturated Fat: 4.2g
- Cholesterol: 34mg
- Sodium: 332mg
- Potassium: 289mg
- Total Carbohydrates: 1.9g
- Fiber: 1.8g
- Sugar: 12.2g
- Protein: 5.4g

Recipe 4: Strawberry Chia Jam

Tips to cook properly
- You can replace strawberries with your favorite fruit

Ingredients
- Fresh strawberries 225g
- Powdered erythritol 24g
- Chia seeds 24g
- Water 70ml

Preparation Method
- Cut the strawberries into small pieces and put in electric pressure cooker pot and Sauté.
- Add erythritol, water and smash the strawberries using potato masher
- Cook it for 10 minutes and add chia seeds and stir well for 5 minutes, before switching off.
- Let it cool for 10 minutes and put in a mason jar and use whenever you need.

Nutritional Information
- Preparation Time: 20 minutes
- Total Servings: 24
- Calories: 84
- Calories from Fat: 34
- Total Fat: 8.9g
- Saturated Fat: 2.6h
- Cholesterol: 21mg
- Sodium: 322mg
- Potassium: 556mg
- Total Carbohydrates: 0.4g
- Fiber: 2.1g
- Sugar: 13.1g
- Protein: 1.3g

Recipe 5: Coconut Cookie Balls

Tips to cook properly
- If desire, sprinkle with extra coconut flakes on top

Ingredients
- 1 cup Almond Flour
- 3 tablespoons Coconut Flour
- 1/4 cup Cocoa Powder
- 1/2 teaspoon Baking Powder
- 1/3 cup Erythritol
- 1/3 cup Unsweetened Shredded Coconut
- 1/4 teaspoon Salt
- 2 large Eggs
- 1/4 cup Coconut Oil
- 1 teaspoon Vanilla Extract

Preparation Method
- Mix together your almond flour, baking powder, erythritol, and unsweetened shredded coconut in a bowl.
- Add coconut flour and cocoa powder to your bowl and continue to mix until all dry ingredients are nicely distributed.
- Add wet ingredients and mix together again. Once the dough starts to harden, use your hands to knead it into a ball. Roll the dough into small balls and keep aside.
- Then, add trivet and 1 cup of water to the inner pot of your electric pressure cooker and press Sauté so it can preheat.
- Then, layer dough balls inside an inner pot of pressure cooker. Once the bottom layer is full, cover with a piece of parchment paper and piece of aluminum foil.
- Both should be cut in a circle to the size of the inner pot. Then put the rest of the muffin cups inside to fill up the second layer. Again, cover with parchment paper and aluminum foil. Close and set a timer of cooker to 10 minutes.
- Once after finishing, let it sit for 10 minutes while it depressurizes naturally.

Nutritional Information
- Preparation Time: 25 minutes
- Total Servings: 20
- Calories:77
- Calories from Fat: 22
- Total Fat: 6.8g
- Saturated Fat: 1.4g
- Cholesterol: 21mg
- Sodium: 198mg
- Potassium: 410mg
- Total Carbohydrates: 1g
- Fiber: 0.3g
- Sugar: 16.3g
- Protein: 2.2g

Recipe 6: Sesame Mug Cake

Tips to cook properly
- If desire, add roasted sesame seeds and lemon zest as a topping

Ingredients
Base:
- 1 large egg
- 2 tablespoons butter
- 2 tablespoons almond flour
- 1/2 teaspoon baking powder

Flavour:
- 1 tablespoon sesame seed
- 1 teaspoon lemon juice
- 1/4 teaspoon cumin
- 1/4 teaspoon pepper
- Pinch salt

Preparation Method
- Get your mug ready, which want to keep in an electric pressure cooker. Add
- Add egg, almond flour, butter, sesame seed, lemon juice, baking powder, cumin, black pepper, and a pinch of salt. Mix well until it looks like smooth.
- Then, add trivet and 1 cup of water to the inner pot of your electric pressure cooker and press Sauté so it can preheat.
- Cover with parchment paper and aluminum foil. Close and set a timer of cooker to 5 minutes.
- Once after finishing, let it sit for 3 minutes while it depressurizes naturally.

Nutritional Information
- Preparation Time: 10 minutes
- Total Servings: 1
- Calories: 412
- Calories from Fat: 287
- Total Fat: 37g
- Saturated Fat: 5.6g
- Cholesterol: 54mg
- Sodium: 398mg
- Potassium: 445mg
- Total Carbohydrates: 3g
- Fiber: 1.3g
- Sugar: 26.6g
- Protein: 11g

Recipe 7: Chocolate Brownies

Tips to cook properly
- If desire, add chopped almonds on top before you cook

Ingredients
- Almond flour 280g
- Unsweetened cocoa powder 55g
- Erythritol 20g
- Coconut oil 60ml
- Maple syrup 24g
- Eggs 2
- Psyllium husk powder 4g
- Torani salted caramel 8g
- Baking powder 4g
- Salt 2g

Preparation Method
- At first, add erythritol, coconut oil, maple syrup, eggs, caramel into a bowl.
- In a separate bowl, combine all almond flour, cocoa powder, husk powder, baking salt, and salt.
- Mix bowl1 and bowl2 mixture using hand mixer and cut batter pan (which you want to keep in an electric pressure cooker).
- Then, add trivet and 1 ½ cup of water to the inner pot of your electric pressure cooker and press Sauté so it can preheat.
- Put your batter pan into the cooker and set the cooking timer for 15 minutes. Once after finishing, let it sit for 10 minutes while it depressurizes naturally.

Nutritional Information
- Preparation Time: 30 minutes
- Total Servings: 4-6
- Calories: 258
- Calories from Fat: 128
- Total Fat: 23.7g
- Saturated Fat: 2.1g
- Cholesterol: 24mg
- Sodium: 456mg
- Potassium: 672mg
- Total Carbohydrates: 4.5g
- Fiber: 2.1g
- Sugar: 13.2g
- Protein: 8g

Recipe 8: Ginger Cookies

Tips to cook properly
- If desire, add dry cherries over cookie before serving and be careful with water measurement

Ingredients
- Almond flour 280g
- Butter 55g
- Erythritol 190g
- Egg 1
- Vanilla extract 5g
- Salt 2g
- Ground ginger 10g
- Ground nutmeg 2g
- Ground cloves 2g
- Ground cinnamon 2g

Preparation Method
- In a large mixing bowl, mix the dry ingredients together.
- In a small bowl, mix the wet ingredients of melted unsalted butter, egg, and vanilla extract until well combined.
- Add the wet ingredients to the dry ingredients. Blend with a hand mixer until combined. The cookie batter will be slightly stiff and crumbly.
- Use a tablespoon to measure out each cookie. Flatten the top of each cookie with a spatula or just use your fingers.
- Then, layer cups inside an inner pot of pressure cooker. Once the bottom layer is full, cover with a piece of parchment paper and piece of aluminum foil.
- Both should be cut in a circle to the size of the inner pot. Then put the rest of the muffin cups inside to fill up the second layer. Again, cover with parchment paper and aluminum foil. For one round of cooking, you can make 8 cookies. Totally you can make 24 cookies.
- Close and set a timer of cooker to 12 minutes on high.

Nutritional Information
- Preparation Time: 15 minutes
- Total Servings: 24
- Calories: 74
- Calories from Fat: 21g
- Total Fat: 6.71g
- Saturated Fat: 0.8mg
- Cholesterol: 4mg
- Sodium: 188mg
- Potassium: 344mg
- Total Carbohydrates: 1.21g
- Fiber: 1.4g
- Sugar: 10.1g
- Protein: 2.25g

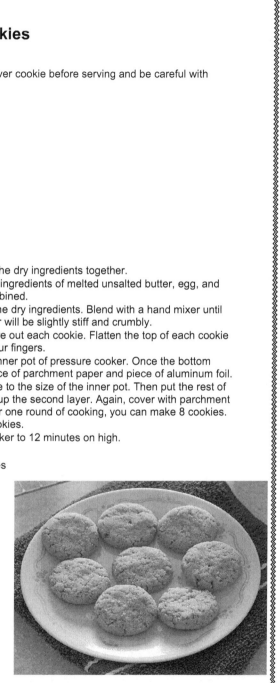

Recipe 9: Cream Pots

Tips to cook properly
- Sprinkle with ground cinnamon powder for extra flavor taste

Ingredients
- Heavy cream 260g
- Powdered erythritol 30g
- Liquid stevia 3g
- Salt (as needed)
- Egg yolks 4
- Water 75g
- Maple syrup 14g
- Vanilla extract 2g
- Maple extract 4g

Preparation Method
- Whisk egg yolks finely and mix water with erythritol in a small pan and start boiling on low heat. After 1 minute, add maple syrup and keep aside
- In another medium bowl, mix cream, stevia, salt, extracts and start boiling on low heat and add water syrup (first bowl) into batter and add whisk egg yolk
- Mix well until it looks smooth and soft
- Add to small cups, then add trivet and 1 cup of water to the inner pot of your electric pressure cooker and press Sauté so it can preheat.
- Slowly put all cups inside the cooker, close and set timer of cooker to 8 minutes.
- Once after finishing, let it sit for 10 minutes while it depressurizes naturally.

Nutritional Information
- Preparation Time: 20 minutes
- Total Servings: 4
- Calories: 359
- Calories from Fat: 79
- Total Fat: 34.9g
- Saturated Fat: 1.1g
- Cholesterol: 34mg
- Sodium: 188mg
- Potassium: 412mg
- Total Carbohydrates: 3g
- Fiber: 1.40g
- Sugar: 16g
- Protein: 2.8g

Recipe 10: Lemon Cup Cake

Tips to cook properly
- If desire, add roasted sesame seeds on top before cooking

Ingredients
- Ricotta 250g
- Eggs 2
- Erythritol 48g
- Lemon Zest 10g
- Fresh Lemon Juice 14g
- Vanilla Extract 5g
- Poppy Seeds 5g

Preparation Method
- Separate 2 eggs into 2 mixing bowls. With a clean, dry electric hand mixer, beat the egg whites until they're foamy.
- Add 2 tablespoons erythritol and beat until the egg whites become shiny and stiff peaks form.
- In the other mixing bowl, cream together the egg yolks, ricotta cheese and the other 2 tablespoons of erythritol.
- Into the egg yolk ricotta bowl, add the zest and juice of half a lemon. Now add the vanilla extract and poppy seeds. Mix well to combine
- Fold the egg whites into the egg yolks half at a time, stirring gently. Grease 4 ramekins and add your batter into each one.
- Then, add trivet and 1 cup of water to the inner pot of your electric pressure cooker and press Sauté so it can preheat.
- Slowly put all ramekins cups inside the cooker, close and set timer of cooker to 8 minutes.
- Once after finishing, let it sit for 10 minutes while it depressurizes naturally.

Nutritional Information
- Preparation Time: 20 minutes
- Total Servings: 4
- Calories: 151
- Calories from Fat: 52
- Total Fat: 20.8g
- Saturated Fat: 2.5g
- Cholesterol: 23mg
- Sodium: 345mg
- Potassium: 221mg
- Total Carbohydrates: 2.9g
- Fiber: 1.2g
- Sugar: 7.2g
- Protein: 9g

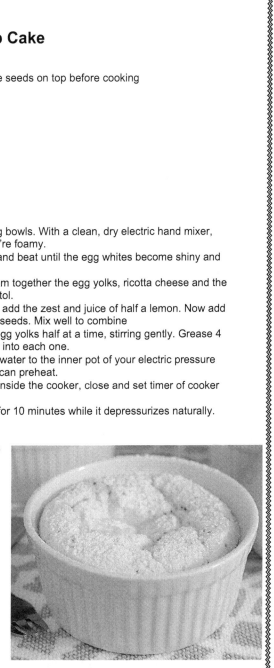

Recipe 11: Keto Cookies

Tips to cook properly

- If desire, add cream over cookie before serving and be careful with water measurement

Ingredients

- Almond flour 140g
- Coconut flour 24g
- Baking powder 3g
- Cinnamon 4g
- Pinch salt
- Erythritol 35g
- Eggs 2
- Coconut oil 30g
- Vanilla extract 2g
- Almond extract 2g
- Sugar-free jam 28g
- Shredded coconut 14g

Preparation Method

- Combine all dry ingredients, egg and mix well. Make it like a paste using a hand mixer.
- Then, add trivet and 1 ½ cup of water to the inner pot of your electric pressure cooker and press Sauté so it can preheat.
- Using a small cookie scoop, fill silicone cups about ⅔ full.
- Then, layer cups inside an inner pot of pressure cooker. Once the bottom layer is full, cover with a piece of parchment paper and piece of aluminum foil.
- Both should be cut in a circle to the size of the inner pot. Then put the rest of the muffin cups inside to fill up the second layer. Again, cover with parchment paper and aluminum foil. For one round of cooking, you can make 8 cookies. Totally you can make 16 cookies.
- Close and set a timer of cooker to 15 minutes on high.

Nutritional Information

- Preparation Time: 20 minutes
- Total Servings: 16
- Calories: 86
- Calories from Fat: 21
- Total Fat: 7.9g
- Saturated Fat:
- Cholesterol: 0.2mg
- Sodium: 298mg
- Potassium: 332mg
- Total Carbohydrates: 1.2g
- Fiber: 2.4g
- Sugar: 8.9g
- Protein: 2.4g

Recipe 12: Mocha Cake

Tips to cook properly
- Garnished with whipped cream or ice cream for extra flavor

Ingredients
- Butter (greasing)
- Butter 180g
- Chopped chocolate 55g
- Heavy cream 120g
- Instant coffee crystals 28g
- Vanilla extract 5g
- Cocoa powder 60g
- Almond flour 50g
- Salt 2g
- Eggs 5
- Stevia/erythritol granulated sweetener 128g
- Optional: Whipped cream or ice cream

Preparation Method
- Grease, cooker pot with butter and in a small saucepan, melt butter and unsweetened chocolate over low heat, whisking occasionally. Remove from heat and allow to cool.
- Whisk together heavy cream, coffee crystals, and vanilla extract in a small bowl. Combine cocoa, almond flour, and salt in a small bowl.
- Beat eggs in a large bowl with an electric mixer on high speed until slightly thickened. Gradually add granulated sweetener and beat on high speed until thick and pale yellow, about 5 minutes.
- Turn mixer speed to low and slowly mix in melted butter and unsweetened chocolate mixture. Stir in cocoa, almond flour and salt mixture.
- Using mixer at medium speed, slowly add in cream, coffee, and vanilla mixture. Pour batter into cooker pot and place a paper towel over the opening of the cooker before placing the lid on top. The paper towel absorbs condensation
- Cook on low for 2 hours. At the end of cooking, the center will have a soft souffle consistency while edges will be more like cake.

Nutritional Information
- Preparation Time: 140 minutes
- Total Servings: 6
- Calories: 434
- Calories from Fat: 211
- Total Fat: 39g
- Saturated Fat: 5.1g
- Cholesterol: 54mg
- Potassium: 399mg
- Total Carbohydrates: 2g
- Fiber: 0.6g
- Sugar: 21.4g
- Protein: 9g

Recipe 13: Fried Broccoli Patties

Tips to cook properly
- For extra taste, add parsley in dough before you make patties

Ingredients
- 1 1/2 cup Almond Flour
- 280g Raw Broccoli Florets
- 125g Cheddar Cheese
- 1/4 cup Coconut Oil
- 2 large Eggs
- 1 teaspoon Salt
- 1 teaspoon Paprika
- 1 teaspoon Garlic Powder
- 1/2 teaspoon Pepper
- 1/2 teaspoon Baking Soda
- 1/2 teaspoon Apple Cider Vinegar

Preparation Method
- Put your broccoli florets into your food processor and blend until it's finely chopped.
- In a large mixing bowl, add Almond Flour, Salt, Paprika, Garlic Powder, Pepper, and Baking Soda.
- Mix the spices and almond flour together, then add eggs and coconut oil. Mix the eggs and oil together with the almond flour until a dough forms.
- Add your broccoli to the mixture. Combine everything well using your hands.
- Grate cheddar cheese and add your cheese to the dough.
- Mix together everything with your hands again, until the cheese is evenly distributed throughout.
- Add oil to your pressure cooker and press Sauté, when oil is hot add your patties and fry until it turns brown both side.
- Put in paper towels to remove excessive oil and serve.

Nutritional Information
- Preparation Time: 20 minutes
- Total Servings: 12
- Calories: 163
- Calories from Fat: 78
- Total Fat: 14.3g
- Saturated Fat: 2.1g
- Cholesterol: 32mg
- Sodium: 198mg
- Potassium: 334mg
- Total Carbohydrates: 2g
- Fiber: 2.0g
- Sugar: 0.6g
- Protein: 6.8g

Recipe 14: Spiced French Toast

Tips to cook properly
- If desire, top with powdered swerve or keto maple syrup

Ingredients
- Pumpkin bread 4 slices
- Egg 1
- Cream 30g
- Orange extract 4g
- Pumpkin pie spice 3g
- Butter 20g

Preparation Method
- In a small container, mix egg, cream, vanilla extract, orange extract and pumpkin pie spice.
- Dip the bread into the mixture and soak for 5 minutes.
- After 5 minutes, again flip the bread and allow it to soak for 5 more minutes.
- Switch on your electric pressure cooker and press Sauté and add butter. When butter is hot, then add soaked toast into the pot and cook until golden brown color
- Flip it and cook another side until browned and serve when it is warm for a nice taste.

Nutritional Information
- Preparation Time: 20 minutes
- Total Servings: 2
- Calories: 428
- Calories from Fat: 223
- Total Fat: 37.4g
- Saturated Fat: 4.5g
- Cholesterol: 21mg
- Sodium: 454mg
- Potassium: 222mg
- Total Carbohydrates: 6.8g
- Fiber: 2.1g
- Sugar: 18.6g
- Protein: 12g

Recipe 15: Flax Flour Pot Cakes

Tips to cook properly
- If desire, add a little honey on top and serve immediately

Ingredients
- Almond flour 70g
- Flax seed meal 70g
- Eggs 4
- Coconut oil 20g
- Coconut milk 120g
- Erythritol 20g
- Butter 30g
- Coconut flour 5g
- Baking powder 5g
- Nutmeg 2g
- Cinnamon 4g
- Pinch salt

Preparation Method
- Mix almond flour, flax seeds, erythritol, salt and baking powder in a bowl.
- Mix all dry ingredients together well so everything is distributed evenly and add eggs to mixture and mix well.
- Mix to a liquid consistency is achieved and add now coconut oil and milk together and mix until more liquid consistency.
- Add coconut flour, spices to the mixture and mix well.
- Switch on your electric pressure cooker and press Sauté. Add butter and coconut oil.
- Add 1/4 cup of pancake mix at a time, cook until brown color appears on both sides and remove from cooker pot.

Nutritional Information
- Preparation Time: 20 minutes
- Total Servings: 8
- Calories: 213
- Calories from Fat: 98
- Total Fat:19.9g
- Saturated Fat: 4.8g
- Cholesterol: 38mg
- Sodium: 256mg
- Potassium: 355mg
- Total Carbohydrates: 1.6g
- Fiber: 0.5g
- Sugar: 22.2g
- Protein: 6.1g

Recipe 16: Buttermilk Pot Cakes

Tips to cook properly
- For extra taste, before serving add maple syrup, walnuts and fresh fruits

Ingredients
- 2 Eggs
- 1/2 Cup liquid egg whites
- 1/2 Cup buttermilk
- 1 teaspoon vanilla extract
- 1 tablespoon vanilla protein powder
- 1/4 Cup coconut flour
- 1 teaspoon baking powder
- Pinch cinnamon
- 1 packet of Splenda or Stevia
- 1 tablespoon Butter (for each pancake)

Preparation Method
- Beat the egg whites with a pinch of salt until they have soft peaks. Mix the buttermilk, egg yolks, liquid egg whites, and vanilla extract in a bowl. Mix well.
- In a separate bowl, whisk the coconut flour, protein powder, baking powder, and cinnamon. Add the dry ingredients to the wet and mix until combined.
- Fold the whipped egg whites into the batter, make sure not to deflate the whites.
- Keep your pressure cooker in Sauté mode and add 1 tablespoon of butter, when butter is hot, pour 1/4 cup of batter.
- Cook until bubbles are visible on top, then flip the pancake over and cook until the other side is golden brown and serve hot with your favorite items.

Nutritional Information
- Preparation Time: 15 minutes
- Total Servings: 4
- Calories: 138.5
- Calories from Fat: 63
- Total Fat: 5.1g
- Saturated Fat: 2.1g
- Cholesterol: 34mg
- Sodium: 667mg
- Potassium: 441mg
- Total Carbohydrates: 10g
- Fiber: 5.12g
- Sugar: 21.2g
- Protein: 12.25g

Recipe 17: Almond Lemon Sandwich

Tips to cook properly
- If desire, before serving garnish with lemon zest and pistachios

Ingredients

Almond Lemon Cakes:
- 1/4 Cup Almond Flour
- 1/4 Cup Coconut Flour
- 1/4 Cup Butter
- 3 Large Eggs
- 1/4 Cup Erythritol
- 1 tablespoon Lemon Juice
- 1 tablespoon Coconut Milk
- 1 teaspoon Cinnamon
- 1/2 teaspoon Almond Extract
- 1/2 teaspoon Vanilla Extract
- 1/2 teaspoon Baking Soda
- 1/2 teaspoon Apple Cider Vinegar
- 1/4 teaspoon Liquid Stevia
- 1/4 teaspoon Salt
- 2 teaspoon Red food Coloring

Preparation Method
- Put a shifter on top of a large mixing bowl. Add almond flour, coconut flour, cinnamon, salt and baking soda. Sift the dry ingredients until everything is fine and powdery.
- In a mixing bowl, crack eggs, then add erythritol, lemon juice, coconut milk, vanilla extract, almond extract, liquid stevia, and apple cider vinegar.
- Add melted butter to the wet ingredients and add food coloring. Stir the ingredients well, making sure that the eggs are thoroughly broken.
- Mix the wet ingredients into the dry ingredients using a hand mixer. Do this until you end with a fluffy looking batter.
- Keep your pressure cooker in Sauté mode and add oil. When oil is hot, add 2/3 cup batter into oil (you can make round patties and add). Cook until both side turns a brown color and serve hot.

Nutritional Information
- Preparation Time: 30 minutes
- Total Servings: 6
- Calories: 180
- Calories from Fat: 67
- Total Fat: 17.5g
- Saturated Fat: 3.2g
- Cholesterol: 36mg
- Sodium: 445mg
- Potassium: 567mg
- Total Carbohydrates: 1.8g
- Fiber: 2.0g
- Sugar: 1.9g
- Protein: 2.8g

Recipe 18: Peanut Butter Cookies

Tips to cook properly
- If desire, serve with extra caramel cream over cookies

Ingredients
- 1/2 Cup Natural Peanut Butter
- 1/3 Cup Erythritol
- 1/3 Cup Coconut Flour
- 1/4 Cup Flaxseed Meal
- 5 tablespoons Salted Butter
- 1 Large Egg
- 1 tablespoon Heavy Whipping Cream
- 1 teaspoon Baking Powder
- 1/4 teaspoon Baking Soda
- Garnish: 1 tablespoon Erythritol

Preparation Method
- In a mixing bowl, add your softened butter and peanut butter. Add your heavy cream and mix thoroughly. Add your flax seed and coconut flour. You can add additional spices here if you'd like to have a different flavor.
- Mix the batter well until it becomes a bit thick and dough-like. Add your baking soda, baking powder, and erythritol and stir in very well.
- Add your egg to the mixture. Continue mixing very well until you get creamy, but still a pliable mixture.
- Roll your cookie dough into balls and place them on a cookie sheet. Make sure they have spread apart at least 1 inch on each side. Press each cookie down with your finger and then lightly trace a pattern on the top.
- Then, add trivet and 1 1/2 cup of water to the inner pot of your electric pressure cooker and press Sauté so it can preheat.
- Cover with a piece of parchment paper and piece of aluminum foil on a trivet and place your cookies on it and again, cover cookies with parchment paper and aluminum foil. Close and set a timer of cooker to 10 minutes.
- Once after finishing, let it sit for 10 minutes while it depressurizes naturally and dry it for 15 to 30 minutes (until it before crispy).

Nutritional Information
- Preparation Time: 30 minutes
- Total Servings: 18-20
- Calories: 97
- Calories from Fat: 34
- Total Fat: 8.5g
- Saturated Fat: 1.3g
- Cholesterol: 32mg
- Sodium: 667mg
- Potassium: 343mg
- Total Carbohydrates:1.5g
- Fiber: 1.3g
- Sugar: 22.2g
- Protein: 2.4g

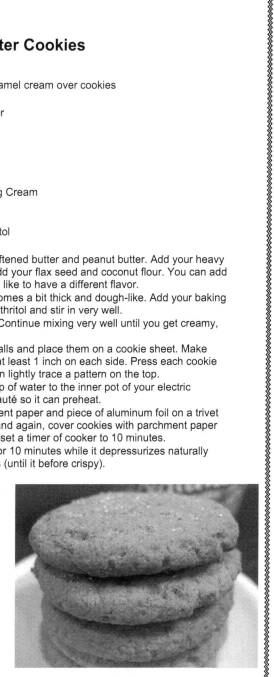

Recipe 19: Pumpkin Pie

Tips to cook properly
- If desire, add cream and enjoy with glass of coffee or tea

Ingredients
- Butter 115g
- Erythritol 30g
- Egg 1
- Liquid stevia 15 drops
- Cinnamon 4g
- Pumpkin puree 40g
- Maple extract 4g
- Pumpkin pie spice 3g
- Almond flour 35g
- Coconut flour 28g
- Chopped pecans 28g

Preparation Method
- Combine your butter and erythritol, mix with hand mixer.
- Add egg, cinnamon, stevia, pumpkin puree, pumpkin pie spice and maple extract, mix well. Lastly, add almond flour and coconut flour and mix until well combined.
- On brownies cups, spray coconut oil and spread batter in an even layer. Chop pecans and sprinkle them over the surface of the blondies.
- hen, add trivet and 2 cups of water to the inner pot of your electric pressure cooker and press Sauté so it can preheat.
- Slowly place all cups into the cooker and set timer 20 minutes on high. Once after finishing, let it sit for 10 minutes while it depressurizes naturally.

Nutritional Information
- Preparation Time: 30 minutes
- Total Servings: 12
- Calories: 112
- Calories from Fat: 34
- Total Fat: 10.8g
- Saturated Fat: 2.1g
- Cholesterol: 45mg
- Sodium: 545mg
- Potassium: 211mg
- Total Carbohydrates: 1.4g
- Fiber: 0.9g
- Sugar: 6.6g
- Protein: 1.4g

Recipe 20: Pumpkin Potcakes

Tips to cook properly
- If desire, add walnuts and raw honey for extra yummy taste

Ingredients
- Almond meal 140g
- Eggs 2
- Pumpkin puree 55g
- Sour cream 50g
- Butter 25g
- Pumpkin pie spice 5g
- Baking powder 4g
- Salt (as needed)

Preparation Method
- Mix eggs, pumpkin puree, cream, and butter together without lumps.
- Mix almond meal, pumpkin pie spice, baking powder and salt together in separate bowl.
- Slowly start adding wet mixture (step1) to get a smooth consistency.
- Switch on your electric pressure cooker and press Sauté and add butter. When butter is hot, then add pancake batter to the pot and cook until bubbles appear on the top.
- Flip it and cook another side until browned and serve when it is warm for a nice taste.

Nutritional Information
- Preparation Time: 15 minutes
- Total Servings: 8
- Calories: 150.9
- Calories from Fat: 67
- Total Fat: 12.8g
- Saturated Fat: 3.6g
- Cholesterol: 54mg
- Sodium: 655mg
- Potassium: 344mg
- Total Carbohydrates: 1.9g
- Fiber: 2.2g
- Sugar: 19.1g
- Protein: 5.4g

Recipe 21: Pumpkin Spice Muffins

Tips to cook properly
- If desire, top with plain cream cheese

Ingredients
- 3/4 cup canned pumpkin
- 1/4 cup sunflower seed butter
- 1 large egg
- 1/2 cup erythritol
- 1/4 cup organic coconut flour, sifted
- 2 tablespoons organic flaxseed meal
- 1 teaspoon ground cinnamon
- 1/2 teaspoon ground nutmeg
- 1/2 teaspoon baking soda
- 1/2 teaspoon baking powder
- 1/4 teaspoon salt

Preparation Method
- In a mixing bowl combine pumpkin, sunflower seed butter, and the egg. Stir until smooth. Add all of remaining dry ingredients. Stir to blend.
- Then, add trivet and 1 cup of water to the inner pot of your electric pressure cooker and press Sauté so it can preheat.
- Then, add trivet and 1 cup of water to the inner pot of your electric pressure cooker and press Sauté so it can preheat. Using a small cookie scoop, fill silicone muffin cups about ⅔ full.
- Then, layer muffin cups inside an inner pot of pressure cooker. Once the bottom layer is full, cover with a piece of parchment paper and piece of aluminum foil.
- Both should be cut in a circle to the size of the inner pot. Then put the rest of the muffin cups inside to fill up the second layer. Again, cover with parchment paper and aluminum foil. Close and set a timer of cooker to 12 minutes.
- Once after finishing, let it sit for 10 minutes while it depressurizes naturally.

Nutritional Information
- Preparation Time: 15 minutes
- Total Servings: 16
- Calories: 42.94
- Calories from Fat: 19g
- Total Fat: 2.9g
- Saturated Fat: 0.9g
- Cholesterol: 45mg
- Sodium: 344mg
- Potassium: 265mg
- Total Carbohydrates: 2.64g
- Fiber: 0.4g
- Sugar: 1.1g
- Protein: 1.84g

Recipe 22: Zucchini Boats

Tips to cook properly
- If desire, garnish with jalapeno pepper slice and additional parsley

Ingredients
- 2 medium zucchini squash
- 4 strips cooked bacon
- ½ cup cheddar cheese
- ¼ cup onion
- ¼ cup sour cream
- 55g cream cheese
- 2 tablespoons butter
- 1 tablespoons minced jalapeno pepper
- Salt & pepper to taste

Preparation Method
- Wash and dry zucchini, cut it in half, then cut each half in half lengthwise. Use a spoon to scoop out most of the insides. Chop the scooped flesh and place in a bowl. Place the zucchini "boats" in the baking dish.
- Add the remaining filling ingredients to the bowl and mash together to combine. Divide mixture evenly between the 8 zucchini sections, filling them completely. Top with a jalapeno slice and crumbled bacon, if desired.
- Then, add trivet and 1 cup of water to the inner pot of your electric pressure cooker and press Sauté so it can preheat.
- Put zucchini into the cooker and set the timer to 12 minutes with quick release, then transfer to serving plates and enjoy the delicious taste.

Nutritional Information
- Preparation Time: 20 minutes
- Total Servings: 4
- Calories: 260
- Calories from Fat: 147
- Total Fat: 22.36
- Saturated Fat: 5.1g
- Cholesterol: 65mg
- Sodium: 678mg
- Potassium: 555mg
- Total Carbohydrates: 3.12g
- Fiber: 0.85g
- Sugar: 0.6g
- Protein: 9.93g

Recipe 23: Vanilla Fried Cookies

Tips to cook properly
- Serve with double cream on top of each cookie

Ingredients
- 1 1/2 cups Almond Flour
- 1/2 cup Unsalted Butter
- 1/3 cup Erythritol
- 2 Large Eggs
- 1 tablespoon Instant Coffee Grounds
- 1 1/2 teaspoon Vanilla Extract
- 1/2 teaspoon Baking Soda
- 1/2 teaspoon Kosher Salt
- 1/4 teaspoon Cinnamon
- 17 Drops Liquid Stevia

Preparation Method
- In a large mixing bowl, add almond flour, instant coffee grounds, baking soda, salt, and cinnamon.
- In 2 bowls, separate your eggs into whites and yolks. Whip your butter with a hand mixer until it's creamy. Once it is, add erythritol and continue creaming the butter until almost white in color.
- Add your 2 egg yolks to the butter and continues mixing until smooth. Mix together your almond flour, coffee grounds, baking soda, salt, and cinnamon until well distributed.
- Add 1/2 of your dry ingredients to your creamed butter mixture and mix well. Once you do this, add vanilla extract and 17 drops liquid stevia. Add the rest of your almond flour mixture and continue mixing until thoroughly combined.
- Beat your 2 egg whites until stiff peaks form. Add your egg whites to the cookie dough and fold them into the dough. Divide your cookie mixture onto a cookie sheet and make patties.
- Keep your pressure cooker in Sauté mode and add oil. When oil is hot, slowly add patties into oil and fry until it turns light brown color. Take out and place on paper towel to remove extra oil from cookies.

Nutritional Information
- Preparation Time:30 minutes
- Total Servings: 10
- Calories: 167
- Calories from Fat: 76
- Total Fat:17.1g
- Saturated Fat: 3.2g
- Cholesterol: 23mg
- Sodium: 456mg
- Potassium: 211mg
- Total Carbohydrates: 1.4g
- Fiber: 1.3g
- Sugar: 4.1g
- Protein: 3.9g

Recipe 24: Mini Vanilla Cakes

Tips to cook properly
- If desire, add frozen cherries on top and serve

Ingredients
Cake:
- Eggs 6
- Cream cheese 90g
- Cream of tartar 2.5g
- Vanilla extract 10g
- Granulated stevia/erythritol mix 48g

Frosting:
- Cream cheese 450g
- Butter 28g
- Granulated stevia/erythritol mix 32g
- Vanilla extract 5g

Preparation Method
- In a medium bowl, beat cream cheese, vanilla extract, sweetener, and egg yolks until smooth.
- In a separate bowl, whip the egg whites and cream of tartar with an electric mixer until stiff peaks form. Next, carefully fold the whipped egg whites into the yolk mixture.
- Scoop about two tablespoons of the mixture into each muffin tins. Then, add trivet and 1 ½ cup of water to the inner pot of your electric pressure cooker and press Sauté so it can preheat.
- Slowly place all cups into the cooker and set timer 20 minutes on high. Once after finishing, let it sit for 10 minutes while it depressurizes naturally.
- On another side, combine all frosting ingredients together in a medium bowl and beat with an electric mixer until smooth.
- Cut cake into 3 layers and then pipe frosting in between each layer of cake.

Nutritional Information
- Preparation Time: 25 minutes
- Total Servings: 8
- Calories: 347
- Calories from Fat: 122
- Total Fat: 30g
- Saturated Fat: 3.2g
- Cholesterol: 32mg
- Sodium: 189mg
- Potassium: 44mg
- Total Carbohydrates: 3.4g
- Fiber: 2.1g
- Sugar: 21.2g
- Protein: 9g

Recipe 25: Fried Mac Cheese

Tips to cook properly
- If desire, eat with steamed spinach leaves

Ingredients
- 1 Head Cauliflower, Riced
- 1 1/2 Cup Shredded Cheddar Cheese
- 3 Large Eggs
- 2 teaspoon Paprika
- 1 teaspoon Turmeric
- 3/4 teaspoon Rosemary

Preparation Method
- Cut and add the cauliflower to your food processor and pulse it until it is the consistency of short grain rice.
- Put your cauliflower into the electric pressure cooker and press Steam and cook for 5 minutes. Once it's done we want to get all the excess moisture out. Lay cauliflower on kitchen towel/ paper towel to wring it out.
- Once you have the cauliflower in the kitchen towel, roll it up tight and apply pressure to the cauliflower. Try to push as much extra moisture out of the cauliflower as you can.
- Once you're finished, extract the mushed cauliflower from the kitchen towel and put it into a bowl. Make sure that its room temperature by this point.
- Add your eggs one at a time to the cauliflower. You don't want a mixture that too watery. Keep in mind that I only did 1/3 of the entire recipe.
- Add your cheese. Finally, your spices to the cauliflower like turmeric, rosemary, and paprika. Mix everything well, using your hands if you want.
- Now add oil to electric pressure cooker and press Sauté button, when oil is very hot. Form your cauliflower mixture into a ball, and then flatten it out in the palm of your hand.
- Add your cauliflower patties into the hot oil and reduce the heat to medium. Allow them to get crisp on one side before flipping them. Continue cooking them until they're crisp on both sides (you can make around 24 patties).

Nutritional Information
- Preparation Time: 40 minutes
- Total Servings: 22-25
- Calories: 41
- Calories from Fat: 18
- Total Fat: 2.9g
- Saturated Fat: 0.6g
- Cholesterol: 0.4mg
- Sodium: 211mg
- Potassium: 445mg
- Total Carbohydrates: 0.9g
- Fiber: 0.9g
- Sugar: 0.3g
- Protein: 2.7g

Recipe 26: Chocolate Zucchini Muffin

Tips to cook properly
- Before serving, add cream cheese as a frosting

Ingredients
- 2 eggs
- ¾ to 1 cup evaporated cane juice
- ½ cup coconut oil
- 2 teaspoons vanilla extract
- 1 tablespoon butter
- 3 tablespoons cocoa powder
- 1 cup sprouted einkorn flour
- ½ teaspoon baking soda
- ¼ teaspoon sea salt
- ¾ teaspoon cinnamon
- 1 cups zucchini (or squash)
- ⅓ cup chocolate chips
- 1 cup water

Preparation Method
- Combine eggs, sweetener, coconut oil, and vanilla extract in a medium-sized mixing bowl. Stir well and add cocoa powder to melted butter.
- Mix until it looks like a thick but smooth dark paste. Then, add chocolate mixture to egg mixture and stir well.
- Add flour, baking soda, sea salt, and cinnamon to the bowl. Stir well. Fold in grated zucchini and chocolate chips.
- Then, add trivet and 1 cup of water to the inner pot of your electric pressure cooker. Press Sauté so it can preheat.
- Using a small cookie scoop, fill silicone muffin cups about ⅔ full. The 6-quart Instant Pot fits 16 muffin cups at a time. Then, layer muffin cups inside an inner pot of pressure cooker.
- Once the bottom layer is full, cover with a piece of parchment paper and piece of aluminum foil. Both should be cut in a circle to the size of the inner pot.
- Then put the rest of the muffin cups inside to fill up the second layer. Try to keep all the muffin cups level. Again, cover with parchment paper and aluminum foil.
- Close the pressure cooker and set to high for 8 minutes, let it sit for 10 to 15 minutes while it depressurizes naturally and add cream cheese frosting.

Nutritional Information
- Preparation Time: 25 minutes
- Total Servings: 24-30
- Calories: 189
- Calories from Fat: 81
- Total Fat: 8.3g
- Saturated Fat: 1.1g
- Cholesterol: 23mg

- Sodium: 150mg
- Potassium: 62mg
- Total Carbohydrates: 24.6g
- Fiber: 0.9g
- Sugar: 16g
- Protein: 2.2g

Recipe 27: Doodle Cookies

Tips to cook properly
- Make sure they are relatively spread out, but they will not spread too much

Ingredients
Cookies:
- 2 Cups Honeyville Almond Flour
- 1/4 Cup Coconut Oil
- 1/4 Cup Homemade Maple Syrup
- 1 tablespoons Vanilla
- 1/4 teaspoon Baking Soda
- 7 Drops Liquid Stevia
- Pinch Salt
- Optional: 1/3 Cup Macadamia Nuts

Topping:
- 2 tablespoons Cinnamon
- 2 tablespoons Erythritol

Preparation Method
- In a bowl, combine melted coconut oil, maple syrup, vanilla, and liquid stevia.
- In a separate bowl, combine almond flour, baking soda, and a pinch of salt.
- Optional: If you are using Macadamia Nuts, add macadamia nuts to your food processor.
- Mix together the wet ingredients until combined well. Mix your wet ingredients into the dry ingredients until a dough is formed.If you are using Macadamia Nuts, add macadamia nuts here.
- In a small metal ramekin, combine 2 tablespoons cinnamon and 2 tablespoons erythritol.
- Roll dough into balls, dip into the cinnamon mixture and then lay them onto a silicone Silpat. Use the bottom side of a mason jar (greased if needed) to flatten the balls. Do this for all your cookies.
- Then, add trivet and 1 cup of water to the inner pot of your electric pressure cooker and press Sauté so it can preheat.
- Then, layer cookies inside an inner pot of pressure cooker. Once the bottom layer is full, cover with a piece of parchment paper and piece of aluminum foil.
- Both should be cut in a circle to the size of the inner pot. Then put the rest of the cookies inside to fill up the second layer. Again, cover with parchment paper and aluminum foil. Close and set a timer of cooker to 10-12 minutes.
- Once after finishing, let it sit for 10 minutes while it depressurizes naturally.

Nutritional Information
- Preparation Time: 25 minutes
- Total Servings: 12
- Calories: 155
- Calories from Fat: 56
- Total Fat: 14.8g

- Saturated Fat: 2.1g
- Cholesterol: 34mg
- Sodium: 455mg
- Potassium: 878mg
- Total Carbohydrates: 2.1g
- Fiber: 3.1g
- Sugar:9.6g
- Protein: 3.6g

Recipe 28: Avocado Muffins

Tips to cook properly
- For better taste, Store in fridge and enjoy cold muffins with hot sauce

Ingredients
- 5 large Eggs
- 5 Sliced roasted Bacon
- 2 tablespoons Butter
- 1/2 cup Almond Flour
- 1/4 cup Flaxseed Meal
- 1 1/2 tablespoons Psyllium Husk Powder
- 2 medium Avocados
- 127g Jack Cheese
- 3 medium Spring Onions
- 1 teaspoon Minced Garlic
- 1 teaspoon Dried Cilantro
- 1 teaspoon Dried Chives
- 1/4 teaspoon Red Chili Flakes
- Salt and Pepper to Taste
- 1 1/2 cup Coconut Milk
- 1 1/2 tablespoons Lemon Juice
- 1 teaspoon Baking Powder

Preparation Method
- In a bowl, mix together eggs, almond flour, flax, psyllium, spices, coconut milk and lemon juice.
- Chop the spring onions and grate the cheese. Add the spring onions, cheese, and baking powder. Then, crumble the bacon. Add the crumbled bacon and melted butter to the batter.
- Slice an avocado in half, remove the pit, and then cube the avocado while it's in the shell. Be careful of the sharp knife as you do this. Scoop out the avocado and fold into the mixture gently.
- Then, add trivet and 1 1/2 cup of water to the inner pot of your electric pressure cooker and press Sauté so it can preheat.
- Using a small cookie scoop, fill silicone muffin cups about ⅔ full. The 6-quart pot fits 16 muffin cups at a time.
- Then, layer muffin cups inside an inner pot of pressure cooker. Once the bottom layer is full, cover with a piece of parchment paper and piece of aluminum foil.
- Both should be cut in a circle to the size of the inner pot. Then put the rest of the muffin cups inside to fill up the second layer. Again, cover with parchment paper and aluminum foil. Close and set a timer of cooker to 10 minutes.
- Once after finishing, let it sit for 10 minutes while it depressurizes naturally.

Nutritional Information
- Preparation Time: 25 minutes
- Total Servings: 16

- Calories: 163
- Calories from Fat: 82
- Total Fat: 14.1g
- Saturated Fat: 4.2g
- Cholesterol: 56mg
- Sodium: 384mg
- Potassium: 455mg
- Total Carbohydrates: 1.5g
- Fiber: 0.4g
- Sugar: 3.3g
- Protein: 6.1g

Recipe 29: Pistachio Chocolate Muffins

Tips to cook properly
- If desire, add extra pistachio on top and serve

Ingredients
- 1 1/2 Cups Honeyville Almond Flour
- 1/2 Cup Pumpkin Puree
- 1/2 Cup Pistachios
- *1/2 Cup* Erythritol
- 2 Large Eggs
- 1/4 Cup Coconut Oil
- 3 Dark choco Bars
- 2 teaspoon Quality Vanilla
- 1 1/2 teaspoon Cinnamon
- 1/2 teaspoon Baking Soda
- 1/2 teaspoon Apple Cider Vinegar
- 1/2 teaspoon Nutmeg
- 1/2 teaspoon Cloves
- 1/2 teaspoon Ginger

Preparation Method
- Grind your cloves with a spice grinder or mortar and pestle. Add all of your dry ingredients to a large mixing bowl, you can also add the ginger here if you are using ground and dried ginger.
- In a separate bowl, add pumpkin puree, 2 eggs, coconut oil, Vanilla, and apple cider vinegar. If you're using minced (wet) ginger, add the 1/2 teaspoon of ginger here.
- Roughly chop your 3 Dark Chocolate Bars. Mix all of the wet ingredients together well.
- Pour 1/2 of your wet ingredients into your dry ingredients and slowly mix them together. Add the second half of your wet ingredients and completely combine them.
- Add your chocolate chunks and 1/2 Cup Pistachios to the mixture and fold them in.
- Then, add trivet and 1 1/2 cup of water to the inner pot of your electric pressure cooker and press Sauté so it can preheat.
- Using a small cookie scoop, fill silicone muffin cups about ⅔ full. The 6-quart pot fits 16 muffin cups at a time.
- Then, layer muffin cups inside an inner pot of pressure cooker. Once the bottom layer is full, cover with a piece of parchment paper and piece of aluminum foil.
- Both should be cut in a circle to the size of the inner pot. Then put the rest of the muffin cups inside to fill up the second layer. Again, cover with parchment paper and aluminum foil. Close and set a timer of cooker to 10 minutes.
- Once after finishing, let it sit for 10 minutes while it depressurizes naturally.

Nutritional Information

- Preparation Time:30 minutes
- Total Servings: 8
- Calories: 231
- Calories from Fat:
- Total Fat: 21.5g
- Saturated Fat: 4.8g
- Cholesterol: 28mg
- Sodium: 445mg
- Potassium: 567mg
- Total Carbohydrates: 4g
- Fiber: 4.5g
- Sugar: 15.1g
- Protein: 6.6g

Recipe 30: Toast Muffins

Tips to cook properly
- Top with 1 tablespoon of sweet cream and some fresh fruits

Ingredients
- 6 Large Eggs
- 2/3 Cup Almond Flour
- 1/4 Cup Peanut Butter
- 1/4 Cup Heavy Cream
- 1/4 Cup Crushed Toasted Almonds
- 2 tablespoons Coconut Oil
- 1 tablespoon Unsalted Butter
- 2 tablespoons Erythritol
- 1 teaspoon Cinnamon
- 1 teaspoon Vanilla
- 1/2 teaspoon Salt
- 1/4 teaspoon Nutmeg
- 10 Drops Liquid Stevia

Preparation Method
- Add 1/4 cup almonds to your food processor. Grind the nuts down into small pieces and roast them.
- In a large mixing bowl, add all dry ingredients and mix well. IN another separate bowl, add all wet ingredients and mix well.
- Slowly mix both separate bowl mixture into one bowl and mix until desire consistency and making sure you have a liquid-like batter.
- Then, add trivet and 1 ½ cup of water to the inner pot of your electric pressure cooker and press Sauté so it can preheat.
- Using a small cookie scoop, fill silicone muffin cups about ⅔ full. The 6-quart pot fits 16 muffin cups at a time. Put some chopped almonds on top of each muffin.
- Then, layer muffin cups inside an inner pot of pressure cooker. Once the bottom layer is full, cover with a piece of parchment paper and piece of aluminum foil.
- Both should be cut in a circle to the size of the inner pot. Then put the rest of the muffin cups inside to fill up the second layer. Again, cover with parchment paper and aluminum foil. Close and set a timer of cooker to 10 minutes.
- Once after finishing, let it sit for 10 minutes while it depressurizes naturally.

Nutritional Information
- Preparation Time: 30 minutes
- Total Servings: 12
- Calories: 171
- Calories from Fat: 71
- Total Fat: 16.3g
- Saturated Fat: 4.3g
- Cholesterol: 44mg

- Sodium: 567mg
- Potassium: 476mg
- Total Carbohydrates: 2g
- Fiber: 1.2g
- Sugar: 15.2g
- Protein: 6.9g

Beginner Dinner Recipes

Recipe 1: Black Beans Soup

Tips to cook properly
- If desired, add little lime juice before you serve

Ingredients
- Water 7 cups
- Black beans 450g
- Chopped onion 1
- Chopped cilantro 20g
- Olive oil 1 tablespoon
- Salt and pepper (as needed)
- Vinegar 2 tablespoons

Preparation Method
- Combine water, black beans, onion, cilantro, olive oil, and salt together in a pressure cooker
- Cook on high according to manufacturer's instructions, about 40 minutes
- Open lid and stir balsamic vinegar into beans

Nutritional Information
- Preparation Time: 50 minutes
- Total Servings: 8
- Calories: 216
- Calories from Fat: 23
- Total Fat: 2.5g
- Saturated Fat: 0.4g
- Cholesterol: 0mg
- Sodium: 450mg
- Potassium: 896mg
- Total Carbohydrates: 37g
- Fiber: 9g
- Sugar: 2.2g
- Protein: 12.5g

Recipe 2: Salt Baked Chicken

Tips to cook properly
- Before serving, add black pepper

Ingredients
- 8 chicken legs
- 2 teaspoons dried ground ginger
- 1¼ teaspoon kosher salt
- ¼ teaspoon five spice powder
- Optional: 1 teaspoon of ground white pepper

Preparation Method
- Season the chicken legs, place the chicken legs in a large mixing bowl. Pour in 2 teaspoons of dried ground ginger, 1 ¼ teaspoon of kosher salt, and ¼ teaspoon of five spice powder. Mix well.
- Wrap the chicken legs, place the seasoned chicken legs on a large piece of parchment paper (don't use aluminum foil). Wrap it up tightly and place it in a shallow dish with the opening side facing upwards. Do not stack more than 2 levels of chicken legs.
- Pressure cook the chicken legs, place a steamer rack in the pressure cooker and pour in 1 cup of water. Carefully place the chicken legs dish onto the rack. Close the lid and cook at high pressure for 18 – 26 minutes or wait for natural release for 20 minutes.
- Remove the dish from the pressure cooker and unwrap the parchment paper carefully and serve immediately.
- The remaining meat juice can be used as a dipping sauce for the chicken.

Nutritional Information
- Preparation Time: 50 minutes
- Total Servings: 4
- Calories: 483
- Calories from Fat:172
- Total Fat: 19.2g
- Saturated Fat: 5.1g
- Cholesterol: 55mg
- Sodium: 1057mg
- Potassium: 198mg
- Total Carbohydrates: 48.6g
- Fiber: 5.2g
- Sugar: 0g
- Protein: 19.1g

Recipe 3: Chicken Curry Soup

Tips to cook properly
- If desire, add chopped cilantro, basil on top before serving

Ingredients
- 1 can coconut milk
- 3 cans water
- 2 portions of curry sauce mix
- 1 teaspoon ground ginger
- 340g frozen blend of broccoli, carrots, sugar snap peas, water chestnut mix
- 170g frozen okra
- 170g cooked chicken breast

Preparation Method
- Put all ingredients in the Instant Pot. Push "Soup" setting. Stir well when done. This is a lite soup with great flavor taste.

Nutritional Information
- Preparation Time: 20 minutes
- Total Servings: 4
- Calories: 179
- Calories from Fat: 39
- Total Fat: 4.4g
- Saturated Fat: 0.7g
- Cholesterol: 0mg
- Sodium: 182mg
- Potassium: 844mg
- Total Carbohydrates: 32.2g
- Fiber: 6.5g
- Sugar: 5.1g
- Protein: 4.4g

Recipe 4: Multi-Grain Fried Rice

Tips to cook properly
- Be careful while adding water

Ingredients
- 3 cups multi-grain rice
- 3 cups of water
- 1 cup of diced ham, chicken, or pork
- 1/4 cup of sliced scallions
- 1 cup grated carrot
- 2 tablespoons of olive oil
- 2 tablespoons of soy sauce

Preparation Method
- Add all ingredients to pressure cooker
- Set pot to Multi-Grain setting
- When cooking cycle is complete, fluff rice and serve

Nutritional Information
- Preparation Time: 25 minutes
- Total Servings: 4
- Calories: 276
- Calories from Fat: 131
- Total Fat: 14.6g
- Saturated Fat: 2.9g
- Cholesterol: 129mg
- Sodium: 367mg
- Potassium: 214mg
- Total Carbohydrates: 16.7g
- Fiber: 3g
- Sugar: 2g
- Protein: 16.1g

Recipe 5: Lentil Chicken Soup

Tips to cook properly
- Before serving, top with freshly chopped cilantro and basil

Ingredients
- 450g dried lentils
- 340g chicken thighs
- 7 cups water
- 1 small onion, chopped
- 2 scallions, chopped
- 1/4 cup chopped cilantro
- 3 cloves garlic
- 1 medium ripe tomato, diced
- 1 teaspoon garlic powder
- 1 teaspoon cumin
- 1/4 teaspoon oregano
- 1/2 teaspoon paprika
- 1/2 teaspoon kosher salt

Preparation Method
- Place all the ingredients into the cooker, stir and cover. Use "Soup" button and cook 30 minutes. When done and the pressure releases, shred the chicken and stir.
- Makes about 11 cups.

Nutritional Information
- Preparation Time: 45 minutes
- Total Servings: 11 cups
- Calories: 129
- Calories from Fat: 55
- Total Fat: 2.5g
- Saturated Fat: 1.2g
- Cholesterol: 36mg
- Sodium: 496mg
- Potassium: 221mg
- Total Carbohydrates: 16g
- Fiber: 5g
- Sugar: 0g
- Protein: 15g

Recipe 6: Marinated Artichokes

Tips to cook properly
- Don't forget to keep overnight and if desire, add little yogurt in marination

Ingredients
- 4 large artichokes
- 2 tablespoons fresh lemon juice
- 2 teaspoons balsamic vinegar
- ¼ cup olive oil
- 1 teaspoon dried oregano
- 2 cloves garlic
- ½ teaspoon sea salt
- ¼ teaspoon fresh ground black pepper

Preparation Method
- Wash artichokes under cold water. Cut off the top inch of the artichoke.
- Place the artichokes in the inner pot of the pressure cooker with 2 cups of water. Choose the "Steam" setting and reduce cooking time to 8 minutes.
- On other side prepare the marinade by mixing lemon juice, balsamic vinegar, olive oil, oregano, garlic, salt, and pepper in a small jar with a lid. Shake well to incorporate all of the ingredients. Set aside.
- Remove the artichokes and cut the artichokes in half. Remove the center cone of purple prickly leaves.
- Drizzle the marinade over the warm artichokes. Turning to make sure to coat them well with marinade. Allow them to sit for 30 minutes to overnight.
- When ready to serve, grill for 3 to 5 minutes and serve.

Nutritional Information
- Preparation Time: 10 minutes
- Total Servings: 4
- Calories: 204
- Calories from Fat: 124
- Total Fat: 13.8g
- Saturated Fat: 1.9g
- Cholesterol: 0mg
- Sodium: 253mg
- Potassium: 630mg
- Total Carbohydrates: 19.3g
- Fiber: 8.9g
- Sugar: 2g
- Protein: 5.5g

Recipe 7: Rice Squash Casserole

Tips to cook properly
- For better taste, add zucchini and natural release

Ingredients
- 2 tablespoons olive oil
- 2 onions
- 2 sticks of celery
- 2 carrots
- 1 red pepper
- 2 cloves of garlic
- 1 teaspoon fresh thyme
- 8 white mushrooms
- 3 cups of vegetable stock
- 300g brown rice
- 760g chopped tomatoes
- 1 squash
- Salt and pepper

Preparation Method
- Put pressure cooker in Sauté function on medium and I heat the oil. Add onions, celery, carrots and red pepper for about 5 minutes.
- Add the garlic, thyme, salt and pepper and heat for another minute. Then add the mushrooms and stir for 1 minute.
- Add the rice, mix it all together. Transfer to metal bowl. Add the tomatoes and the 2-3 cups of stock for a sticky rice.
- Now stir in the squashes. Put about an inch and a half of water into the pressure cooker. Place the bowl with all the ingredients mixed on a flat trivet into the pot and press rice setting button, wait for the natural release and enjoy the taste.

Nutritional Information
- Preparation Time: 15 minutes
- Total Servings: 5
- Calories: 368.9
- Calories from Fat: 54
- Total Fat: 6.1g
- Saturated Fat: 2.4g
- Cholesterol: 8.8mg
- Sodium: 614.2mg
- Potassium: 482mg
- Total Carbohydrates: 67.2g
- Fiber: 7.1g
- Sugar: 10.1g
- Protein: 12.2g

Recipe 8: Pressure Cooker Jambalaya

Tips to cook properly
- Add and stir prawns before serving

Ingredients
- 2 tablespoons olive oil
- 450g chicken breasts and thighs diced
- 450g prawns
- 2 cups yellow onions
- 2 cups tri-color bell peppers
- 2 tablespoons garlic
- 1 1/2 cups rice
- 3 1/2 cups chicken stock
- 1 cup crushed tomatoes
- 1 tablespoon creole seasoning
- 1 tablespoon Worcestershire sauce
- 450g andouille sausage (pre-cooked and sliced)

Preparation Method
- Set pressure cooker to Sauté. Coat chicken with 1 tablespoon creole seasoning, and brown the meat on all sides. Remove the chicken from heat and set aside.
- Add onions, peppers, and garlic, and Sauté until the onions are translucent. Add rice, and sauce for 2 minutes. Add tomato puree, creole seasoning, Worcestershire, and chicken. Close the lid and press Rice.
- When the rice is cooked, release steam, remove the lid, and add sausage and prawns. Place lid back on the pressure cooker and press Manual, and cook an additional 2 minutes.

Nutritional Information
- Preparation Time: 20 minutes
- Total Servings: 8-10
- Calories: 348
- Calories from Fat: 124
- Total Fat: 13.8g
- Saturated Fat: 4.5g
- Cholesterol: 72mg
- Sodium: 1143mg
- Potassium: 536mg
- Total Carbohydrates: 32.3g
- Fiber: 2.2g
- Sugar: 1.4g
- Protein: 22.1g

Recipe 9: Spinach Soup

Tips to cook properly
- Add spinach at the end and top with chopped bacon

Ingredients
- 1200g navy beans, rinsed and drained
- 4 slices center cut bacon, chopped
- 1 medium onion, chopped
- 1 large carrot, chopped
- 1 large celery stalk, chopped
- 2 tablespoons tomato paste
- 4 cups reduced sodium chicken broth
- 2 bay leaves
- 1 sprig fresh rosemary
- 3 cups baby spinach

Preparation Method
- In a blender, blend beans with 1 cup of water.
- Press Sauté button then cook the bacon until crisp. Set aside on paper towels.
- Add the onion, carrots, and celery to the pot and cook until soft, about 5 minutes. Stir in the tomato paste then add the pureed beans, beans, broth, rosemary and bay leaves.
- Cook on high pressure 15 minutes. Let the pressure release, remove rosemary and bay leaves.
- Place 2 cups of the soup in the blender and puree to thicken, then add back to the soup along with the spinach and stir until wilted. To serve, ladle into 6 bowls and top with bacon.

Nutritional Information
- Preparation Time: 20 minutes
- Total Servings: 6 cups
- Calories: 211
- Calories from Fat:
- Total Fat: 1.5g
- Saturated Fat: 0.5g
- Cholesterol: 2mg
- Sodium: 1150mg
- Potassium: 666mg
- Total Carbohydrates: 39g
- Fiber: 12g
- Sugar: 4g
- Protein: 15g

Recipe 10: Electric Pressure Cooker Picadillo

Tips to cook properly
- You can serve with brown rice or half boiled rice

Ingredients
- 1/2 large chopped onion
- 2 cloves garlic
- 1 tomato
- 1 teaspoon kosher salt
- 1/2 red bell pepper
- 2 tablespoons cilantro
- 450g lean ground beef
- 110g tomato sauce
- 1 teaspoon ground cumin
- 2 bay leaf
- 2 tablespoons alcaparrado

Preparation Method
- Press Sauté button when hot brown meat on high heat in large Sauté pan and season with salt and pepper. Use a wooden spoon to break the meat up into small pieces until no longer pink.
- Add onion, garlic, pepper, salt, tomato and cilantro and stir 1 minute, add alcaparrado or olives and about 2 tablespoons cumin, and bay leaf. Add tomato sauce and 3 tablespoons of water and mix well.
- Cover and cook high pressure 15 minutes. Natural or quick release and enjoy the taste.

Nutritional Information
- Preparation Time: 30 minutes
- Total Servings: 6
- Calories: 207
- Calories from Fat: 76
- Total Fat: 8.5g
- Saturated Fat: 0g
- Cholesterol: 74mg
- Sodium: 0g
- Potassium: 245mg
- Total Carbohydrates: 5g
- Fiber: 1g
- Sugar: 3g
- Protein: 25g

Recipe 11: Spicy Vegetable Soup

Tips to cook properly
- Right before you serve, add freshly chopped cilantro and basil for extra flavor

Ingredients
- 1 cup celery
- 1/2 cup carrots
- 1 medium onion
- 1-inch long fresh jalapeno
- 2 tablespoons olive oil
- 1 teaspoon coriander seeds
- 1/2 teaspoon cumin seed
- 3 big russet potatoes
- 2 tablespoons chicken broth
- 4 cups of water
- 1/4 teaspoon ground turmeric
- 1 teaspoon ground cumin
- 2 tablespoons chopped jalapenos
- Optional: chopped cilantro

Preparation Method
- Set pressure cooker on Sauté. Add 2 tablespoons olive oil to the cooker and let warm up for a minute.
- Drop in coriander seeds and cumin seeds and heat until the coriander seeds pop. Put in the chopped celery, carrots onion, and jalapeno.
- Sauté until the onions become translucent, about 5 minutes. Add the turmeric, cumin, and pickled jalapenos. Once those have released some nice aroma, put in the potatoes and chicken broth.
- Change the setting to soup and set for 30 minutes. Let pressure return to normal. Right before serving add in the chopped cilantro. Serve with good bread.

Nutritional Information
- Preparation Time: 35 minutes
- Total Servings: 4
- Calories: 155
- Calories from Fat:101
- Total Fat: 11.2g
- Saturated Fat: 4.9g
- Cholesterol: 27mg
- Sodium: 1058mg
- Potassium: 334mg
- Total Carbohydrates: 9.9g
- Fiber: 2.7g
- Sugar: 3.4g
- Protein: 5.4g

Recipe 12: Mushroom Gravy Soup

Tips to cook properly
- All purpose flour can be replaced with 2 tablespoons of cornstarch

Ingredients
- 2 tablespoons olive oil or vegetable oil
- 225g mushrooms
- ¼ cup chicken broth or beef broth
- 2 ¾ cup water
- 4 tablespoons all-purpose flour
- 4 tablespoons butter
- ¼ cup milk

Preparation Method
- Add oil to pressure cooker and press Sauté button. Add sliced mushroom to cooker. Add chicken or beef broth. Continue to cook down until mushroom appears darker in color.
- Add water and close lid. Slide lever to the "Pressurize" mode. As soon as the cooker is pressurized, switch to quick release. Drain broth and mushroom in a colander and save broth. Place mushrooms back.
- Add 4 tablespoons of butter to a saucepan and melt to a slight simmer. Add the 4 tablespoons of all-purpose flour slowly and whisking constantly until the mixture smells like pie crust.
- Slowly add in mushroom broth until all clumps are dissolved and there is a creamy texture. Add milk and bring to a boil. Add mushrooms and bring to a simmer. Continue to whisk occasionally and simmer for about 8 min.
- Remove from pan and enjoy the taste. Serve over noodles, rice or as soup. It tastes like cream of mushroom soup.

Nutritional Information
- Preparation Time: 25 minutes
- Total Servings: 4
- Calories: 278
- Calories from Fat: 116
- Total Fat: 6.8g
- Saturated Fat: 1.9g
- Cholesterol: 95mg
- Sodium: 521mg
- Potassium: 399mg
- Total Carbohydrates: 24.1h
- Fiber: 1.6g
- Sugar: 3.7g
- Protein: 14g

Recipe 13: Mediterranean Tuna Pasta

Tips to cook properly
- Before serving, add extra grated feta cheese

Ingredients
- 1 Tablespoon of olive oil
- ½ cup of chopped red onion
- 225g egg pasta (uncooked)
- 400g diced tomatoes
- 1 Tablespoon basil
- 1 Tablespoon garlic
- 1 Tablespoon oregano
- 1-1/4 cups of water
- ¼ teaspoon of salt
- 1/8 teaspoon of pepper
- 200g tuna fish
- 210g marinated artichoke
- Crumbled feta cheese
- Fresh chopped parsley

Preparation Method
- Sauté the red onion for about 2 minutes. Add the dry noodles, tomatoes, water, salt, and pepper then set your cooker to soup for 10 minutes.
- Turn off the warm setting and add tuna, artichokes and your reserved liquid from the artichokes and Sauté on normal while stirring for about 4 more minutes till hot.
- Top with a little feta cheese and parsley for your taste.

Nutritional Information
- Preparation Time: 20 minutes
- Total Servings: 6
- Calories: 330
- Calories from Fat: 70
- Total Fat: 7.7g
- Saturated Fat: 2g
- Cholesterol: 10mg
- Sodium: 710mg
- Potassium: 396mg
- Total Carbohydrates: 48g
- Fiber: 2.8g
- Sugar: 4.7g
- Protein: 14.7g

Recipe 14: Potato Garlic Soup

Tips to cook properly
- Before serving, add roasted garlic (fried in purified butter) for delicious taste

Ingredients
- 900g potatoes
- 3/4 cup baby carrots
- 12 roasted garlic cloves
- 1/2 cup celery
- 1/2 cup fresh baby spinach leaves
- 1 cup onion
- 1 cup vegetable broth
- 1 tablespoon fresh basil leaves
- 1/8 teaspoon crushed red pepper
- 1/8 teaspoon paprika
- 1 tablespoon ground flax or chia seeds
- 1/2 teaspoon salt
- Garnish: cheddar cheese, fresh basil leaves

Preparation Method
- Place all ingredients into the pressure cooker and stir. Press the soup button and leave the time set to 30 minutes.
- When the cooker beeps that it is finished cooking, throw a kitchen towel over the lid and then do a quick pressure release. Insert an immersion blender, and apply short zaps until the soup is thick but still has some chunky potato and carrot pieces.
- Taste the soup and then add salt, if desired. Ladle into bowls and garnish with cheese and basil
- Serve with freshly baked whole grain wheat bread or cornbread.

Nutritional Information
- Preparation Time: 35 minutes
- Total Servings: 8 cups
- Calories: 150
- Calories from Fat: 67
- Total Fat: 3.2g
- Saturated Fat: 1.2g
- Cholesterol: 10mg
- Sodium:445mg
- Potassium: 396mg
- Total Carbohydrates: 34.3g
- Fiber: 3g
- Sugar: 4.1g
- Protein: 8.4g

Recipe 15: Pepe Soup

Tips to cook properly
- Don't forget to garnish with grated cheese and chopped basil leaves

Ingredients
- 450g lean ground beef
- 1/2 teaspoon kosher salt
- 1/2 cup diced onion
- 1/2 cup diced celery
- 1/2 cup diced carrot
- 780g diced tomatoes
- 900g beef stock
- 2 bay leaves
- 110g small pasta
- optional: grated parmesan cheese

Preparation Method
- Press the Sauté button, when it's very hot add the ground beef and salt and cook until browned breaking the meat up into small pieces as it cooks. When browned, add the onion, celery, and carrots and Sauté 3 to 4 minutes.
- Add the tomatoes, beef stock and bay leaves, close and using pressure cooker press soup (35 minutes).
- After that use the quick release, once the pressure is out to open, add the pasta and stir, cover and press manual pressure 6 minutes. Remove bay leaves and serve.

Nutritional Information
- Preparation Time: 45 minutes
- Total Servings: 6
- Calories: 249
- Calories from Fat: 122
- Total Fat: 8g
- Saturated Fat: 1.1g
- Cholesterol: 49mg
- Sodium: 593mg
- Potassium: 367mg
- Total Carbohydrates: 23g
- Fiber: 3g
- Sugar: 4g
- Protein: 21g

Recipe 16: Mashed Potatoes

Tips to cook properly
- Before serving add purified butter, it gives delicious taste

Ingredients
- 4 potatoes
- 1 cup water
- 100ml milk
- 2 tablespoons unsalted butter
- 2 cloves garlic
- 2 tablespoons parmesan cheese
- Kosher salt & pepper for taste

Preparation Method
- Fill the pressure cooker with 1 cup of water. Place the steamer trivet in the cooker and add quartered potatoes in the steamer trivet.
- Cook at high pressure for 8 minutes with an Electric Pressure Cooker, then quick release.
- While the potatoes are cooking, heat a small saucepan over medium heat. Melt the butter and add the garlic. Add a pinch of kosher salt. Sauté the garlic for 1 to 2 minutes until fragrant and golden in color.
- Add the milk and deglaze the pan. Remove mixture from heat when it is hot. Remove the lid. Mash the cooked potatoes in a medium mixing bowl with a potato masher.
- Add half of the garlic butter mixture to the bowl. Continue to mash, stir, and add the mixture until desired consistency. Add Parmesan cheese. Taste and season with salt and pepper. Serve warm.

Nutritional Information
- Preparation Time: 25 minutes
- Total Servings: 2-4
- Calories: 226
- Calories from Fat: 63
- Total Fat: 7g
- Saturated Fat: 4.3g
- Cholesterol: 16mg
- Sodium: 237mg
- Potassium: 102mg
- Total Carbohydrates: 36g
- Fiber: 2.9g
- Sugar: 1.9g
- Protein: 6g

Recipe 17: Italian Pulled Pork

Tips to cook properly
- If desire, add grated cheese before serving with pasta or noodles

Ingredients
- 510g pork tenderloin
- 1 teaspoon kosher salt
- black pepper, to taste
- 1 teaspoon olive oil
- 5 cloves garlic, smashed with the side of a knife
- 800g crushed tomatoes
- 200g roasted red peppers
- 2 sprigs fresh thyme
- 2 bay leaves
- 1 tablespoon chopped fresh parsley

Preparation Method
- Season pork with salt and pepper. Press Sauté button to warm, add oil and garlic and Sauté until golden brown, 1 to 1 1/2 minutes, remove with a slotted spoon.
- Add pork and brown about 2 minutes on each side. Add the remaining ingredients and garlic, reserving half of the parsley.
- Cook high pressure 45 minutes. Natural release, remove bay leaves, shred the pork with 2 forks and top with remaining parsley. Serve over your favorite pasta.

Nutritional Information
- Preparation Time: 55 minutes
- Total Servings: 10
- Calories: 93
- Calories from Fat: 34
- Total Fat: 1.5g
- Saturated Fat:
- Cholesterol: 33mg
- Sodium: 347mg
- Potassium: 247mg
- Total Carbohydrates: 6.5g
- Fiber: 0g
- Sugar: 3g
- Protein: 11g

Recipe 18: Mango Dal

Tips to cook properly
- It taste delicious with basmati rice and garnish with chopped parsley

Ingredients
- 1 tablespoon coconut oil
- 1 teaspoon ground cumin
- 1 medium onion
- 4 cloves garlic
- 1 tablespoon minced fresh ginger
- 1 teaspoon ground coriander
- 1/8 teaspoon cayenne pepper
- 1 teaspoon sea salt
- 1 cup chana dal
- 4 cups chicken broth
- 1 teaspoon ground turmeric
- 2 mangos peeled and diced
- Juice of ½ lime
- ½ cup chopped fresh cilantro

Preparation Method
- Place dal in a colander and rinse until water runs clear.
- Set the pressure cooker to Sauté to heat up the insert. Heat coconut oil until melted, add cumin and Sauté until fragrant, about 30 seconds.
- Add onion, Sauté until soft and starting to brown about 5 minutes. Add garlic, ginger, coriander, cayenne and sea salt and Sauté for 1 minute more.
- Add the dal, chicken broth, and turmeric to the pot. Keep on the Sauté feature and bring to a boil and boil for about 10 minutes.
- Add mangoes. Place the lid on the pressure cooker. Press the Beans/Chili button, adjust the time to 20 minutes. After naturally released, stir in lime juice and cilantro.
- Serve over cooked rice.

Nutritional Information
- Preparation Time: 30 minutes
- Total Servings: 4-6
- Calories: 177
- Calories from Fat: 22
- Total Fat: 2.5g
- Saturated Fat: 0.4g
- Cholesterol: 0mg
- Sodium: 36mg
- Potassium: 326mg
- Total Carbohydrates: 26.4g
- Fiber: 4.6g
- Sugar: 1.3g
- Protein: 8.1g

Recipe 19: Chickpea Stew

Tips to cook properly
- It will take more time because yu have to cook soup and couscous separately

Ingredients
- 1 tablespoon butter
- 1 1/2 cups yellow onion
- 1/2 cup carrot
- 3/4 cup green bell pepper
- 3/4 cup red bell pepper
- 1 tablespoon ginger
- 1 tablespoon garlic
- 425g chickpeas
- 1 tablespoon coriander seeds
- 1 tablespoon cumin
- 1 tablespoon smoked paprika
- 2 teaspoons turmeric
- 2 teaspoons salt
- 800g stewed tomatoes
- 360ml coconut milk

Couscous:
- 2 cups water
- 1 1/3 cups couscous
- 1 tablespoon olive oil
- 1/2 teaspoons salt

Preparation Method
- Set the cooker to Sauté. Add butter and Sauté onions, carrots, peppers, ginger, garlic, and cauliflower, and Sauté until onions are translucent.
- Add the chickpeas, spices, salt, tomatoes, and coconut milk, and close the lid.
- Press "soup", then manually reduce time to 10 minutes. Remove the lid, and set aside stew to keep warm.
- After cleaning the cooker, make the couscous. Place all ingredients in the cooker and close the lid. Press "Manual" and set to cook for 10 minutes.

Nutritional Information
- Preparation Time: 30 minutes
- Total Servings: 6-8
- Calories: 155
- Calories from Fat: 43
- Total Fat: 4.8g
- Saturated Fat: 0.4g
- Cholesterol: 0mg
- Sodium: 508mg
- Potassium: 343mg
- Total Carbohydrates: 21.2g
- Fiber: 4.2g
- Sugar: 2.1g
- Protein: 4.4g

Recipe 20: Lentil Split Pea Soup

Tips to cook properly
- Garnish with freshly chopped coconut, basil, and cilantro

Ingredients
- Red lentil 1 cup
- Yellow split peas 1 cup
- Chopped onion 1
- Chopped carrots 2
- Chopped garlic cloves 5
- Ground cumin 1 ½ teaspoon
- Chicken broth 8 cups
- Salt and pepper (as needed)
- Lemon juice 1 teaspoon

Preparation Method
- Place the lentils, split peas, onion, carrots, garlic, and cumin into a pressure cooker, and stir in the chicken broth.
- Cook under pressure for 30 minutes. Remove from heat, and allow pressure to cool.
- When the cooker is at normal, open and season with salt and pepper and stirs in lemon juice to serve.

Nutritional Information
- Preparation Time: 40 minutes
- Total Servings: 10
- Calories: 170
- Calories from Fat: 7
- Total Fat: 0.7g
- Saturated Fat: 0g
- Cholesterol: 4mg
- Sodium: 780mg
- Potassium: 264mg
- Total Carbohydrates: 29.4g
- Fiber: 6.6g
- Sugar: 3.2g
- Protein: 11.6g

Recipe 21: Chicken Adobo

Tips to cook properly
- After opening pressure cooker, remove all bay leaves

Ingredients
- 2 pounds chicken
- 1 tablespoon oil
- Green onions (for garnish)
Sauce:
- ¼ cup Filipino soy sauce
- ½ cup light soy sauce
- ¼ cup Filipino vinegar
- 1 tablespoon fish sauce
- 1 tablespoon sugar
- 10 crushed cloves garlic
- 1 small onion
- 1 teaspoon ground black peppercorn
- 1 dried red chili
- 4 dried bay leaves

Preparation Method
- Combine Filipino soy sauce, light soy sauce, vinegar, fish sauce and sugar in a medium mixing bowl.
- Add oil to the pot and brown the chicken for 1 to 2 minutes with the skin side down first. (Instant Pot users: press Sauté button) Then, remove the chicken from the pot.
- Sauté garlic and onion in the pot until fragrant and golden in color. Then, add ground black peppercorn, red chili, and bay leaves to the pot and Sauté for 30 seconds. Add the Sauce mixture and deglaze the pot.
- Cook at high pressure for 9 minutes with an Electric Pressure Cooker, then natural release.

Nutritional Information
- Preparation Time: 35 minutes
- Total Servings: 2-4
- Calories: 520
- Calories from Fat: 277
- Total Fat: 30.7g
- Saturated Fat: 8.3g
- Cholesterol: 188mg
- Sodium: 886mg
- Potassium: 438mg
- Total Carbohydrates: 2.2g
- Fiber: 0.3g
- Sugar: 0.2g
- Protein: 44.5g

Recipe 22: Pressure Cooker Minestrone Soup

Tips to cook properly

- Before serving garnish with freshly chopped cilantro and basil leaves

Ingredients

- 1 cup cooked white beans
- 450g cooked ground beef
- 1 potato diced
- 2 carrots diced
- 2 stalks celery diced
- 1 chopped onion
- 2 cloves garlic
- 900g chicken broth
- 800g crushed tomatoes
- 2 teaspoon tomato paste
- Italian seasoning (as needed for taste)
- 1 teaspoon salt

Preparation Method

- Add all ingredients to pressure cooker and stir. Put pressure cooker on manual high pressure for 20 minutes. Let depressurize for 10-minutes.

Nutritional Information

- Preparation Time: 30 minutes
- Total Servings: 4-6
- Calories: 367
- Calories from Fat: 188
- Total Fat: 14.2g
- Saturated Fat: 1.9g
- Cholesterol: 122mg
- Sodium: 998mg
- Potassium: 394mg
- Total Carbohydrates: 45.6g
- Fiber: 12.2g
- Sugar: 3.9g
- Protein: 18.2g

Recipe 23: Basil Chicken Thighs

Tips to cook properly
- Before serving sprinkle with chopped cilantro

Ingredients
- 450g Chicken thighs
- 2 tablespoons of fresh cilantro
- 1-1/2 teaspoons of minced garlic
- 1 teaspoon of dried basil
- 1/2 teaspoon of salt
- 1/2 teaspoon of pepper
- 2 tablespoons of minced green onion
- 1 teaspoon of garlic powder
- 2 tablespoons olive oil
- 1/2 cup of balsamic Vinegar
- 1 teaspoon of Worcestershire sauce
- 1/3 cup of cream sherry wine

Preparation Method
- In a plastic bag, mix the basil, salt, pepper, sherry, Worcestershire sauce, garlic powder, minced onion and balsamic vinegar.
- Mix it up, then add chicken to the mixture, be sure to cover the chicken in this sauce and set aside.
- Set your Instant Pot to Sauté, add the olive oil and Sauté the minced garlic, stirring frequently.
- Set your Instant Pot to the Poultry setting, add the chicken and sauce from bag to the existing olive oil and garlic that is already in there. Close the lid, and cook for 15 minutes.
- When serving, sprinkle the chopped cilantro on top for a tasty treat. Serve with white Jasmine rice and your favorite vegetable.

Nutritional Information
- Preparation Time: 30 minutes
- Total Servings: 4
- Calories: 238
- Calories from Fat: 110
- Total Fat: 12.2g
- Saturated Fat: 3.4g
- Cholesterol: 72mg
- Sodium: 352mg
- Potassium: 451mg
- Total Carbohydrates: 10.8g
- Fiber: 2.6g
- Sugar: 4g
- Protein: 20.6g

Recipe 24: Sweet and Sour Spareribs

Tips to cook properly
- Cornstarch helps to thicken the sauce

Ingredients
- 1 tablespoon olive oil
- 1 medium onion sliced
- 1/4 cup ketchup
- 1/4 soy sauce
- 1/3 cup brown sugar
- 1/3 cup rice wine vinegar
- 560g pineapple
- 2 cloves garlic chopped
- 1 teaspoon finely chopped ginger
- 1 teaspoon fish sauce (optional)
- 1 teaspoon chili powder
- 1 teaspoon ground coriander
- Pinch of smoked paprika
- Salt and pepper to taste
- 1800g of ribs
- Corn starch slurry

Preparation Method
- In a pressure cooker, add oil, Sauté onions until just translucent. Add the rest of the ingredients except cornstarch slurry. Make sure spareribs are submerged in sauce. You can marinate refrigerated in the pot for several hours.
- Pressure cook on Stew for 12 minutes, leave on keep warm for 3 minutes. Release pressure. Check meat for doneness and moisture. If needs more time set timer to Stew for a few more minutes.
- When meat is done, remove meat to a bowl and adjust seasoning (if needed). Set to Sauté, when sauce starts to boil, add cornstarch slurry to thicken to desired taste and stir for one minute.
- Serve with rice and veggies of your choice. Variation, brown meat in oil on Sauté before cooking. After pressure cooking, basting with strained sauce.

Nutritional Information
- Preparation Time: 25 minutes
- Total Servings: 4
- Calories: 668
- Calories from Fat: 303
- Total Fat: 33.7g
- Saturated Fat: 11.6g
- Cholesterol: 120mg
- Sodium: 2482mg
- Potassium: 407mg
- Total Carbohydrates: 59.1g
- Fiber: 0.6g
- Sugar: 44g
- Protein: 31.9g

Recipe 25: Pressure Cooker Mac and Cheese Bowl

Tips to cook properly
- Aluminum foil can be used to keep food moist and make clean-up easier

Ingredients
- 454g elbow macaroni
- 1000g cold running water
- 60g unsalted butter
- 397g sharp cheddar, freshly grated
- 70g mild cheddar or American cheese, freshly grated
- Kosher salt and ground black pepper
- 2 large beaten eggs
- 355ml evaporated milk
- 1 teaspoon Sriracha sauce
- 1 teaspoon ground mustard

Preparation Method
- Add elbow macaroni, 4 cups water, and a pinch of kosher salt in pressure cooker. Close the lid and pressure cook at high pressure for 4 minutes (quick release).
- While the macaroni is pressure cooking, in a medium mixing bowl, beat 2 large eggs and mix in ground mustard, sriracha, and 355ml evaporated milk. Mix well.
- Keep the heat on low or medium low. Place 4 tablespoons of unsalted butter in the pressure cooked macaroni. Mix well with a silicone spatula and let the butter melt.
- Pour in the wet ingredients and mix well. Add grated cheese (1/3 portion at a time) and stir constantly until the cheese fully melt.
- If the mac and cheese are too runny, turn the heat to medium to reduce it down. Taste and season with kosher salt and ground black pepper
- Mac and Cheese need to be served piping hot, so serve immediately.

Nutritional Information
- Preparation Time: 35 minutes
- Total Servings: 6
- Calories: 701
- Calories from Fat: 301
- Total Fat: 33.5g
- Saturated Fat: 20.4g
- Cholesterol: 103mg
- Sodium: 552mg
- Potassium: 348mg
- Total Carbohydrates: 64.9g
- Fiber: 3.4g
- Sugar: 7.8g
- Protein: 34g

Recipe 26: Pressure Cooker Pozole

Tips to cook properly
- Before serving avocado is optional

Ingredients
- 550g 4-inch pieces boneless pork shoulder
- Kosher salt and fresh cracked pepper
- 1 tablespoons olive oil
- 1 medium white onion
- 4 garlic cloves
- 2 tablespoons chili powder
- 4 cups low sodium chicken broth
- 2 cups water
- 850g hominy drained and rinsed
- 110g diced avocado and lime wedges, for serving
- cilantro for garnish

Preparation Method
- Season the pork with salt. In a pressure cooker, heat half of the oil over medium-high heat. Add the pork and cook until pieces are browned on all sides, about 8 minutes, transfer to a plate.
- Add remaining oil, onion, garlic, and chili powder and Sauté until soft, 4 minutes. Add broth and water, cook, stirring and scraping up browned bits with a wooden spoon. Return pork to the pressure cooker.
- Secure lid. Bring to high pressure over medium-high heat; reduce heat to maintain pressure and cook until meat is tender about 45 minutes. Remove from heat, vent pressure, then remove the lid. Skim fat if any.
- Using two forks, shred pork; then stir in hominy and heat through. Serve with avocado and lime and garnish with cilantro.

Nutritional Information
- Preparation Time: 55 minutes
- Total Servings: 6
- Calories: 365
- Calories from Fat:122
- Total Fat: 16g
- Saturated Fat: 0.9g
- Cholesterol: 60mg
- Sodium: 882mg
- Potassium: 344mg
- Total Carbohydrates: 33g
- Fiber: 7g
- Sugar: 2g
- Protein: 22g

Recipe 27: Mushroom Meatloaf

Tips to cook properly
- Aluminum foil can be used to keep food moist, cook it evenly, and make cleanup easier.

Ingredients
- 450g ground meat
- 1 chopped onion
- 1 egg
- 1 cup cooked rice
- 10 small mushrooms
- 1 cup milk
- 1 sliced potatoes (about 1/2 " slices)
- Sea salt (as needed)
- Dry garlic (as needed)
- Topping:
- 3/4 cup ketchup
- 4 tablespoons brown sugar

Preparation Method
- Spray inner pot with non-stick spray. Mix meatloaf ingredients, shape into a round loaf and place inside the pot, forming to fit.
- I like to form meatloaf more to one side of the pot and add thick potato slices stacked up in the remaining area next to the loaf. (If you decide to add potatoes, season them now with sea salt/garlic.)
- Make your meatloaf topping and add to the top of your loaf. Choose the slow cook key and adjust time and cook on low for 6-8 hours or on HIGH 4-6 hours.

Nutritional Information
- Preparation Time: 6-8 hours
- Total Servings: 2
- Calories: 665
- Calories from Fat: 357
- Total Fat: 30.4g
- Saturated Fat: 14.9g
- Cholesterol: 223mg
- Sodium: 1001mg
- Potassium: 678mg
- Total Carbohydrates: 26.2g
- Fiber: 2g
- Sugar: 6.2g
- Protein: 32.6g

Recipe 28: Indian Style Goat Meat

Tips to cook properly
- Taste delicious with hot basmati rice

Ingredients
- 500g frozen goat meat
- 8 garlic cloves
- 2 small onions
- 1 medium shallot
- 1 tablespoon ginger
- 1 medium potato
- 1 tablespoon cilantro
- 2 tablespoons olive oil
- 3 tablespoons curry powder
- ¼ teaspoon chili powder
- 125ml tomato paste
- 1 ¼ cup water
- Kosher salt and black pepper

Preparation Method
- Press Sauté button and add 1 tablespoon of olive oil into the cooker.
- Add the goat meat into the cooker. Add in 2 pinches of kosher salt and black pepper. Cook for 5 minutes. Remove and set aside.
- Add 1 tablespoon of olive oil, then add in the sliced onion, minced ginger, garlic, and shallot, then stir for roughly a minute. Stir for roughly 30 seconds until fragrant.
- Add 3 tablespoons of curry powder and ¼ teaspoon of Indian chili pepper, then stir for roughly 1 to 2 minutes. Add in the remaining 1 cup of water.
- Add meat and add 125 ml of tomato paste on top of the meat. Do not stir. Add in the quartered potatoes. Keep pressure cook at high pressure for 35 to 40 minutes. Turn off the heat and fully natural release (roughly 15 minutes).
- Garnish with chopped cilantro. Serve immediately.

Nutritional Information
- Preparation Time: 80 minutes
- Total Servings: 2-4
- Calories: 256
- Calories from Fat: 91
- Total Fat: 10.1g
- Saturated Fat: 2g
- Cholesterol: 66mg
- Sodium: 219mg
- Potassium: 677mg
- Total Carbohydrates: 13.2g
- Fiber: 1.9g
- Sugar: 2.2g
- Protein: 22.8g

Recipe 29: Honey Soy Chicken Sauce

Tips to cook properly
- Before serving to add honey and soy sauce for better taste

Ingredients
- 680g chicken wings
- 4 cloves garlic
- ½ large onion
- 2-star anise
- 1 tablespoon ginger
- 1 tablespoon honey
- ½ cup warm water
- 1 tablespoon peanut oil
- 1 ½ tablespoon cornstarch
- Chicken Wing Marinade:
- 2 tablespoons light soy sauce
- 1 tablespoon dark soy sauce
- 1 tablespoon Shaoxing wine
- 1 teaspoon sugar
- ¼ teaspoon salt

Preparation Method
- Marinate the Chicken Wings: Marinate the chicken wings with the Chicken Wing Marinade for 20 minutes.
- Heat Up the Pressure Cooker: Heat up your pressure cooker. Make sure your pot is as hot as it can be when you place the chicken wings into the pot. This will prevent the chicken wings from sticking to the pot.
- Brown the Chicken Wings: Add 1 tablespoon of peanut oil into the pot. Ensure to coat the oil over the whole bottom of the pot. Add the marinated chicken wings into the pot. Then, brown the chicken wings for roughly 30 seconds on each side. Flip a few times as you brown them as the soy sauce and sugar can be burnt easily. Remove and set aside.
- Sauté the onions, star anise, ginger, garlic by pressing Sauté button.
- Mix 1 tablespoon of honey with a ½ cup of warm water, then add it to the pot and deglaze the bottom of the pot.
- Place all the chicken wings with all the meat juice and the leftover chicken wing marinade into the pot and pressure cook at High Pressure for 5 minutes.
- Open the lid carefully and taste one of the honey soy chicken wings and the honey soy sauce. Season with more salt or honey if desired.
- Thicken the Honey Soy Sauce: Remove all the chicken wings from the pot and set aside. Turn on the heat to medium (Instant pot: press Sauté button).
- Mix 1 ½ tablespoon of cornstarch with 1 tablespoon of cold running tap water. Keep mixing and add it into the honey soy sauce one-third at a time until desired thickness.
- Coat and Serve: Turn off the heat and add the chicken wings back into the pot. Coat well with the honey soy sauce and serve immediately.

Nutritional Information
- Preparation Time: 30 minutes
- Total Servings: 2-4
- Calories: 437
- Calories from Fat: 142
- Total Fat: 15.8g
- Saturated Fat: 7g
- Cholesterol: 101mg
- Sodium: 750mg
- Potassium: 302mg
- Total Carbohydrates: 38.2g
- Fiber: 0.6g
- Sugar: 42.2g
- Protein: 30.3g

Recipe 30: Portuguese Chicken with Rice

Tips to cook properly
- Garnish with grated cheese and serve hot

Ingredients
- 3 chicken drumsticks and thighs
- 1 medium carrot
- 2 small potatoes
- 1 small onion
- 1 small shallot
- 3 garlic cloves
- 1 green bell pepper
- 2 small bay leaves
- 200 ml coconut milk
- 1 tablespoon light soy sauce
- 1 tablespoon peanut oil
- 1 ½ teaspoon turmeric powder
- 1 teaspoon ground cumin
- Kosher salt and ground black pepper
- 1 ½ tablespoon cornstarch mixed with 2 tablespoons water

Chicken Marinade:
- 1 tablespoon light soy sauce
- 1 tablespoon rice wine
- ½ teaspoon sugar
- A dash of ground white pepper

Rice:
- 230ml water
- 250g jasmine rice

Preparation Method
- Marinate chicken with ½ teaspoon of sugar, a dash of ground white pepper, 1 tablespoon of light soy sauce, and 1 tablespoon of Shaoxing wine for 20 minutes.
- Instant Pot, press Sauté button and Sauté the onion and garlic. Add 1 tablespoon of peanut oil into the pressure cooker. Add sliced onion, garlic, salt, and black pepper Sauté until brown & fragrant.
- Pour in the chicken, Sauté until slightly browned. Add in 1 ½ teaspoon of turmeric powder and 1 teaspoon cumin powder. Add quartered potatoes, carrots, and 2 small bay leaves. Mix well. Pour in 200 ml of coconut milk and 1 tablespoon of light soy sauce.
- Place a steamer rack into the pressure cooker and carefully place a bowl with 250g jasmine rice onto the rack. Pour 230ml water into the bowl of rice. Make sure all the rice are soaked with water. Cook at high pressure for 4 minutes.
- Turn heat to medium and add green pepper, cook for one minute, taste the seasoning. Add more light soy sauce, coconut milk, or salt if desired. Mix the cornstarch with water and mix it into the coconut sauce one-third at a time until desired thickness. Turn off the heat.

- Fill up the container with Portuguese chicken and vegetables. Add grated cheese (as much as you like!) over the top and place into oven for 5 – 10 minutes. Remove from oven and serve immediately.

Nutritional Information
- Preparation Time: 60 minutes
- Total Servings: 2
- Calories: 301
- Calories from Fat: 150
- Total Fat: 16.7g
- Saturated Fat: 5.8g
- Cholesterol: 56mg
- Sodium: 540mg
- Potassium: 524mg
- Total Carbohydrates: 14.8g
- Fiber: 1.5g
- Sugar: 2.1g
- Protein: 18.4g

DESSERT RECIPES
Beginners Dessert Recipes

Recipe 1: Black Chocolate Cake

Tips to cook properly
- If desire, top with cream and enjoy the taste

Ingredients
- 200g black chocolate
- 100g butter
- 100g sugar
- 25g all-purpose flour
- 3 eggs

Preparation Method
- Melt chocolate and butter together.
- In a medium bowl, add sugar, flour, eggs and mix well.
- Add 250ml water in the electric pressure cooker.
- Cook 6 minutes on "manual", then quick release.

Nutritional Information
- Preparation Time: 10 minutes
- Total Servings: 4-8pieces
- Calories: 500
- Calories from Fat: 255
- Total Fat: 30.2g
- Saturated Fat: 10.4g
- Cholesterol: 71mg
- Sodium: 387mg
- Potassium: 278ng
- Total Carbohydrates: 52.4g
- Fiber: 2.4g
- Sugar: 40g
- Protein: 6.1g

Recipe 2: Tapioca Pearls Pudding

Tips to cook properly
- Try using a liner in your pressure cooker for easier cleanup

Ingredients
- 60g seed tapioca pearls
- 300g whole milk
- 115g water
- 100g sugar
- ½ lemon zest

Preparation Method
- Prepare the pressure cooker by adding one cup of water and the steamer basket and set aside.
- Rinse tapioca pearls in a fine-mesh strainer. To a 4-cup capacity, heat-proof bowl add the tapioca pearls, milk, water, lemon zest, and sugar.
- Mix well until the sugar has dissolved and you no longer feel the grit of it at the base.
- Set electric pressure cookers for 8 minutes at high pressure and refrigerate it for at least 3 hours, or overnight. Before serving top with seasonal fruit.

Nutritional Information
- Preparation Time: 25 minutes
- Total Servings: 4-6
- Calories: 187
- Calories from Fat: 0
- Total Fat: 2.5g
- Saturated Fat:
- Cholesterol: 6.3 mg
- Sodium: 39.2mg
- Potassium: 212mg
- Total Carbohydrates: 39.6g
- Fiber: 0.1g
- Sugar: 28.9g
- Protein: 2.5g

Recipe 3: Pumpkin Brown Rice Pudding

Tips to cook properly
- You can substitute 1 teaspoons of vanilla bean for the vanilla extract

Ingredients
- 1 cup short grain brown rice
- 3 cups dairy-free milk
- ½ cup water
- ½ cup pitted dates, cut into small pieces
- 1/8 teaspoon salt
- 1 stick cinnamon
- 1 cup pumpkin puree
- 1 teaspoon pumpkin spice mix
- ½ cup maple syrup
- 1 teaspoon vanilla extract

Preparation Method
- Bring the milk and water to a boil in an electric pressure cooker pot. Add the soaked rice, dates, cinnamon stick, and salt. Set a cooking timer for 20 minutes.
- When the pressure has released, stir in the pumpkin puree, maple syrup, and pumpkin spice mix. Cook, stirring constantly for 3 to 5 minutes, to thicken the pudding and cook out the raw pumpkin flavor. Remove from the heat and discard the cinnamon stick. Stir in the vanilla.
- Transfer to a bowl and cover the surface with plastic wrap, so it touches the hot pudding, to prevent a skin from forming, and so the steam from the hot pudding doesn't condense and create water on the surface. Let cool about 30 minutes. The pudding will thicken as it cools.
- Spoon into serving cups. Serve warm, or cold, topped with maple-syrup sweetened coconut cashew whipped cream or fresh whipped cream. Sprinkle with pumpkin spice mix and enjoy the taste.

Nutritional Information
- Preparation Time: 25 minutes
- Total Servings: 6
- Calories: 310
- Calories from Fat: 4
- Total Fat: 0.5g
- Saturated Fat: 0.2g
- Cholesterol: 3mg
- Sodium: 315mg
- Potassium: 512mg
- Total Carbohydrates: 69g
- Fiber: 3.3g
- Sugar: 28g
- Protein: 9.3g

Recipe 4: Berry Compote

Tips to cook properly
- Wait until it comes to room temperature and later refrigerate

Ingredients
- 2 cups sliced fresh strawberries
- 1 cup blueberries
- 3/4 cup sugar
- 2 tablespoons lemon juice
- 1 tablespoon cornstarch
- 1 tablespoon water

Preparation Method
- Add strawberries, 1/3 cup blueberries, sugar, and lemon juice to electric pressure cooking pot and stir to combine.
- Select High Pressure and 3 minutes cooking time, use a natural pressure release for 10 minutes.
- In a small bowl, whisk together cornstarch and water. Add to compote in electric pressure cooking pot. Bring to a boil using the Sauté function, stirring constantly.
- Stir in remaining blueberries. Put in a storage container and cool to room temperature. Refrigerate until ready to serve.

Nutritional Information
- Preparation Time: 15 minutes
- Total Servings: 2
- Calories: 134
- Calories from Fat: 0.9
- Total Fat: 0.1g
- Saturated Fat: 0g
- Cholesterol: 0g
- Sodium: 5mg
- Potassium: 53mg
- Total Carbohydrates: 35g
- Fiber: 2g
- Sugar: 28.1g
- Protein: 0.3g

Recipe 5: Chestnut Truffles with Hazelnut

Tips to cook properly
- Overnight refrigeration gives better taste than eating in 1-3 hours

Ingredients
- 1000g fresh chestnuts
- 150g sugar
- 150g butter
- 1 cup hazelnuts
- 125ml rum flavoring
- ¼ cup sweet chocolate powder

Preparation Method
- Wash the chestnuts well, place in your electric pressure cooker and cook for 8 minutes at high pressure.
- Disengage the "keep warm" mode or unplug the cooker and open when the pressure indicator finished. The chestnuts are the easiest to work with while they are still warm and moist.
- Slice each chestnut in half and with a small, rounded object (I used the handle of my teaspoon) insert, twist and get most of the pulp out - leaving the brown fuzzy skin in the shell or picking it out of your chestnut pulp bowl if they fall in.
- Mix in the liquor melted butter and sugar and mash finely with a potato masher.
- If the mix is too wet, let it rest for up to an hour while the chestnut pulp absorbs the excess liquid. Then, form a small ball in your hand, tuck in the whole hazelnut, place the little ball in a plate that is already dusted with cocoa powder to keep them from sticking.
- Drizzle a little cocoa powder on top and then roll again, in your hands, into a tighter ball. Refrigerate for an hour or overnight before serving. Makes 30-48 balls.

Nutritional Information
- Preparation Time: 25 minutes
- Total Servings: 30-48 balls
- Calories: 98
- Calories from Fat: 23
- Total Fat: 12g
- Saturated Fat: 1g
- Cholesterol: 45mg
- Sodium: 233mg
- Potassium: 312mg
- Total Carbohydrates: 23.4g
- Fiber: 2.4g
- Sugar: 10.7g
- Protein: 4.3g

Recipe 6: Lemon Creme Cupcake

Tips to cook properly
- You can replace blackberries with any other fresh available fruits

Ingredients
- 250ml Whole Milk
- 250ml Fresh Cream
- 6 Egg Yolks
- 1 Lemon
- 150g White Sugar
Garnish:
- ½ cup of Fresh blackberries

Preparation Method
- Peel the skin of the lemon with the potato peeler to get wide strips of zest. Then, in a heavy-bottomed saucepan, on medium heat, add the milk, cream and lemon zest. Stir occasionally until the mixture begins to bubble. Turn off the heat and let cool (about 20-30 minutes).
- While the mixture is cooling prepare your electric pressure cooker by adding the minimum amount of water and set it aside.
- In a mixing bowl, add the egg yolks and sugar, whisk until the sugar is dissolved. Then, when the cream & milk mixture has cooled a bit, pour it slowly and incorporate it into the yolks.
- Stir with your whisk just enough to get everything mixed together well. Next, pour the mixture slowly through a strainer into a spouted container. Pour into cups or ramekins, cover with foil and arrange in steamer basket so that all are sitting straight.
- Lower the basket into the pressure cooker carefully, and cook for 10 minutes for ramekins and only 5 minutes for espresso cups.
- Remove the custards and leave to cool uncovered for about 30-45 minutes and serve with fresh fruit and fruit syrup drizzled on top.

Nutritional Information
- Preparation Time: 40 minutes
- Total Servings: 6
- Calories: 344
- Calories from Fat: 68
- Total Fat: 7.3g
- Saturated Fat: 1.1g
- Cholesterol: 1g
- Sodium: 389mg
- Potassium: 64mg
- Total Carbohydrates: 78.1g
- Fiber: 0.7g
- Sugar: 56.2g
- Protein: 2.6g

Recipe 7: Chestnut Jam

Tips to cook properly
- Peeled chestnuts are available in supermarkets

Ingredients
- 750g fresh peeled chestnuts
- 300g white sugar
- 300g water
- Optional: 1/8 cup rum liquor

Preparation Method
- Put all ingredients in pressure cooker and cook for 20 minutes at high pressure.
- Disengage the "keep warm" mode or unplug the cooker and open when the pressure indicator has gone down (20 to 30 minutes).
- Add an optional splash or rum to taste (⅛th of a cup) and blending with an immersion blender until desired consistency. Serve to use as a spread, like jam, on bread, cakes, and sweets.

Nutritional Information
- Preparation Time: 85 minutes
- Total Servings: 10
- Calories: 247
- Calories from Fat:
- Total Fat: 2g
- Saturated Fat:
- Cholesterol: 1mg
- Sodium: 177mg
- Potassium: 344mg
- Total Carbohydrates: 4g
- Fiber: 5g
- Sugar: 18g
- Protein: 4.5g

Recipe 8: Chocolate Fondue

Tips to cook properly
- Before serving, add freshly chopped fruits for better taste

Ingredients
- 100g Swiss Dark Bittersweet Chocolate
- 100g Fresh Cream
- 1 teaspoon Sugar
- 1 teaspoon Amaretto liquor (optional)

Preparation Method
- Prepare the pressure cooker by adding two cups of water and the rack or trivet and set aside.
- In a small ceramic heat-proof container, such as a small fondue pot or ramekin or mug, add the chocolate in large chunks and measure their weight. Then, add the same amount of fresh cream, sugar, and liquor.
- Lower the uncovered container into the pressure cooker. Close and lock the lid of the pressure cooker. Punch in 2 minutes pressure cooking time at high pressure.
- Serve immediately or transfer to a fondue stand with the heat/flame set at medium. Serve with fresh fruit cut into bite-sized pieces, small long cookies or bread cubes.

Nutritional Information
- Preparation Time: 11 minutes
- Total Servings: 2-4
- Calories: 216
- Calories from Fat: 0
- Total Fat: 20.3g
- Saturated Fat: 1.1g
- Cholesterol: 34.3 mg
- Sodium: 9.5mg
- Potassium: 112mg
- Total Carbohydrates: 11.7g
- Fiber: 2.6g
- Sugar: 6.5g
- Protein: 1.8g

Recipe 9: Baked Apples

Tips to cook properly
- Serve apples with lot of liquid

Ingredients
- 6 fresh apples
- 30g raisins
- 250ml red wine
- 100g sugar
- 1 teaspoon cinnamon powder

Preparation Method
- Add the apples to the base of the pressure cooker. Pour in wine, sprinkle raisins, sugar and cinnamon powder. Close and lock the lid of the pressure cooker.
- For electric pressure cookers: Cook for 10 minutes at high pressure. Disengage the "keep warm" mode or unplug the cooker and open when the pressure indicator has gone down (20 to 30 minutes).
- Scoop out of the pressure cooker and serve in a small bowl with lots of cooking liquid.

Nutritional Information
- Preparation Time: 40 minutes
- Total Servings: 6
- Calories: 188.7
- Calories from Fat: 98
- Total Fat: 11.5g
- Saturated Fat: 0.3g
- Cholesterol: 31 mg
- Sodium: 91mg
- Potassium: 197mg
- Total Carbohydrates: 41.9g
- Fiber: 3.8g
- Sugar: 34.7g
- Protein: 0.6g

Recipe 10: Lemon Candies

Tips to cook properly
- After removing, place them in parchment paper and let it dry completely

Ingredients
- 500g organic lemons (about 5 lemons)
- 450g white granulated sugar
- 1.25 liters water

Preparation Method
- Wash the lemons well, using a scrubby sponge to clean the surface. Slice the lemon in half lengthwise and juice - reserve the juice for another use as indicated in the introduction.
- Slice off the nub at the tip, and then slice each half in quarters. Hold the quarters flat on the cutting board peel or slice out the out the pulp. Slice the de-pulped lemon quarters into thin strips.
- To the pressure cooker add the lemon peel strips and four cups of water and cook for 3 minutes at high pressure. Strain the lemon peel strips and rinse them. Then, discard cooking water and rinse out the pressure cooker.
- Add sugar, 1 cup water, lemon strips on medium heat and cook for 10 minutes at high pressure.
- Strain peels, saving the delicate syrup if you like for another use and spread the peels on a parchment paper to cool for 15 minutes or more.
- Gently toss four to five peels at a time in a small plate of sugar to coat. Put the sheet pan with the sugared-coated candied lemon peels in the refrigerator uncovered for at least 4 hours to dry completely -overnight is even better.
- Move the strips to a glass jar for storage in a cool dry place for 6-8 weeks - or keep refrigerated for up to six months.

Nutritional Information
- Preparation Time: 50 minutes
- Total Servings: 80 pieces
- Calories: 6.2
- Calories from Fat: 0
- Total Fat: 0g
- Saturated Fat: 0g
- Cholesterol: 0 mg
- Sodium: 10mg
- Potassium: 17mg
- Total Carbohydrates: 1.7g
- Fiber: 0.1g
- Sugar: 1.5g
- Protein: 0.2g

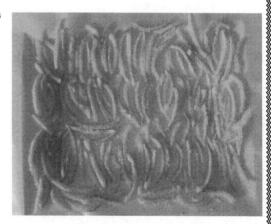

Recipe 11: Cheese Flan

Tips to cook properly
- Add caramel after removing from cooker and before serving

Ingredients
- 400g sweetened condensed milk
- 340g evaporated milk
- 225g cream cheese
- 5 eggs
- 1 teaspoon vanilla extract
- 1/2 teaspoon cinnamon
- 1/2 teaspoon nutmeg
- caramel: 6 tablespoons sugar

Preparation Method
- Make the caramel; use your flan pan to melt the sugar. Stir until it is melted and a medium brown color. Don't let it burn. Remove from heat and swirl the liquid sugar to coat the sides of the pan. Make the custard while it cools.
- Put the cream cheese in a medium sized bowl. Add each egg one at a time until nicely blended. Add remaining ingredients and put in your caramelized pan.
- Put a couple inches of water in the pressure cooker and place the flan on a trivet, cook it on manual for 15 minutes. Let the pressure drop naturally. Remove flan from cooker and let cool to room temp, then refrigerate for 6 – 8 hours or longer if you want.
- Run a knife around the edge of the pan, flip onto a plate that has a rim to catch the caramel. Slice and enjoy.

Nutritional Information
- Preparation Time: 25 minutes
- Total Servings: 8
- Calories: 475
- Calories from Fat: 194
- Total Fat: 21.5g
- Saturated Fat: 12.3g
- Cholesterol: 201mg
- Sodium: 252mg
- Potassium: 425mg
- Total Carbohydrates: 58g
- Fiber: 0g
- Sugar: 55.3g
- Protein: 14.3g

Recipe 12: Zucchini Nut Bread

Tips to cook properly
- Wait until natural release and remove cake slowly from cooker

Ingredients
- 3 eggs
- 1 cup applesauce
- 2 cups sugar
- 1 tablespoon vanilla extract
- 2 cups grated zucchini
- 2 1/2 cups flour
- 1/2 cups cocoa powder
- 1 teaspoon salt
- 1 teaspoon baking soda
- 1 teaspoon cinnamon or pumpkin pie spice
- 1/4 teaspoon baking powder
- 1/2 cup chopped walnuts
- 1/2 cup chocolate chips

Preparation Method
- Beat eggs, applesauce, sugar, and vanilla. Stir in zucchini.
- Combine all dry ingredients. Add zucchini mixture and blend well.
- Pour into greased pan to fit your pressure cooker, I used an 8″ bundt pan.
- Pour 1 1/2 cups water into the pot and put the trivet in the bottom. Lower pan into a pressure cooker in a foil sling to facilitate removal after the cake is done and set it on the trivet.
- Cook for 25 minutes on manual (high)
- Natural release for 10 minutes and then open the lid and remove cake to cool.

Nutritional Information
- Preparation Time: 40 minutes
- Total Servings: 12
- Calories: 276
- Calories from Fat:111
- Total Fat: 12.4g
- Saturated Fat: 1.2g
- Cholesterol: 31mg
- Sodium: 253mg
- Potassium: 123mg
- Total Carbohydrates: 35.6g
- Fiber: 1.1g
- Sugar: 16.7g
- Protein: 4g

Recipe 13: Creamy Rice Pudding

Tips to cook properly
- If desire, add little cream on top before serving

Ingredients
- 1 cups rice
- 3/4 cups sugar
- 1/2 teaspoon salt
- 5 cups milk
- 2 eggs
- 1 teaspoons vanilla extract
- 1 cup golden raisins
- 1 teaspoon cinnamon

Preparation Method
- In a pressure cooker add rice, sugar, salt, and milk. Press the Sauté button. Stir and bring to a boil. Stir constantly to dissolve the sugar. It does not take long to come to a boil.
- As soon as the mixture comes to a boil. Turn to the stream release. Press the rice button.
- While the rice is cooking, in a bowl whisk the eggs, half and half, and the vanilla extract.
- When you hear the beep sound telling you that the rice is finished cooking, press cancel. Wait 15 minutes.
- After the 15 minutes, use the quick pressure release. Stir the egg mixture into the pot. You can add the raisins here if you wish.
- Press the Sauté button. Cook uncovered till the mixture begins to boil. Press Cancel to turn off the cooker. Stir in the raisins. Serve immediately or chill.

Nutritional Information
- Preparation Time: 35 minutes
- Total Servings: 4
- Calories: 384
- Calories from Fat: 121
- Total Fat: 14.1g
- Saturated Fat: 7.4g
- Cholesterol: 127mg
- Sodium: 245mg
- Potassium: 591mg
- Total Carbohydrates: 56g
- Fiber: 1g
- Sugar: 31.2g
- Protein: 12.6g

Recipe 14: Smoked Salmon Cheesecake

Tips to cook properly
- Don't forget to refrigerate

Ingredients
- 450g cream cheese
- 2 small Boursin kinds of cheese
- 1 tablespoon sour cream
- 4 eggs
- 1 tablespoon chopped parsley
- 1 tablespoon fresh dill
- 1/2 tablespoon half chopped chives
- 225g smoked salmon
- 80g grated parmesan cheese
- 1 lemon juice

Preparation Method
- Placed all of the cheeses, cream, eggs and herbs into a food processor and whizzed briefly until mixed. Added the lemon juice and chopped smoked salmon and whizzed briefly.
- Poured into the cake tin (it was very liquid) and wrapped the outside of the tin in foil (not covering the top) and made a sling of folded foil to lift the cheesecake in and out.
- One cup of water in the pot, trivet, and cheesecake on top of the trivet. Cook for 25 minutes and quick release when it finished and I left to cool then placed in the fridge overnight.

Nutritional Information
- Preparation Time: 30 minutes
- Total Servings: 4-8 pieces
- Calories: 375
- Calories from Fat: 265
- Total Fat: 29.5g
- Saturated Fat:16.2g
- Cholesterol: 117mg
- Sodium: 209mg
- Potassium: 119mg
- Total Carbohydrates: 23.1g
- Fiber: 0.6g
- Sugar: 17g
- Protein: 6g

Recipe 15: Chocolate Bean Cake

Tips to cook properly
- If desire, garnish with chopped cashews and walnuts

Ingredients
- 1 cup borlotti beans
- ½ cup cocoa powder
- ½ cup raw honey
- ⅛ teaspoon pure almond extract
- 3 tablespoons olive oil
- 2 large eggs
- 1/8 teaspoon sea salt
- 2 teaspoon baking powder
- Garnish: ¼ cup sliced almonds

Preparation Method
- In a pressure cooker, add the soaked rinsed and strained beans and water and cook for 12 minutes at high pressure.
- Strain the beans and place into a food processor and blend to almost a puree.
- In the meantime, rinse out the pressure cooker and add one cup of water and steamer basket, and set aside.
- Lightly coat a 4-cup capacity heat-proof bowl with olive oil, and an optional sprinkle of cocoa powder, and set aside.
- Into the processor add the cocoa powder, honey, almond extract, olive oil, eggs, and salt. Puree the contents of the processor at high speed until well combined, then add the baking powder and process for about a minute.
- Using a spatula plop the contents of the processor into the heat-proof bowl. Lower the uncovered heat-proof bowl onto the steamer basket. Cook for 20 minutes at high pressure in an electric pressure cooker.
- Remove the cake and let cool for about 5 minutes before unmoulding the cake onto a serving dish and garnish with sliced almonds.

Nutritional Information
- Preparation Time: 60 minutes
- Total Servings: 8
- Calories: 163.4
- Calories from Fat: 0
- Total Fat: 7.8g
- Saturated Fat: 1.2g
- Cholesterol: 53.8 mg
- Sodium: 187.7mg
- Potassium: 166mg
- Total Carbohydrates: 24.4g
- Fiber: 3.9g
- Sugar: 16.1g
- Protein: 4.4g

Recipe 16: Apple and Ricotta Cake

Tips to cook properly
- Make sure that steamer basket fits properly into electric pressure cooker

Ingredients
- 2 cups water
- 2 apples
- 1 tablespoon lemon juice
- ¼ cup raw sugar
- 1 egg
- 1 cup ricotta cheese
- ⅓ cup sugar
- 3 tablespoons olive oil
- 1 teaspoon vanilla extract
- 1 cup all-purpose flour
- ⅛ teaspoon cinnamon
- 2 teaspoons baking powder
- 1 teaspoon baking soda

Preparation Method
- Prepare pressure cooker by adding water to the base, plus steamer basket and set aside.
- Slice one apple and dice the other and cover with lemon juice. Prepare a shallow and wide 4-cup capacity heat-proof bowl by adding a disk of wax paper at the bottom and oiling and dusting the interior with flour.
- Sprinkle the base of the bowl with raw sugar and arrange the sliced apples artistically. In a small mixing bowl, mix the egg, ricotta, sugar, olive oil and vanilla using a fork. Then, sprinkle the flour, cinnamon, baking powder and baking soda in the mixing bowl using a flour sifter, or fine mesh strainer.
- Blend well with a fork and then stir in the apple dices. Pour into prepared bowl and lower into the pressure cooker
- Cook for 15 to 20 minutes at high pressure. Turn the cake out onto a serving plate. Serve warm or chilled.

Nutritional Information
- Preparation Time: 30 minutes
- Total Servings: 6
- Calories: 160
- Calories from Fat: 53
- Total Fat: 5.9g
- Saturated Fat: 2.1g
- Cholesterol: 4.1g
- Sodium: 68mg
- Potassium: 64mg
- Total Carbohydrates: 22.9g
- Fiber: 0.5g
- Sugar: 15.3g
- Protein: 4.4g

Recipe 17: Crema Catalana

Tips to cook properly
- Before serving, add little cream and nutmeg

Ingredients
- 500ml fresh cream
- 6 egg yolks
- 80g white sugar
- 1 cinnamon stick
- 1 orange zested

Garnish:
- 1 teaspoon nutmeg
- 4 tablespoons raw sugar for caramelizing

Preparation Method
- Begin by heating up the cream, citrus zest and cinnamon stick on low heat in the small saucepan and stirring occasionally. When the cream begins to boil turn off the heat and let the ingredients infuse (about 30 minutes).
- In the meantime, prepare your pressure cooker by adding two cups of water, and steamer basket. Set aside.
- In a mixing bowl, add the egg yolks and sugar, whisk until the sugar is dissolved. Then, when the cream has cooled to room temperature, add the yolks and stir with your whisk just enough to get everything mixed together well.
- Next, pour the mixture slowly through a strainer into a spouted container. Pour the mixture into ramekins, cover tightly with foil and arrange in the steamer basket, close pressure cooker.
- Put 8 minutes cooking time for ramekins and only 5 minutes cooking time for espresso cups, after that press cancel button.
- If they are still very liquid, set pressure cook for an additional 5 minutes with the same opening procedure noted above.
- Remove the custards and once the custards are cooled, cover them with plastic wrap and place them in the refrigerator to chill for 3-4 hours or overnight. Before serving, grate a little nutmeg and sprinkle a layer of sugar.

Nutritional Information
- Preparation Time: 85 minutes
- Total Servings: 4
- Calories: 410
- Calories from Fat: 132
- Total Fat: 14.7g
- Saturated Fat: 8.8g
- Cholesterol: 83mg
- Sodium: 319mg
- Potassium: 91mg
- Total Carbohydrates: 66.4g
- Fiber: 0.7g
- Sugar: 45.4g
- Protein: 4.6g

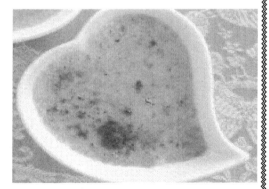

Recipe 18: Chocolate Bread Pudding

Tips to cook properly
- If desire, add scoop of vanilla, strawberry ice cream before serving

Ingredients
- 2 cups water
- 2 tablespoons butter
- 2 large eggs
- 5 tablespoons white sugar
- 1 cup whole milk
- 1 teaspoon vanilla extract
- 1/8 teaspoon kosher salt
- 200 grams multi-grain bread
- 100 grams bittersweet chocolate
- 1 tablespoon raw sugar
- 1 tablespoon butter

Preparation Method
- Prepare the pressure cooker by adding two cups of water and the trivet.
- In a large bowl, whisk the eggs and sugar then add the milk, vanilla extract, and salt. Pour the bread cubes into the mixing bowl and lightly mix with your fingers and let stand 5 minutes.
- Then, mix again and pour bread cubes and any remaining custard mixture into the buttered heat-proof dish. Add the chocolate chunks, again mixing lightly to ensure even distribution.
- Let stand again for another 5 minutes and give everything a final mix. Place 2 cups water in the pressure cooker and cook for 10-15 minutes at high pressure.
- Carefully lift out the pudding from the pressure cooker and sprinkle the top with raw sugar, and lastly with little dots of butter. Slide under the broiler for about 5 minutes or until the top has crisped and the sugar has caramelized.
- Serve with a drizzle of heavy cream or a scoop of vanilla ice cream.

Nutritional Information
- Preparation Time: minutes
- Total Servings: 4-6
- Calories: 306
- Calories from Fat: 163
- Total Fat: 18.2g
- Saturated Fat: 8.5g
- Cholesterol: 90mg
- Sodium: 169mg
- Potassium: 180mg
- Total Carbohydrates: 33.9g
- Fiber: 1.6g
- Sugar: 23.4g
- Protein: 5.5g

Recipe 19: Orange Ricotta Cake

Tips to cook properly
- Don't forget, foil lifter for keeping in and taking out from cooker

Ingredients
- 1000g Ricotta
- 4 eggs
- 1/4 cup of white sugar
- 1/4 cup of organic honey
- 1 cup of dates soaked for 20 minutes
- 1/2 lemon zest and juice
- 1/4 teaspoon vanilla extract

Preparation Method
- Beat ricotta until smooth and in a separate bowl/food processor.
- Beat eggs and sugar for 3 minutes then combine with ricotta.
- Add warm honey and whisk in with orange juice, add vanilla and zest then whisk into cheese mixture followed with the chopped dates.
- Combine well for at least a few minutes to distribute dates and create a smooth batter and pour into a buttered pan or a heatproof dish suitable for the electric pressure cooker.
- Cover with foil and make a foil lifter 3 fold and long enough to go under and up the sides of you cake pan/dish.
- Place a trivet at the bottom of your pressure cooker and add approximately 2 cups of water, place the foil lifter under your pan lower into pressure cooker pan folding the foil handles inwards.
- Set pressure to high for 20 minutes and quick release. Serve dusted with icing sugar or sweetener cocoa powder, warm or well chilled.

Nutritional Information
- Preparation Time: 40 minutes
- Total Servings: 6
- Calories: 250
- Calories from Fat: 87
- Total Fat: 9.6g
- Saturated Fat: 5.3g
- Cholesterol: 96mg
- Sodium: 94mg
- Potassium: 144mg
- Total Carbohydrates: 31g
- Fiber: 0.7g
- Sugar: 19.3g
- Protein: 6.2g

Recipe 20: Eggnog Cheesecake

Tips to cook properly
- Refrigerating overnight gives delicious taste

Ingredients
Crust:
- 2 teaspoons butter
- 1/2 cup ground ginger snap cookies
Filling:
- 450g regular cream cheese
- 1/2 cup sugar
- 2 large eggs
- 1 teaspoon pineapple flavoring
- 1/2 teaspoon ground nutmeg
- 1/2 teaspoon vanilla

Preparation Method
- Prepare a foil strip to lower cake into the pressure cooker. Cut off an 18″ long piece of standard-width aluminum foil and set aside.
- Grease the bottom and sides of the springform pan with melted butter. Before butter sets, quickly coat the sides of the pan with the crumbs and distribute the remaining crumbs on the bottom.
- Using an electric mixer or food processor, blend the cream cheese and sugar till smooth. Blend in eggs, nutmeg, pineapple flavoring and vanilla. (Do not over mix the batter) Pour the batter into the prepared pan.
- Pour 2 cups water into a 6-quart or larger cooker. Set a trivet on the bottom of the cooker to raise the cheesecake above the water.
- Center the uncovered pan on the foil strip and lower it onto the trivet. Fold down the ends of the strip.
- Manually set electric pressure timer for 15 minutes and cook.
- Remove and refrigerate for at least 4 hours or overnight. Serve the cheesecake with your favorite topping.

Nutritional Information
- Preparation Time: 24 minutes
- Total Servings: 8
- Calories: 410
- Calories from Fat: 303
- Total Fat: 33.6g
- Saturated Fat: 18.1mg
- Cholesterol: 182mg
- Sodium: 301mg
- Potassium: 112mg
- Total Carbohydrates: 21.5g
- Fiber: 0.2g
- Sugar: 16.7g
- Protein: 5.6g

Recipe 21: Fruit Clafoutis Cake

Tips to cook properly
- Don't add frozen fruits, try to get and add fresh fruits for delicious taste

Ingredients
- 300g fruits
- 2 eggs
- 100g sugar
- 100g all-purpose flour
- 250ml milk
- 1 tablespoon vanilla extract
- powdered sugar
- olive oil

Preparation Method
- Prepare your electric pressure cooker by adding a trivet, or steamer basket, to keep the form from touching the bottom of the pan.
- Add two cups of water to the pressure cooker and set aside. Wash and de-seed, stem and prepare the fruit of your choice.
- In a mixing bowl, add the eggs, sugar, and vanilla and mix them well with a whisk or fork. Next, add the flour and milk. Oil the form and line with wax paper. Pour the mixture, and then sprinkle the fruit into the mixture evenly. Cover tightly with tin foil.
- Place in pressure cooker and set pressure cooker timer to 20 minutes and cook. When it is ready, remove the form the pressure cooker, let it cool and then pull out the dessert. Move to a serving dish and sprinkle with powdered sugar right before serving. Serve warm or chilled.

Nutritional Information
- Preparation Time: 25 minutes
- Total Servings: 6-8
- Calories: 223
- Calories from Fat: 34
- Total Fat: 3.8g
- Saturated Fat: 1.4g
- Cholesterol: 97mg
- Sodium: 57mg
- Potassium: 167mg
- Total Carbohydrates: 41
- Fiber: 1.6g
- Sugar: 27.4g
- Protein: 5.9g

Recipe 22: Triple Chocolate Cheesecake

Tips to cook properly
- Wait minimum 60 minutes before serving

Ingredients
Crust:
- 4 tablespoons butter
- 1 ½ cups chocolate cookie crumbs
Cheesecake Filling:
- 225g packages cheese cream
- 1 cup sugar
- 2 tablespoons cornstarch
- 3 large eggs
- ½ cup plain greek yogurt
- 1 tablespoon vanilla extract
- 110g milk chocolate
- 110g white chocolate
- 110g dark chocolate
Topping: sugared cranberries

Preparation Method
- Spray a deep dish 7-inch springform pan with nonstick cooking spray.
- Line the bottom of the pan with parchment paper for easy removal of the cake once it's done.
- Stir cookie crumbs and melted butter together and press evenly across the bottom and halfway up the sides of the pan. Place in the freezer to set (this can be done 2-3 days in advance).
- Cream the cream cheese with a handheld mixer on low speed until very smooth, scrape the bowl and mix again.
- Add sugar and cornstarch, continue to scrape and mix the ingredients together on low speed until well combined and smooth.
- Add eggs, one at a time, continuing to mix and scrape bowl as needed. Finally, add yogurt and vanilla and mix just until blended. Scrape the bowl and continue to stir by hand until smooth, if needed.
- Divide batter into 3 separate bowls (about 2 cups each). Melt the milk chocolate in the microwave for 30 seconds, stir. Return the chocolate to the microwave for another 15-30 seconds and stir until it is completely melted and smooth.
- Whisk into one of the bowls of cheesecake batter. Repeat with the white and dark chocolate (each being stirred into a different bowl of batter).
- Refrigerate the 3 bowls for 15-20 minutes so they will be more firm for layering. Remove the bowls from the fridge and take the pan with the crust out of the freezer. Time to layer!
- Pour dark chocolate batter into the center of the crust and smooth to form an even layer. Very carefully spoon dollops of the white chocolate batter on top of the dark chocolate, gently smooth over the top. Repeat with milk chocolate batter.

- Add 1 cup of water to the electric pressure cooker and place trivet inside. Carefully lower the prepared pan onto the trivet. Cook at high pressure for 45 minutes.
- Remove pan from the pressure cooker and let cool for 10 minutes. Slowly remove the spring form ring, being careful not to break the crust.
- Allow the cake to cool completely and then cover and place in the refrigerator (at least 4 hours, overnight is best).
- Before serving, let stand at room temperature 30-60 minutes. Decorate with sugared cranberries, if desired.

Nutritional Information

- Preparation Time: 15 minutes
- Total Servings: 8-10
- Calories: 415
- Calories from Fat: 204
- Total Fat: 22.7g
- Saturated Fat: 11.6g
- Cholesterol: 73mg
- Sodium: 258mg
- Potassium: 264mg
- Total Carbohydrates: 45.2g
- Fiber: 1.9g
- Sugar: 37.2g
- Protein: 7.2g

Recipe 23: Cinnamon Poached Pears

Tips to cook properly
- Cut bottom of pears to make it stand properly in plate

Ingredients
- 1 lemon
- 3 cups water
- 2 cups white wine
- 2 cups organic cane sugar
- 6 cinnamon sticks
- 6 Bartlett pears

Chocolate Sauce:
- 250g dark chocolate
- 1/2 cup coconut milk
- ¼ cup coconut oil
- 2 tablespoons maple syrup or honey

Preparation Method
- Put the water, wine, sugar, and cinnamon sticks in the electric pressure cooking pot. Select Sauté and bring to a simmer, stirring until the sugar dissolves.
- Switch to the Keep Warm setting so the liquid stays hot until the pears are peeled and ready.
- Peel the pears, keeping them whole, with the stems intact. Rub them immediately with the cut lemon to keep from turning brown. Squeeze the remaining lemon juice into the wine/sugar syrup and drop the juiced lemon into the syrup.Slip the pears into the hot syrup, lock the lid and bring to high pressure for 3 minutes.
- Carefully remove the pears with a slotted spoon and let cool. When the syrup has cooled a bit, pour it over the pears.
- To make the Chocolate Sauce, place the chocolate in a bowl. In a small saucepan, over medium flame, heat the coconut milk, coconut oil, and maple syrup just to the boil. Pour it over the chocolate and let sit a minute. Whisk until smooth. Keep warm until you serve the pears.
- To serve, slice a little piece off the bottom of each pear and so they will stand up. Place each pear on a plate and pour the warm chocolate sauce over.

Nutritional Information
- Preparation Time: 10 minutes
- Total Servings: 6
- Calories: 400
- Calories from Fat: 43
- Total Fat: 4.8g
- Saturated Fat: 2.1g
- Cholesterol: 0.56g
- Sodium: 183mg
- Potassium: 399mg
- Total Carbohydrates: 65.2g

- Fiber: 6.2g
- Sugar: 45.4g
- Protein: 4g

Recipe 24: Orange Cheesecake

Tips to cook properly
- Garnish with whipped cream, grated orange candy melts, and Oreo cookie crumbs.

Ingredients
- 1 cup crushed Oreo cookie crumbs
- 2 tablespoons butter melted
Filling:
- 450g cream cheese
- 1/2 cup sugar
- 2 tablespoons sour cream
- 1 teaspoon vanilla extract
- 2 eggs
- 1/2 cup orange candy melts
- 1 tablespoon orange zest

Preparation Method
- Prepare a 7-inch springform pan by coating it with a non-stick spray.
- In a small bowl, combine the Oreo cookie crumbs and butter. Spread evenly on the bottom and 1 inch up the side of the pan. Place in the freezer for 10 minutes.
- Place 8 ounces of cream cheese into a mixing bowl. Add 1/4 cup sugar and beat at medium speed until smooth. Blend in sour cream, and vanilla. Mix in one egg just until blended.
- In a second mixing bowl, place 8 ounces of cream cheese and add 1/4 cup sugar and beat until smooth. Gradually beat in melted candy melts. Mix in one egg just until blended. Stir in orange zest.
- Scatter dollops of vanilla batter on top of the crust alternating with dollops of orange batter. Use a skewer to swirl the orange and vanilla batters together.
- Pour 1 cup of water into the electric pressure cooking pot, and place the trivet in the bottom. Carefully center the filled pan on a foil sling and lower it into the pressure cooking pot. Fold the foil sling down so that it doesn't interfere with closing the lid.
- Lock the lid in place. Select High Pressure and set the timer for 25 minutes, use a natural pressure release for 10 minutes, and then do a quick pressure release to release any remaining pressure. When valve drops carefully remove the lid.
- Remove cheesecake and check the cheesecake to see if the middle is set but slightly jiggly like a set jello. If not, cook the cheesecake an additional 5 minutes. Use the corner of a paper towel to soak up any water on top of the cheesecake.
- Remove the springform pan to a wire rack to cool. When cheesecake is cooled, refrigerate covered with plastic wrap for at least 4 hours or overnight. Refrigerate until ready to serve.
- Decorate with whipped cream, grated orange candy melts, and Oreo cookie crumbs.

Nutritional Information

- Preparation Time: minutes
- Total Servings: 6
- Calories: 516
- Calories from Fat: 223
- Total Fat: 26g
- Saturated Fat: 10.3g
- Cholesterol: 98mg
- Sodium: 254mg
- Potassium: 127mg
- Total Carbohydrates: 55g
- Fiber: 0.6g
- Sugar: 39.2g
- Protein: 7.1g

Recipe 25: Raspberry Cheesecake

Tips to cook properly
- Use the corner of a paper towel to soak up any water on top of the cheesecake

Ingredients
- 1 cup crushed Oreo cookie crumbs (12 Oreos)
- 2 tablespoons butter melted

Filling:
- 450g cream cheese
- 1/4 cup sugar
- 1/2 cup seedless raspberry jam
- 1/4 cup sour cream
- 1 tablespoon all-purpose flour
- 2 eggs

Topping:
- 170g milk chocolate
- 1/3 cup heavy cream
- Fresh raspberries

Preparation Method
- Prepare a 7-inch springform pan by coating it with a non-stick spray. Line with parchment paper if desired.
- In a small bowl, combine the Oreo cookie crumbs and butter. Spread evenly on the bottom and 1 inch up the side of the pan. Place in the freezer for 10 minutes.
- In a mixing bowl mix cream cheese and sugar at medium speed until smooth. Blend in jam, sour cream, and flour. Mix in eggs one at a time just until blended. Pour batter into the springform pan on top of the crust.
- Pour 1 cup of water into the electric pressure cooking pot, and place the trivet in the bottom. Carefully center the filled pan on a foil sling and lower it into the pressure cooking pot. Fold the foil sling down so that it doesn't interfere with closing the lid.
- Select High Pressure and set the timer for 25 minutes. Remove cheesecake and check the cheesecake to see if the middle is set. If not, cook the cheesecake an additional 5 minutes. Use the corner of a paper towel to soak up any water on top of the cheesecake.
- Remove the springform pan to a wire rack to cool. When cheesecake is cooled, refrigerate covered with plastic wrap for at least 4 hours or overnight.
- When cheesecake is chilled, prepare topping, place half of the chocolate in a mixing bowl. Heat heavy cream on medium-high heat until it comes to a boil.
- Remove from heat and immediately pour cream over chocolate and stir until chocolate is completely melted. Add remaining chocolate and stir until chocolate is completely melted.
- Cool until ganache is thickened but still thin enough to drip down the sides of the cheesecake. Spoon chocolate ganache on top of the cheesecake, spreading to edges and letting the ganache drip down the sides. Decorate top with raspberries. Refrigerate until ready to serve.

Nutritional Information
- Preparation Time: 25 minutes
- Total Servings: 6
- Calories: 412
- Calories from Fat: 254
- Total Fat: 28.3g
- Saturated Fat: 16.4g
- Cholesterol: 95mg
- Sodium: 226mg
- Potassium: 109mg
- Total Carbohydrates: 34.4g
- Fiber: 1g
- Sugar: 29g
- Protein: 6.8g

Recipe 26: Mini Egg Cakes

Tips to cook properly
- Before refrigerate, cover cakes with plastic wrap for overnight for delicious taste

Ingredients
Crust:
- 1 cup graham cracker crumbs (8 crackers)
- 3 tablespoons butter
- 1 tablespoon sugar

Filling:
- 340g cream cheese
- 1/4 cup granulated sugar
- 2 tablespoons sour cream
- 1/2 teaspoon vanilla extract
- pinch of salt
- 1 large egg
- 1 cup eggs malted milk candies
- Whipped cream

Preparation Method
- Prepare six 6-ounce glass custard cups by spraying them with non-stick cooking spray.
- In a small bowl, combine the graham cracker crumbs, butter, and sugar. Divide evenly between the six custard cups. Press evenly into the bottom and up the side of the pans about 1/2 inch. Place in the freezer for 10 minutes.
- In a mixing bowl, mix cream cheese and sugar at medium speed until smooth. Add sour cream, vanilla, and salt and mix just until blended. Add egg and mix just until blended. Gently fold in egg candies. Divide batter evenly between the six cups.
- Pour 1 cup of water into the electric pressure cooking pot, and place the trivet in the bottom. Place three cups on the trivet. Place the second trivet on top of the cups and place the remaining three cups on top.
- Select High Pressure and set the timer for 5 minutes. Remove the cups to a wire rack to cool. If necessary, remove any water drops from the top of the cheesecake with a corner of a paper towel.
- When cheesecake is cooled, refrigerate covered with plastic wrap for at least 4 hours or overnight. Serve topped with whipped cream.

Nutritional Information
- Preparation Time: 15 minutes
- Total Servings: 6
- Calories: 204
- Calories from Fat: 135
- Total Fat: 15g
- Saturated Fat: 7.8g
- Cholesterol: 72mg

- Sodium: 141mg
- Potassium: 63mg
- Total Carbohydrates: 13.7g
- Fiber: 0.1g
- Sugar: 5.7mg
- Protein: 4.1g

Recipe 27: Apple Crumb Cake

Tips to cook properly
- Before serving, sprinkle with powdered sugar

Ingredients
- 6 small red apples
- 170g Butter
- 1 square of butter
- 2 tablespoons all-purpose flour
- ¼ cup raw sugar
Crumb Filling:
- 150g dry breadcrumbs
- 120g Sugar
- 1 teaspoon cinnamon
- 1 teaspoon ginger powder
- ½ lemon, juice, and rind

Preparation Method
- Prepare the ingredients for the crumb filling by combining the breadcrumbs, sugar, cinnamon, ginger, lemon juice, zest and melted butter.
- Mix well and set aside while you work on your apples and prepare your container. Take your unpeeled well-washed apples and remove their core. Then, slice them very thinly- use a mandolin, if you can, for really nice, even, thin slices.
- Butter the interior of the container all the way up to the edge. Next, put the tablespoons of flour in the container and swoosh the flour around so that you have an even coat of flour stuck to the butter inside the container.
- Begin layering the apple slices. The bottom layer will become the top when you flip the cake out of the container so arrange the apple slices carefully for this first layer. I laid them in a fan shape, being careful that the hole from the core did not show.
- Add a layer of bread crumb mixture. Alternate apple and breadcrumb layers until your container is full or you run out of ingredients. Don't worry, the other layers of apples do not need to be so carefully laid - just ensure that you have apple slices all the way to the edge of the container and in a relatively even layer.
- When you are finished filling your container, cover tightly with tin foil. Prepare the electric pressure cooker by adding the minimum amount of water required, usually 1 to 2 cups, and placing the trivet.
- Lower the container in the pressure cooker onto the steamer basket/trivet. Cook for 20 minutes at high pressure.
- Open the pressure cooker with the Natural release method and disengage the "keep warm" mode or unplug the cooker.
- Now, sprinkle the top of the cake with a nice layer of raw sugar and grill until the sugar has melted and the top of the cake is a beautiful golden brown.

Nutritional Information
- Preparation Time: 30 minutes

- Total Servings: 6
- Calories: 212
- Calories from Fat: 86
- Total Fat: 9.5g
- Saturated Fat: 2.5g
- Cholesterol: 24mg
- Sodium: 59mg
- Potassium: 41mg
- Total Carbohydrates: 28.3g
- Fiber: 0.4g
- Sugar: 17.2g
- Protein: 2.7g

Recipe 28: Brulee Cheesecake

Tips to cook properly
- Be careful, before removing the cheesecakes from the baking cups

Ingredients
Cheesecake Crust:
- 90g graham crackers
- 56g butter
- Pinch of sea salt
- 19g brown sugar
- 32g all-purpose flour
Cheesecake Mixture:
- 454g cream cheese
- 2 large eggs
- 133g white sugar
- 120g sour cream
- 16g cornstarch
- 10ml vanilla extract
- Pinch of sea salt
Crackable Caramel:
- 2 teaspoons white sugar per cheesecake bite

Preparation Method
- Make the Cheesecake Crust: Finely ground the graham crackers in a food processor. Finely ground graham crackers with rolling pin to create cheesecake crust
- In a small mixing bowl, mix ground graham crackers, sea salt, and 2 brown sugar together with a fork. Add all-purpose flour, butter and mix until the mixture sticks together.
- Place about 1 tbsp graham cracker crumbs into each silicone baking cups. Gently press down the crumbs with a spoon to form a nice, even layer. Place the baking cups in the freezer while making the cheesecake mixture.
- Cheesecake Crust: Place the baking cups in a 325°F oven for 12-15 minutes.
- Make the Cheesecake Mixture: Mix cornstarch, sea salt, white sugar together.
- In a medium mixing bowl, beat cream cheese on low speed with a hand mixer until creamy. Add in half of the sugar mixture and beat until incorporated using low speed.
- Scrape down the sides and the hand mixer with a silicone spatula every time a new ingredient is added. Add the remaining sugar mixture and beat until incorporated using low speed.
- Add sour cream and vanilla extract to the cream cheese mixture. Beat until incorporated using low speed. Blend in two eggs using low speed, one at a time. Mix well after adding each egg. Fill the baking cups to ⅔ full with cream cheese mixture.
- For Smooth Surface: Tap the baking cups against the counter a few times to let the air bubbles rise to the surface. Burst the air bubbles with a toothpick. Tap it a few more times until no air bubbles rise to the surface.

- Pressure Cook the Cheesecake: Pour 1 cup (250 ml) of cold running tap water into the Electric Pressure Cooker. Place the baking cups on top of a trivet that doesn't touch the water. At High Pressure for 7 minutes and Full Natural Release. The natural release will take roughly 7 minutes. Open the lid carefully.
- Cool the Cheesecake: Remove the baking cups from the Pressure Cooker and place them on a wire rack. After a few minutes, carefully run your thumb against the rim of the baking cups to avoid the cheesecake from sticking.
- Chill the Cheesecake in the Fridge: Once the cheesecake baking cups have completely cooled, loosely cover them with aluminum foil. Then, place it in the refrigerator for at least 4 – 6 hours.
- Serve: Carefully remove the cheesecakes from the baking cups. Spread roughly 1 ½ - 2 teaspoons white sugar evenly on top of each cheesecake bite.

Nutritional Information
- Preparation Time: 35 minutes
- Total Servings: 10
- Calories: 423
- Calories from Fat: 290
- Total Fat:34.3g
- Saturated Fat: 10.2g
- Cholesterol: 34mg
- Sodium: 261mg
- Potassium: 200mg
- Total Carbohydrates: 34g
- Fiber: 3.6g
- Sugar: 22.2g
- Protein: 8.1g

Recipe 29: Christmas Pudding Cake

Tips to cook properly
- Be careful, while lifting the cake out of the pressure cooker

Ingredients
- 100g cranberries
- 100g dry apricots
- ⅛ teaspoon olive oil
- 125g all-purpose flour
- 200g sugar
- 11g baking powder
- 2 grams ginger powder
- 1 gram cinnamon powder
- 1 pinch salt
- 200g butter
- 4 large eggs
- 50g maple syrup
- 100g carrot

Preparation Method
- Put the dried cranberries and apricots, in a small deep bowl and cover with boiling water.
- Prepare a pudding mold, or 5-cup capacity heat-proof bowl by adding a drop of olive oil, and then spreading it around with a paper towel until the inside of the bowl is well covered, and set aside.
- Prepare the pressure cooker base with two cups of cold water and the steamer basket or trivet. Into a food processor bowl add the flour, sugar, baking powder, cinnamon, ginger, and salt. Pulse a few times to mix. Then, add the chopped butter and pulse a few more times until evenly distributed.
- Next, add the eggs and maple syrup, and pulse the processor a few times until well blended. Strain the dried fruit, and give it a quick rinse under cold water if it's still a little bit hot. Sprinkle the dried fruit and grated carrot on top of the mixture. Coax the pudding batter into the prepared bowl using the spatula. Lower the uncovered bowl onto the steamer basket and close the pressure cooker lid.
- Electric pressure cookers: turn on the Brown/Sauté setting and when steam starts to sneak out of the pressure cooker (in about 10 minutes), start counting down 15 minutes of steam without pressure pre-cooking time. Cook for 35 minutes at high pressure.
- Lift the pudding out of the pressure cooker and cover tightly until ready to invert and serve. Serve with an optional dousing of fresh cream.

Nutritional Information
- Preparation Time: 70 minutes
- Total Servings: 12 pieces
- Calories: 314.3
- Calories from Fat: 45
- Total Fat: 15.7g

- Saturated Fat: 2.2g
- Cholesterol: 115.5mg
- Sodium:165.8mg
- Potassium: 345mg
- Total Carbohydrates: 38.8g
- Fiber: 1.7g
- Sugar: 27.9g
- Protein: 3.8g

Recipe 30: Chocoflan

Tips to cook properly
- If desire, sprinkle ground pistachios and be careful before while lifting the cake from cooker

Ingredients

For Caramel:
- 1 cup sugar

For Flan:
- 2 eggs
- 225g whole milk
- 225g condensed milk
- 1 teaspoon vanilla extract

For Cake:
- 150g sugar
- 110g flour
- 35g cocoa powder
- ¼ teaspoon baking soda
- ½ teaspoon baking powder
- 1/8 teaspoon salt
- 1 egg
- 125ml yogurt
- 3 tablespoons vegetable oil

Preparation Method
- Prepare the pressure cooker with 2 cups of water and trivet or steamer basket and set aside.
- Prepare the caramel as instructed in the Creme Caramel recipe, and then quickly pour it into the tube pan.
- In a medium mixing bowl make the flan by breaking up the eggs well with a fork and mix in the milk, sweetened condensed milk, and vanilla. Set aside.
- In another medium mixing bowl mix all of the dry ingredients for the cake. Add the sugar, flour, cocoa powder, baking soda, baking powder and salt and mix well with a clean fork and set aside.
- In a small bowl break up the egg with a fork and then mix in the yogurt and oil. Using a spatula scrape out all of the egg and yogurts from the small bowl and combine with the flour/cocoa mixture using a fork and mixing only until the ingredient is just combined - the mixture will be like a thick paste.
- To construct the whole dessert, spatula out the chocolate cake mixture into the caramel coated tube pan and flatten into a somewhat flat and even layer.
- Next, pour the flan mixture on top of that. Set the tube pan in the middle of the foil sling and lower into the electric pressure cooker.
- Cook for 15-20 minutes at high pressure - it may take longer for silicone or ceramic containers to pressure cook. Open with the Natural release method
- Lift the dessert out of the cooker and let it cool. Then cover with plastic wrap and refrigerate and chill for 6-24 hours. Top with an upside-down serving plate

and quickly flip. Remove the tube pan from the cake and serve with an optional sprinkling of ground pistachios or pecans.

Nutritional Information

- Preparation Time: 45 minutes
- Total Servings:6- 8
- Calories: 249
- Calories from Fat: 113
- Total Fat: 12.6g
- Saturated Fat: 4.2g
- Cholesterol: 70mg
- Sodium: 266mg
- Potassium: 139mg
- Total Carbohydrates: 31g
- Fiber: 0.5g
- Sugar: 21.6g
- Protein: 5.1g

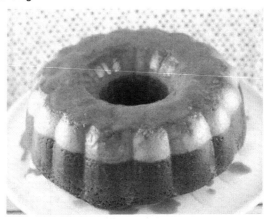

SUPER BOOST HEALTH RECIPES

Recipe 1: Sushi Rice

Tips to cook properly
- If you do not have a bamboo sushi mat, the easiest way to roll the sushi is to use a clean dish towel

Ingredients
- 200g sushi rice
- 375ml water
- 3 tablespoons rice wine vinegar
- Pinch of sugar

Preparation Method
- To the pressure cooker add the rinsed sushi rice and water and mix to evenly distribute the rice.
- Set electric pressure cookers cooking time for 7 minutes at high pressure.
- When cooking time is up, count 5 minutes of Natural pressure release.
- Stir the rice wine vinegar into the rice and tumble the rice into a large wooden bowl or wooden cutting board and smooth out into an even layer. Let cool for about 10 minutes, and it's ready to be used to make sushi.

Nutritional Information
- Preparation Time: 23 minutes
- Total Servings: 18 pieces
- Calories: 188.7
- Calories from Fat:56
- Total Fat: 0g
- Saturated Fat: 0g
- Cholesterol: 0mg
- Sodium: 7.5mg
- Potassium: 215mg
- Total Carbohydrates: 44.8g
- Fiber: 0g
- Sugar: 0.8g
- Protein:2.9g

Recipe 2: Eggplant Spread Paste

Tips to cook properly
- Before serving sprinkle with freshly chopped thyme and cilantro

Ingredients
- 4 tablespoons olive oil
- 900g eggplant
- 4 garlic cloves
- 1 teaspoon salt
- 125ml water
- 1 lemon juice
- 1 tablespoons tahini
- ¼ cup black olives
- 1 tablespoon fresh thyme
- Fresh extra virgin olive oil

Preparation Method
- Peel the eggplant in alternating stripes of skin and no skin, slice the biggest chunks possible to cover the bottom of your electric pressure cooker. The rest can be roughly chopped.
- Keep electric pressure cooker on medium heat and add the olive oil. When the oil has heated, carefully place the large chunks of eggplant "face down" to fry and caramelize on one side, about 5 minutes, add garlic cloves with the skin on. Then, flip over the eggplant add the remaining uncooked eggplant, salt, and water.
- Set electric pressure cookers timer for 3 minutes at high pressure.
- Take the pressure cooker base to the sink, and tip it to remove and discard most of the brown liquid.
- Add the Tahini, lemon juice, cooked and uncooked garlic cloves and black olives and puree everything together using an immersion blender.
- Pour out into the serving dish and sprinkle with fresh Thyme, remaining black olives and a dash of fresh olive oil before serving.

Nutritional Information
- Preparation Time: 23 minutes
- Total Servings: 4-6
- Calories: 155.5
- Calories from Fat: 34
- Total Fat: 11.7g
- Saturated Fat: 1.8g
- Cholesterol: 0mg
- Sodium: 820.6mb
- Potassium: 455mg
- Total Carbohydrates: 16.8g
- Fiber: 4.5g
- Sugar: 5.6g
- Protein: 2g

Recipe 3: Steamed Artichokes

Tips to cook properly
- Use mayonnaise as a dipping sauce

Ingredients
- 2 medium artichokes
- 1 lemon
- 2 tablespoons mayonnaise
- 1 teaspoon Dijon mustard
- 1 pinch paprika

Preparation Method
- Add one cup of water to the electric pressure cooker pot and lower the steamer basket inside.
- Place artichokes facing upwards and then spritz any remaining lemon on top of each.
- set cooking time for 10 minutes at high pressure. When time is up, open the pressure cooker with the Natural release method
- Mix mayonnaise with mustard and place in small dipping container, then sprinkle with paprika. Serve warm.

Nutritional Information
- Preparation Time: 25 minutes
- Total Servings: 4
- Calories: 77.5
- Calories from Fat: 34
- Total Fat: 5g
- Saturated Fat: 4.8g
- Cholesterol: 31mg
- Sodium: 155mg
- Potassium: 162mg
- Total Carbohydrates: 7.1g
- Fiber: 3.5g
- Sugar: 0g
- Protein:2g

Recipe 4: Borlotti Bean Salad

Tips to cook properly
- Instead of vinegar add 1 tablespoon of lemon juice

Ingredients
- ¼ small red onion
- 1 tablespoon white wine vinegar
- 900g fresh Borlotti beans
- 4 cups water
- 2 garlic cloves
- 1 bay leaf
- 3 anchovies
- 2 tablespoons olive oil
- fresh ground black pepper
- 1 teaspoon salt

Preparation Method
- Put sliced onions in serving bowl and drizzle with the vinegar and set aside.
- In an electric pressure cooker add shelled beans, garlic, bay leaf, and water.
- Set electric pressure cooker timer for 9 minutes at high pressure.
- Strain the beans and rinse under cold water to cool off. Mix beans with onions (and their vinegar), anchovies, olive oil, black pepper, and salt.

Nutritional Information
- Preparation Time: 20 minutes
- Total Servings: 8
- Calories: 111
- Calories from Fat: 42
- Total Fat: 4.7g
- Saturated Fat: 0.6g
- Cholesterol: 0g
- Sodium: 299mg
- Potassium: 12mg
- Total Carbohydrates: 15.9g
- Fiber: 2.4g
- Sugar: 10.6g
- Protein: 2g

Recipe 5: Chickpea Hummus

Tips to cook properly
- Before serving sprinkle freshly chopped parsley

Ingredients
- 180g dry chickpeas
- 1 bay leaf
- 4 garlic cloves
- 2 tablespoons tahini
- 1 lemon
- ¼ teaspoon powdered cumin
- ½ teaspoon sea salt
- ½ bunch Parsley
- 1 teaspoon paprika
- 1 tablespoon extra virgin olive oil

Preparation Method
- Rinse the chickpeas and put them in your pressure cooker. Cover with about 6 cups of water. Add two crushed garlic cloves and the Bay Leaf.
- Set electric pressure timer for 18 minutes at high pressure. Drain the chickpeas, reserving all of the cooking liquid.
- Pour chickpeas into a food processor and add back ½ a cup of cooking liquid along with Tahini, lemon juice, cumin and 1 or 2 fresh garlic cloves.
- When the hummus has reached the right consistency, add salt to taste and puree again to mix well. Place either in individual serving dishes or communal dipping bowl.
- Make a nice deep round groove in the middle with a spatula and pour a generous helping of your best olive oil.
- Sprinkle with paprika and fresh parsley, and a few whole cooked chickpeas and serve.

Nutritional Information
- Preparation Time: 30 minutes
- Total Servings: 6-8
- Calories: 109.1
- Calories from Fat:45
- Total Fat: 3.8g
- Saturated Fat: 0.5g
- Cholesterol: 0 mg
- Sodium: 332.9mg
- Potassium: 299mg
- Total Carbohydrates: 22g
- Fiber: 3.3g
- Sugar: 0.2g
- Protein: 4.1g

Recipe 6: Chinese Tea Eggs

Tips to cook properly
- If you are not eating immediately, don't open shells

Ingredients
- 3 Eggs (hard-boiled and cooled)
- ¼ cup soy sauce
- 1 Lemon zested
- 2 teabags (Black tea)
- 1 tablespoon cloves
- 1 tablespoon black peppercorns
- 1 tablespoon juniper berries
- 2 bay leaves

Preparation Method
- Crack the exterior of the shell of the hard-boiled egg by tapping them with the back of a teaspoon and set aside.
- In a separate pan, add all of the ingredients with a cup of water except for the soy sauce.
- Bring to a boil, then add the soy sauce eggs and any additional water to cover.
- Cover with tin foil. Prepare your electric pressure cooker by adding one cup of water, and the steamer basket.
- Set electric pressure timer for 20 minutes. When the time is up, remove tin foil and let cool further if you wish.
- Serve for your guests to peel! The eggs can also be done ahead of time and stored in the refrigerator in a plastic back or darkened even further stored in the tea mixture.

Nutritional Information
- Preparation Time: 34 minutes
- Total Servings: 3
- Calories: 76
- Calories from Fat: 45
- Total Fat: 5g
- Saturated Fat: 1.6g
- Cholesterol: 186mg
- Sodium: 659mg
- Potassium: 94mg
- Total Carbohydrates: 1.2g
- Fiber: 0.3g
- Sugar: 0.4g
- Protein: 6.6g

Recipe 7: Steamed Mussels

Tips to cook properly
- Properly clean mussels with sponge

Ingredients
- 900g Mussels
- 1 White Onion
- 1 Small head of Radicchio
- 450g Baby Spinach
- 1 clove of Garlic
- ½ cup dry white wine
- ½ cup of water
- 1 tablespoon olive oil

Preparation Method
To clean the mussels:
- Right before cooking, hold the mussel with the round end towards you and pull on the little "beard" sliding it in the opening toward you as you pull. Then, clean the shells by scrubbing with a nylon brush or scrubby sponge.

Prepare the dish:
- Prepare individual deep appetizer plates by laying a layer of baby spinach and radicchio strips and set aside.
- Prepare the mussels, by arranging them in the steamer basket, and set aside.
- Keep electric pressure cooker in Sauté, add a swirl of olive oil. Add the onion and garlic clove. When those have softened, deglaze with red wine and quickly add the steamer basket with the mussels.
- Set electric pressure cooker for 10 minutes and when the cooking time is up, open the cooker and serve the steaming liquid! This is now your briny broth and separate mussels in plates and serves immediately (you can hot steaming broth over the mussels).

Nutritional Information
- Preparation Time: 15 minutes
- Total Servings: 4
- Calories: 158
- Calories from Fat:59
- Total Fat: 6.6g
- Saturated Fat: 3.7g
- Cholesterol: 42mg
- Sodium: 196mg
- Potassium: 360mg
- Total Carbohydrates: 5.4g
- Fiber: 0.3g
- Sugar: 1.9g
- Protein: 10.7g

Recipe 8: Braised Peas with Bacon

Tips to cook properly
- If desire, add little cheese on top of serving bowl

Ingredients
- 100g Bacon
- 1 Green Onion
- 450g Peas
- ¼ cup of Beer
- 1 tablespoon mint
- 1 tablespoon butter
- Salt and Pepper to taste

Preparation Method
- Prepare your pressure cooker by adding a trivet, or steamer basket, to keep the heat proof dish from touching the bottom of the cooker.
- Add two cups of water to the electric pressure cooker and set aside.
- Layout the pancetta and half of the green onion in the heat-proof and flame-proof dish. Put the dish directly on the heat at the lowest flame to melt the fat.
- When the pancetta starts to sizzle (in about 5 minutes) turn off the flame and add the beer. Scrape lightly on the bottom to incorporate the brown juicy bits in the liquid.
- Add a pinch of salt, and peas. Mix well and cover with tin foil. Before lowering the heat proof dish insert into the electric pressure cooker. Set timer to 1 minutes. Open lid and add butter, mint, pepper and any additional salt to taste. Transfer to serving dish immediately.

Nutritional Information
- Preparation Time: 8 minutes
- Total Servings: 3-4
- Calories: 281
- Calories from Fat: 192
- Total Fat: 21.2g
- Saturated Fat: 3.6g
- Cholesterol: 21mg
- Sodium: 284mg
- Potassium: 244mg
- Total Carbohydrates: 15.6g
- Fiber: 3.8g
- Sugar: 8.4g
- Protein: 7.4g

Recipe 9: Chicken Liver Spread

Tips to cook properly
- For more delicious taste add 1 teaspoon of purified butter

Ingredients
- 350g Chicken livers
- 1 Onion
- 1 Bay leaf
- ¼ cup Red wine
- 2 Anchovies in oil
- 1 tablespoon capers
- 1 tablespoon butter
- 1 teaspoon rum
- Salt and pepper to taste

Preparation Method
- Put pressure cooker in Sauté mode and add olive oil, onions with a little salt and pepper. Then, add the chicken livers and bay leaf.
- Set pressure cooker timer to 5 minutes. After that open cooker and add the red wine and stir well with a wooden spoon.
- Again set pressure cooker timer for 5 minutes at high pressure and after natural release, remove and discard the Bay Leaf and add the Anchovies and Capers.
- Puree the contents of the cooker with a stick blender, add seasoning and butter, mix well.
- Transfer to a serving container and sprinkle with fresh herbs to garnish. Spread on toasted french bread slices and enjoy the taste.

Nutritional Information
- Preparation Time: 15 minutes
- Total Servings: 8-10
- Calories: 139
- Calories from Fat: 87
- Total Fat: 9.7g
- Saturated Fat: 5.6g
- Cholesterol: 158mg
- Sodium: 266mg
- Potassium: 146mg
- Total Carbohydrates: 4.2g
- Fiber: 0.6g
- Sugar: 2.1g
- Protein: 7.1g

Recipe 10: Sweet & Sour Pearl Onions

Tips to cook properly
- For better taste, make small hole in middle of the onions

Ingredients
- 500g Cipolline
- 125ml Water
- 1 Bay leaf
- Pinch of Salt
- 4 tablespoons Balsamic Vinegar
- 1 tablespoon Honey
- 1 tablespoon all-purpose flour

Preparation Method
- Clean the pearl onions by cutting both ends. Put the onions in the electric pressure cooker with half a cup of water, a pinch of salt and the bay leaf.
- Set pressure cooker, cooking timer for 5 minutes at low pressure.
- While the baby onions are cooking, you can make the sweet and sour sauce, In a small saucepan, put the flour, honey, and balsamic vinegar.
- Turn on the heat very low and start stirring quickly with a wooden spoon and as soon as all the lumps are out to turn off the heat - the whole process should only take about 30 seconds.
- Pour the sweet and sour sauce in the pressure cooker and mix in with the baby onions. Transfer to serving dish and serve, or let sit overnight in refrigerator prior to serving to intensify the flavor.

Nutritional Information
- Preparation Time: 20 minutes
- Total Servings: 6
- Calories: 168
- Calories from Fat: 106
- Total Fat: 11.8g
- Saturated Fat: 7.4g
- Cholesterol: 31mg
- Sodium: 952mg
- Potassium: 237mg
- Total Carbohydrates: 14.6g
- Fiber: 2.6g
- Sugar: 6.9g
- Protein: 2.4g

Recipe 11: Italian Rice Salad

Tips to cook properly
- Make sure that eggs are hard boiled

Ingredients
For the Rice:
- 2 cups of Arborio Rice
- 4 cups water
- 1 pinch of salt
- 1 teaspoon olive oil

For the Salad:
- 2 Fresh Tomatoes
- 3 Boiled Eggs (2 chopped and 1 wedged for decoration)
- 1 cup Black or Green Olives
- 1 bunch Basil, chopped
- 110g Tuna fish
- 1 Mozerella ball
- 3 tablespoons capers in vinegar
- 1 tablespoon Olive Oil

Preparation Method
- To the pressure cooker add the rice, water, salt and olive oil.
- Set pressure cooker, cooking timer for 4 minutes at high pressure. When time is up, immediately pour out the rice into the strainer in the sink.
- In a mixing bowl, mix the rice with the rest of the salad ingredients and serve immediately.

Nutritional Information
- Preparation Time: 20 minutes
- Total Servings: 6
- Calories: 324
- Calories from Fat: 145
- Total Fat: 20.2g
- Saturated Fat: 2.4g
- Cholesterol: 121mg
- Sodium: 541mg
- Potassium: 254mg
- Total Carbohydrates: 26.1g
- Fiber: 2.4g
- Sugar: 4.1g
- Protein: 15.4g

Recipe 12: Peperonata Salad

Tips to cook properly
- Roasted butter garlic gives extra flavor

Ingredients
- 2 Red Peppers
- 2 Yellow Peppers
- 1 Green Pepper
- 2 Tomatoes
- 1 Red Onion
- 2 Garlic cloves
- 1 bunch fresh basil or parsley
- 1 tablespoon olive oil
- Salt and pepper

Preparation Method
- Rinse and remove the stems and seeds from the peppers. Slice the peppers into thin strips. Rinse the tomatoes, put them in a chopper, and chop them 'til pulpy.
- Put pressure cooker in Sauté, add a little oil and onions. When onions begin to soften the onions then, add the peppers, and one garlic clove wrapper on, and, without stirring, let one side of the peppers brown (approximately 5 minutes).
- Add the tomato puree, if needed, salt and pepper, mix well. Set pressure cooker, cooking time to 6 minutes at high pressure. After that remove and put them immediately in a serving bowl.
- Add one clove of raw, pressed, garlic, chopped basil, and a little swirl of fresh olive oil. Mix and serve.

Nutritional Information
- Preparation Time: 10 minutes
- Total Servings: 4
- Calories: 196
- Calories from Fat: 87
- Total Fat: 9.6g
- Saturated Fat: 1.5g
- Cholesterol: 0mg
- Sodium: 510g
- Potassium: 393g
- Total Carbohydrates: 28.6g
- Fiber: 3.7g
- Sugar: 7.7g
- Protein: 4g

Recipe 13: Vegetable Medley

Tips to cook properly
- Add only 1 cup of water

Ingredients
- 1 large Eggplant
- 1 teaspoon salt
- ¼ cup olive oil
- 1 medium pepper
- 2 medium Zucchini
- 1 onion
- 2 medium potatoes
- 10 cherry tomatoes
- 1 tablespoon Capers
- 2 tablespoons pine nuts
- 1 tablespoons raisins
- ¼ cup olives
- 1 bunch basil
- Salt and Pepper to taste

Preparation Method
- Put it in a strainer and sprinkle the cubes with salt. To get all of the bitter liquid out: add a plate on top of the cubed eggplant and some kind of weight on top of that to push it down and leave them to rest for about half an hour.
- In the meantime, wash and slice the other vegetables. Set pressure cooker on Sauté mode and add the olive oil and brown the vegetables, adding them in the following order, stirring them constantly with a wooden spoon.
- First, add the eggplant and potatoes (stir and cook for 3 minutes), peppers and onions (wait another 3 minutes and keep stirring), Zucchini (stir for another 3 minutes).
- Finally, add half the chopped basil, pine nuts, raisins, olives, capers, salt, and pepper to taste. Add one cup of water. Set electric pressure cooker, cooking timer for 4 minutes at high pressure.
- When time is up, open the pressure cooker and transfer the contents of the pressure cooker to a serving dish immediately and before serving, mix cherry tomatoes and dressing with a little fresh olive oil, balsamic vinegar, fresh basil and pine nuts.

Nutritional Information
- Preparation Time: 20 minutes
- Total Servings: 6
- Calories: 191
- Calories from Fat: 45
- Total Fat: 5g
- Saturated Fat: 0.7g
- Cholesterol: 0mg
- Sodium: 257mg

- Potassium: 1022mg
- Total Carbohydrates: 34.6g
- Fiber: 7.5g
- Sugar: 5.5g
- Protein: 4g

Recipe 14: Potato Cheese Soup

Tips to cook properly
- In final stage, don't boil just bring to heat

Ingredients
- 2 tablespoons butter
- 1/2 cup chopped onion
- 6 cups peeled and cubed potatoes
- 500g chicken broth
- 1 teaspoon salt
- 1/2 teaspoon black pepper
- 1/8 teaspoon red pepper flakes
- 2 tablespoons dried parsley
- 2 tablespoons cornstarch
- 2 tablespoons water
- 85g cream cheese
- 1 cup shredded cheddar cheese
- 2 cups half and half
- 1 cup frozen corn
- 6 slices crisp-cooked bacon

Preparation Method
- Select Sauté and add butter to the pressure cooker. When butter is melted, add the onion and cook, stirring occasionally until the onion is tender, about 5 minutes.
- Add 250g chicken broth, salt, pepper, red pepper flakes, and parsley to the onions.
- Put the steamer basket in the pressure cooker pot. Add the diced potatoes. Select High Pressure and 4 minutes cooking time.
- When timer beeps, turn off the pressure cooker, wait 5 minutes, then do a quick pressure release. Carefully remove potatoes and steamer basket from the pressure cooking pot.
- In a small bowl, dissolve cornstarch in 2 tablespoons water. Select Simmer and add cornstarch mixture to the pot stirring constantly. Add cubed cream cheese and shredded cheese. Stir until cheese is melted.
- Add remaining 250g of chicken broth, half, and a half, corn, crumbled bacon, and cooked potatoes, and heat through but do not bring to a boil.

Nutritional Information
- Preparation Time: 20 minutes
- Total Servings: 6-8
- Calories: 311
- Calories from Fat: 118
- Total Fat: 13.1g
- Saturated Fat: 8.2g
- Cholesterol: 40mg
- Sodium: 638mg

- Potassium: 836mg
- Total Carbohydrates: 37.1g
- Fiber: 4.1g
- Sugar: 7.8g
- Protein: 12.1g

Recipe 15: Chilled Fruit Soup

Tips to cook properly
- Using spoon, carefully remove pulp from cantaloupe

Ingredients
- 1/2 cantaloupe
- 1 large orange
- 2 peaches
- 450g pineapple juice
- 225g plain Greek yogurt
- 1/2 teaspoon vanilla
- 1 tablespoon powdered sugar
- 1 tablespoon chia seeds

Preparation Method
- Add prepared fruit and pineapple juice to pressure cooker.
- Set pressure cooker, cooking timer for 5 minutes on high pressure and quick release when time is up.
- Use an immersion blender or pour into blender and puree until completely smooth. Pour through a strainer to remove any bulky pulp.
- Cool to room temperature then add Greek yogurt, vanilla, and powdered sugar and whisk to combine.
- Chill in refrigerator and serve cold swirled with extra yogurt and sprinkled with chia seeds.

Nutritional Information
- Preparation Time:15 minutes
- Total Servings: 4
- Calories: 96
- Calories from Fat: 3
- Total Fat: 0.3g
- Saturated Fat: 0.1g
- Cholesterol: 0mg
- Sodium: 16mg
- Potassium: 399mg
- Total Carbohydrates: 16.4g
- Fiber: 1g
- Sugar: 12.6g
- Protein: 1.8g

Recipe 16: Farro and Cherry Salad

Tips to cook properly
- If desire, add freshly chopped parsley and cilantro before serving

Ingredients
- 1 cup raw whole grain farro
- 1 tablespoon apple cider vinegar
- 1 teaspoon freshly squeezed lemon juice
- 1 tablespoon olive oil
- ¼ teaspoon sea salt
- ½ cup dried cherries
- ¼ cup finely minced chives or green onions
- 8 or 10 mint leaves
- 2 cups cherries

Preparation Method
- Rinse farro. Put in the pressure cooker with 3 cups water. Set timer for 40 minutes and automatic release. The grain should be plump and tender, but chewy.
- Drain the farro. (If you wish, save the extra liquid for soup stock.) Put the cooked farro in a bowl. Stir in vinegar, lemon juice, oil, salt, dried cherries, chives, and mint.
- Refrigerate until cold. Just before serving, stir in fresh cherries.

Nutritional Information
- Preparation Time:45minutes
- Total Servings: 6
- Calories: 334g
- Calories from Fat: 123
- Total Fat: 13.7g
- Saturated Fat: 1.6g
- Cholesterol: 2g
- Sodium: 600mg
- Potassium: 231mg
- Total Carbohydrates: 48g
- Fiber: 2.4g
- Sugar: 16.7g
- Protein: 5.7g

Recipe 17: Kale with Baked Tofu

Tips to cook properly
- Kale can be replaced with spinach

Ingredients
- 1 leek
- 1 bunch Lacinato kale
- 1 tablespoon olive oil
- 1 teaspoon sweet paprika
- ½ cup vegetable broth or water
- ½ teaspoon sea salt
- Pinch cayenne pepper
- 2 teaspoons sherry vinegar
- 85g baked tofu
- ¼ cup chopped almonds

Preparation Method
- Cut the leek in half lengthwise, then very thinly slice crosswise into half-moons. You should have about 1 ½ cups. Stack 5 kale leaves, one on top of the other.
- As best you can roll into a tube shape and slice ¼-inch thick into ribbons. Repeat with the remaining kale.Heat the olive oil in the pressure cooker. Sauté the leeks until tender, 3 to 5 minutes.
- Stir in the paprika and cook another minute. Add the vegetable broth, kale ribbons, salt, and cayenne. Lock the lid in place and cook on high pressure 2 minutes. Quick release the pressure. If you wish, drain off the excess liquid and save for soup.
- Stir in the sherry vinegar and tofu. Taste and add more salt if needed. Transfer to a serving dish and sprinkle with the almonds. Serve immediately.

Nutritional Information
- Preparation Time: 15 minutes
- Total Servings: 4
- Calories: 114
- Calories from Fat: 71
- Total Fat: 7.9g
- Saturated Fat: 1.1g
- Cholesterol: 0mg
- Sodium: 116mg
- Potassium: 162mg
- Total Carbohydrates: 4.3g
- Fiber: 0.7g
- Sugar: 2g
- Protein: 8.9g

Recipe 18: Red Chile Posole

Tips to cook properly
- Before serving garnish with freshly chopped parsley and cilantro

Ingredients
- 900g frozen posole
- 900g lean boneless pork
- 1 onion
- 1 teaspoon garlic
- 1 tablespoon cumin
- 4 cups chicken broth/stock
- 1/2 cup ground red chile
- 340g bottle of beer
- 1 tablespoon Mexican oregano
- 2 bay leaves
- 1 teaspoon sea salt
- Fresh ground pepper

Garnishes:
- cilantro, lime, queso fresco, avocado

Preparation Method
- Add the posole to the cooker pot. Cover with water to the "maximum" line. Pressure cook on "beans" setting medium (about 15 minutes) or about 15 minutes if doing it on the cook top. Do a natural release for about 5 minutes, then release the pressure.
- Drain posole, and set aside. It should be tender but firm. Rinse and dry the pot. Brown pork cubes with chopped onion, garlic, and cumin on the Sauté or browning setting.
- Whisk red chile powder into the chicken broth/stock. Add to the pot along with the beer, Mexican oregano, bay leaves, salt, and pepper.
- Set to the "stew" setting or on the cooktop for about 20 minutes. While the pork cooks, prepare the garnishes.
- Add the posole into the pot with the tender pork. Stir to combine. Ladle the posole into bowls, and top with preferred garnishes.

Nutritional Information
- Preparation Time: 25 minutes
- Total Servings: 4
- Calories: 321
- Calories from Fat: 92
- Total Fat: 10.6g
- Saturated Fat: 2.7g
- Cholesterol: 37mg
- Sodium: 748mg
- Potassium: 348mg
- Total Carbohydrates: 31.8g
- Fiber: 5.5g
- Sugar: 5.7g
- Protein: 15.4g

Recipe 19: Chicken Tinga

Tips to cook properly
- Preheat and apply little butter to tortillas before you put chicken mixture

Ingredients
- 1 tablespoon vegetable oil
- 1/ 2 large sweet onion
- 2 cloves garlic
- 1 large tomatillo
- 1 teaspoon ground cumin
- 1 teaspoon dried Mexican oregano
- 1 teaspoon salt
- 425g diced tomatoes
- 1/4 cup water
- 2 chipotle chiles in adobo sauce
- 1 tablespoon cayenne pepper sauce
- 3 large uncooked chicken breasts
- 425g black or pinto beans
- 6 (12-inch) flour tortillas
- 110g cheddar cheese

Preparation Method
- Preheat electric pressure cooking pot. Add oil and onion and cook until softened, about 3 minutes. Add garlic and cook for 1 minute. Add tomatillo, cumin, oregano, and salt and cook, stirring constantly, another 3 minutes.
- Add tomatoes, water, chipotles, and cayenne pepper sauce. Puree mixture until it's very smooth (I used my blender and pureed it in the pressure cooker pot).
- Stir in chicken. Select electric pressure cooker, cooking time for 4 minutes. When timer beeps, turn pressure cooker off and do a quick pressure release.
- Select Sauté and cook, stirring occasionally and gently, until sauce clings to chicken and most of the liquid has evaporated.
- Mash beans with a potato masher or fork, until chunky. Assemble burritos by spooning chicken mixture onto tortillas. Add beans and sprinkle with cheese. Roll burritos as desired.

Nutritional Information
- Preparation Time: 30 minutes
- Total Servings: 4
- Calories: 402
- Calories from Fat: 180
- Total Fat: 20g
- Saturated Fat: 5.7g
- Cholesterol: 91mg
- Sodium: 395
- Total Carbohydrates: 20.5g
- Fiber: 2.3g
- Sugar: 2.7g
- Protein: 26.9g

Recipe 20: Creamy Enchilada Soup

Tips to cook properly
- Before serving only sprinkle ground cheese

Ingredients
- 4 cups chicken broth
- 3 chicken breasts
- 100g chopped green chilies
- 1 yellow onion, coarsely chopped
- 3 large russet potatoes
- 1 red bell pepper, cored, seeded and coarsely chopped
- 680g butternut squash
- 3 cloves garlic
- 2 teaspoons salt
- 2 teaspoons cumin
- 225g tomato sauce
- 2 tablespoons allspice seasoning
- 425g cannellini beans
- Additional toppings: pico de gallo, sour cream, shredded cheese, fresh or canned corn, diced avocado, Cholula hot sauce, whole grain tortilla chips

Preparation Method
- Whisk together taco seasoning, add chicken broth, chicken, green chilies, onion, potatoes, pepper, squash, garlic, salt, cumin, tomato sauce and 2 tablespoons of taco seasoning to the pressure cooker pot and gently stir.
- Set pressure cooker, cooking time for 20 minutes. When cooking is complete, use a natural release.
- Remove chicken and place on a cutting board, cover with foil. Using an immersion blender, blend soup until very smooth.
- Chop or shred chicken and return it to the pot of soup. Add cannellini beans and stir. To serve, ladle soup into a bowl, immediately sprinkle with cheese and top with desired toppings.

Nutritional Information
- Preparation Time: 30 minutes
- Total Servings: 8
- Calories: 290
- Calories from Fat: 147
- Total Fat: 16.3g
- Saturated Fat: 8.6g
- Cholesterol: 74mgSodium: 512mg
- Potassium: 284mg
- Total Carbohydrates: 16.8g
- Fiber: 3.3g
- Sugar: 1.1g
- Protein: 18g

Recipe 21: Pumpkin Chicken Corn Chowder

Tips to cook properly
- If desire, add crumbled bacon and freshly chopped parsley

Ingredients
- 2 tablespoons butter
- 1 cup diced onion
- 1 garlic clove
- 820g chicken broth
- 425g Pumpkin Puree
- 1/2 teaspoon Italian seasoning
- 1/4 teaspoon freshly ground black pepper
- 1/8 teaspoon dried red pepper flakes
- 1/8 teaspoon freshly grated nutmeg
- 2 large russet potatoes, cubed
- 2 large chicken breasts
- 2 cup frozen corn
- 1/2 cup half and half
- Salt and ground pepper (as needed)

Preparation Method
- Keep cooker in Sauté mode and add butter to the pressure cooking pot. When butter is melted, add the onion and cook, stirring occasionally until the onion is tender, about 5 minutes. Add garlic and cook 1 minute more.
- Add chicken broth, pumpkin puree, Italian seasoning, pepper, red pepper flakes, and nutmeg to the pressure cooking pot. Stir to combine.
- Add the diced potatoes and diced chicken. Set electric pressure cooker, cooking timer for 4 minutes with natural release. When timer beeps, turn off the pressure cooker.
- Stir in corn and a half and a half. Add salt and pepper to taste. Serve topped with crumbled bacon and chopped parsley.

Nutritional Information
- Preparation Time: 25 minutes
- Total Servings: 6
- Calories: 352
- Calories from Fat: 206
- Total Fat: 21.6g
- Saturated Fat: 7.2g
- Cholesterol: 21mg
- Sodium: 1377
- Potassium: 480mg
- Total Carbohydrates:28.6g
- Fiber: 3.9g
- Sugar: 3.2g
- Protein: 7.9g

Recipe 22: Sweet Potato Cheese Soup

Tips to cook properly
- Make sure that, potatoes and sweet potatoes are cut into small cubed size

Ingredients
- 2 tablespoons butter
- 1/2 cup chopped onion
- 400g chicken broth
- 1 teaspoon salt
- 1/2 teaspoon black pepper
- 1/8 teaspoon red pepper flakes
- 2 tablespoons dried parsley
- 3 cups peeled and cubed sweet potatoes
- 3 cups peeled and cubed russet potatoes
- 2 tablespoons cornstarch
- 2 tablespoons water
- 85g cream cheese
- 1 cup shredded cheddar cheese
- 2 cups half and half
- 1 cup frozen corn
- 6 slices crisp-cooked bacon

Preparation Method
- Select Sauté and add butter to the pressure cooker pot. When butter is melted, add the onion and cook, stirring occasionally until the onion is tender, about 5 minutes. Add 1 can chicken broth, salt, pepper, red pepper flakes, and parsley to the onions.
- Put the steamer basket in the pressure cooker pot. Add the sweet potatoes to the steamer basket. Select High Pressure and 2 minutes cook time and start.
- When timer beeps, carefully remove sweet potatoes and set aside. Add the russet potatoes to the steamer basket. Select High Pressure and 4 minutes cook time and start. When timer beeps, turn off pressure cooker and remove potatoes and steamer basket from the pressure cooking pot.
- In a small bowl, dissolve cornstarch in 2 tablespoons water. Select Simmer and add cornstarch mixture to the pot stirring constantly. Add cubed cream cheese and shredded cheese. Stir until cheese is melted. Add remaining can of chicken broth, half and half, corn, and heat through but do not bring to a boil. Add crumbled bacon and potatoes.

Nutritional Information
- Preparation Time: 30 minutes
- Total Servings: 6
- Calories: 289
- Calories from Fat: 143
- Total Fat: 15.9g
- Saturated Fat: 8.8g
- Cholesterol: 44mg

- Sodium: 182mg
- Potassium: 449mg
- Total Carbohydrates: 25.7g
- Fiber: 4.4g
- Sugar: 7.4g
- Protein: 5.9g

Recipe 23: Korean Chicken Thighs

Tips to cook properly
- You can substitute sriracha sauce instead of ketchup

Ingredients

Korean BBQ Sauce:
- 1/2 cup gochujang
- 1/4 cup hoisin sauce
- 1/4 cup ketchup
- 1/4 cup mirin
- 1/4 cup soy sauce
- 1/4 cup sake rice wine
- 1 tablespoon unseasoned rice vinegar
- 1 tablespoon fresh ginger
- 1/2 tablespoon garlic

Chicken:
- 2 tablespoons vegetable oil
- 900g chicken thighs
- 1 medium onion
- 1 tablespoon ginger
- 1 teaspoon garlic
- 1 cup chicken broth
- 2 teaspoons cornstarch
- 1/4 cup water

Preparation Method

Korean BBQ Sauce:
- Whisk the ingredients in a medium bowl. Remove and set aside 1 cup for finishing the sauce.

Chicken:
- Sauté the pressure cooker and brown the chicken pieces on both sides in the vegetable oil. Set aside.
- Add the onion, ginger, and garlic. Cook until the onion is soft. Add the chicken pieces and onion mixture to the pressure cooker.
- Mix the chicken broth with the Korean BBQ sauce remaining in the prep bowl. Add to the pressure cooker pot. Set pressure cooker timer for 15 minutes and cook on high pressure.
- Remove 1 cup of cooking liquid to a medium saucepan. Mix the cornstarch with broth or water. Bring the cooking liquid to a boil, and add the cornstarch slurry a bit at a time until thickened as desired. Add in the reserved BBQ sauce. Stir until combined and bubbly.

To Serve:
- Using a slotted spoon, remove chicken pieces to a platter. Pour the sauce over the top, and garnish with slice scallions. Serve with jasmine rice.

Nutritional Information
- Preparation Time: 35 minutes

- Total Servings: 4
- Calories: 476
- Calories from Fat: 214
- Total Fat: 23.8g
- Saturated Fat: 4.8g
- Cholesterol: 71mg
- Sodium: 1150mg
- Potassium: 227mg
- Total Carbohydrates: 39g
- Fiber: 1.6g
- Sugar: 2.3g
- Protein: 18.5g

Recipe 24: Almond Rice

Tips to cook properly
- Soak saffron in milk for 10 minutes and add to rice including milk gives extra flavor

Ingredients
- 400g chicken broth
- 1 1/4 cup water
- Pinch of saffron threads
- 1 tablespoon butter
- 1 medium onion
- 1 celery stalk
- 2 cups long grain white rice
- 1/2 teaspoon salt
- 1/2 cup sliced almonds

Preparation Method
- Heat broth and water in a small saucepan over moderate heat until hot, then crumble saffron into liquid and stir. Remove from heat.
- Place the butter in the pressure cooking pot. Select Sauté when the butter is melted and sizzling, add the chopped onions and celery. Cook, stirring occasionally until vegetables are tender, about 3 to 5 minutes.
- Stir in rice and cook, stirring frequently, until rice becomes opaque, about 1 to 2 minutes. Add saffron broth and salt.
- Select High Pressure and set the timer for 3 minutes. When beep sounds wait 5 minutes and fluff rice, stir in almonds, and serve immediately.

Nutritional Information
- Preparation Time: 20 minutes
- Total Servings: 4
- Calories: 263
- Calories from Fat: 58
- Total Fat: 6.5g
- Saturated Fat: 2.2g
- Cholesterol: 10mg
- Sodium: 383mg
- Potassium: 129mg
- Total Carbohydrates: 44.6g
- Fiber: 1.6g
- Sugar: 1.6g
- Protein: 5.5g

Recipe 25: Chicken Marsala

Tips to cook properly
- Freshly chopped chives adds delicious taste for chicken

Ingredients
- 4 slices peppered bacon
- 1350g chicken thighs
- Salt and pepper
- 1/2 cup sweet Marsala wine
- 1 cup chicken broth
- 1 tablespoon vegetable oil
- 3 tablespoon butter
- 225g mushrooms
- 2 tablespoon cornstarch
- 3 tablespoon cold water
- Garnish: chopped parsley or chives

Preparation Method
- Select Browning and add diced bacon to electric pressure cooker pot. Brown the bacon until crisp, stirring frequently. Remove bacon to a plate, leaving the bacon fat in the pot.
- Season chicken with salt and pepper. Add the chicken to the pot and brown on both sides in the bacon fat. Cook the chicken in batches. Remove the chicken to a platter, leaving the fat in the pan.
- Add the marsala to deglaze the pot and let it almost completely evaporate to concentrate the flavor and remove most of the liquid.
- Add the chicken broth and browned chicken to the pot, along with any juices that have collected on the platter. Close and Select High Pressure and 10 minutes cook time.
- While the chicken is cooking, heat a large Sauté pan over medium-high heat until hot. Add oil and 1 tablespoon butter. When butter is melted, add the mushrooms and cook until golden. Season with salt and pepper.
- When the timer beeps, do a quick pressure release and remove the chicken from the pressure cooker pot to a serving dish.
- Combine the cornstarch and water, whisking until smooth. Add cornstarch mixture to the sauce to the pot stirring constantly. Select Simmer and bring to a boil, stirring constantly. Stir in remaining two tablespoons butter. Add mushrooms and stir to coat with sauce.
- Taste, adjust seasoning if desired. Combine sauce with chicken in the serving bowl. Serve topped with crumbled bacon and chopped parsley.

Nutritional Information
- Preparation Time: 45 minutes
- Total Servings: 4
- Calories: 448
- Calories from Fat: 26.6
- Total Fat: 26.6g

- Saturated Fat: 7.6g
- Cholesterol: 99mg
- Sodium: 543
- Potassium: 411mg
- Total Carbohydrates: 13.3g
- Fiber: 0.5g
- Sugar: 2.8g
- Protein: 28.8g

Recipe 26: Chicken Burrito

Tips to cook properly
- Make sure you apply purified butter for tortillas before you wrap it

Ingredients
- 1 cup long grain white rice
- 1 1/4 cups water
- 1/2 teaspoon salt
- 3 cups chicken
- 1 cup salsa
- 1 teaspoon chili powder
- 1/2 teaspoon ground ginger
- 1/3 cup peanut butter
- 2 tablespoons teriyaki sauce
- 2 tablespoons water
- 1/4 cup packed sugar
- 8 flour tortillas for burritos

Preparation Method
- Add the rice, 1 1/4 cups water and salt to the electric pressure cooker pot. Stir and select high pressure and 3 minutes cook time. When timer beeps, turn off pressure cooker and use a quick pressure release.
- Add chicken, salsa, chili powder, ginger, peanut butter, teriyaki sauce, 2 tablespoons water and brown sugar to the rice in the cooking pot. Stir.
- Select Sauté and bring to a boil. Cook 3 minutes until rice is tender and chicken is heated through.
- Heat tortillas as directed on package. Spoon 1/2 cup chicken filling in the middle of each tortilla and roll up burrito style. Serve topped with salsa and sour cream.

Nutritional Information
- Preparation Time: 20 minutes
- Total Servings: 8
- Calories: 555
- Calories from Fat: 199
- Total Fat: 22.2g
- Saturated Fat: 8.1g
- Cholesterol: 102mg
- Sodium: 988mg
- Potassium: 401mg
- Total Carbohydrates: 48.2g
- Fiber: 3.4g
- Sugar: 3.1g
- Protein: 29.1g

Recipe 27: Mozzarella Chicken

Tips to cook properly
- Try to add ground mozzarella over the chicken

Ingredients
- 1 tablespoon olive oil
- 4 chicken breasts
- 2 cloves garlic
- 400g tomatoes puree
- 1 cup water
- 1 teaspoon dried basil
- 1/4 teaspoon red pepper flakes
- 1/4 teaspoon salt
- 1 cup grated Mozzarella

Preparation Method
- Salt and pepper chicken breasts. Add oil to the electric pressure cooking pot, select Browning. When oil is hot, brown the chicken breasts in two batches, Remove to a plate.
- When all the chicken is browned, add more oil if necessary and add garlic and Sauté for 1 minute. Add tomatoes, water, basil, red pepper flakes and salt to the pressure cooking pot. Stir to combine. Add chicken breasts to the pressure cooking pot.
- Select 5 minutes cook time. When timer beeps, turn off and use a quick pressure release. Check and make sure the chicken is cooked through and no longer pink in the middle.
- Preheat the broiler and spray a small glass casserole dish with non-stick spray. Place the chicken in the dish. Select simmer and cook sauce until sauce thickens and is desire consistency. Pour sauce over chicken.
- Sprinkle Mozzarella over chicken and put the dish under the broiler until the cheese is melted and starting to lightly brown. Watch it closely once it starts to brown it can brown quickly.

Nutritional Information
- Preparation Time: 25 minutes
- Total Servings: 4
- Calories: 363
- Calories from Fat: 98
- Total Fat: 10.9g
- Saturated Fat: 3.9g
- Cholesterol: 87mg
- Sodium: 1377mg
- Potassium: 1301mg
- Total Carbohydrates: 25.4g
- Fiber: 5g
- Sugar: 9.2g
- Protein: 29.3g

Recipe 1: Butter Chicken

Tips to cook properly
- Don't forget to add cornstarch, it will thicken your sauce in chicken

Ingredients
- 10 boneless skinless chicken thighs
- 800g diced tomatoes and juice
- 2 jalapeno peppers
- 2 tablespoons fresh ginger root
- 1/2 cup unsalted butter
- 2 teaspoons ground cumin
- 1 tablespoon paprika
- 2 teaspoons kosher salt
- 3/4 cup heavy cream
- 3/4 cup Greek yogurt
- 2 teaspoons garam masala
- 2 teaspoons ground roasted cumin seeds
- 2 tablespoons cornstarch
- 2 tablespoons water
- 1/4 cup cilantro

Preparation Method
- Put tomatoes, jalapeno, and ginger in a blender or food processor and blend to a fine puree.
- Add butter to electric pressure cooking pot, select Browning. When butter is melted and foam begins to subside, add the chicken pieces, a few at a time, and sear until they are nicely browned all over. Remove them with a slotted spoon into a bowl and put aside.
- Add ground cumin and paprika to the butter in the pot and cook, stirring rapidly, for 10-15 seconds. Add the tomato mixture, salt, cream, yogurt and chicken pieces to the pot. Gently stir the chicken to coat the pieces. Close and select 5 minutes cook time.
- When timer beeps, turn off and use a natural pressure release for 10 minutes. After 10 minutes use a quick pressure release to release any remaining pressure.
- Stir in the garam masala and roasted cumin. Whisk together cornstarch and water in a small bowl. Stir into sauce in the pot. Select Sauté and bring to a boil. Turn off pressure cooker and stir in minced cilantro. Serve with rice and naan.

Nutritional Information
- Preparation Time: 60 minutes
- Total Servings: 8-10
- Calories: 880
- Calories from Fat: 741

- Total Fat: 81.1g
- Saturated Fat: 32.1g
- Cholesterol: 303mg
- Sodium: 1461mg
- Potassium: 567mg
- Total Carbohydrates: 12.8g
- Fiber: 2.6g
- Sugar: 4.6g
- Protein: 26.4g

Recipe 2: Cheesy Chicken Rice

Tips to cook properly
- Aluminum foil can be used to keep food moist, cook it evenly, and make cleanup easier

Ingredients
- 1 tablespoon vegetable oil
- 450g chicken breasts
- 1 yellow onion
- 1⅓ cups long grain white rice
- 1½ cups chicken broth
- ¾ teaspoon salt
- ¼ teaspoon pepper
- ¼ teaspoon garlic powder
- 1½ tablespoons all-purpose flour
- ½ cup milk
- 1½ cups shredded cheddar cheese
- 2 cups frozen broccoli florets

Preparation Method
- Keep electric pressure cooker in Sauté mode and add oil, when oil starts sizzling, add the cubed chicken and onion and Sauté until chicken is lightly golden and onion is translucent.
- Add rice, chicken broth, salt, pepper, and garlic powder, then secure the lid and set cooker timer for 5 minutes.
- Perform a quick release and whisk together the flour and milk, add flour mixture. Again set cooker timer for 2 minutes.
- Stir in cheddar cheese and broccoli florets, and Again set cooker timer for 2 minutes or until combined and broccoli is warm throughout.

Nutritional Information
- Preparation Time: 30 minutes
- Total Servings: 4
- Calories: 756
- Calories from Fat: 277
- Total Fat: 30.4g
- Saturated Fat: 9.9g
- Cholesterol: 110mg
- Sodium: 1642mg
- Potassium: 485mg
- Total Carbohydrates: 72.4g
- Fiber: 3g
- Sugar: 7.6g
- Protein: 31.2g

Recipe 3: Italian Chicken Parmigiana

Tips to cook properly
- This recipe more suitable for pasta

Ingredients
- 1 chopped onion
- 2 cups of mushrooms
- ¼ cup of Red Wine
- ½ cup of Chicken Stock
- 1 tablespoon Crushed Garlic
- 3 Cups Spaghetti Sauce
- 1 Cup Shredded Parmesan Cheese
- 6 Chicken Breasts
- ¼ Cup White Flour
- ¼ teaspoon Dried Rosemary
- ¼ teaspoon Dried Basil
- ¼ teaspoon Garlic Powder
- Salt and Pepper to taste

Preparation Method
- Cut mushrooms and onion into small pieces. Put in pressure cooker pot and press Sauté button. When it is turning to brown color, add olive oil and Sauté them until they are slightly cooked, though. Press cancel and turn off the pressure cooker.
- Now take the white flour, rosemary, basil and garlic powder and mix them up in a shallow dish. Dip the chicken breasts into the mixture and coat each breast well. You can choose to mix up one egg and make the batter thicker but I chose not to.
- Pan fry the chicken breasts with olive oil on a hot pan on the stove. It should be just about 2-minutes on each side to get it nicely browned and a bit crusty. Remember you're not going to "cook" the chicken on the pan, just get it browned. The center of the chicken should still be raw.
- While the chicken is browning on the pan. You can go back to the mushroom and onion mixture. Add the marinara sauce, chicken stock, red wine, half of the parmesan cheese and crushed garlic all into the pot. Give it a nice mix.
- You can now take the chicken breasts from the pan and transfer it into the red sauce in the electric pressure cooker. Coat each breast with the sauce evenly.
- Close pressure cooker and adjust cooking time to 10 minutes. In meantime, you can make some pasta or rice or whatever you want to eat with chicken.

Nutritional Information
- Preparation Time: 20 minutes
- Total Servings: 4
- Calories: 528
- Calories from Fat: 164
- Total Fat: 18.3g

- Saturated Fat: 7.6g
- Cholesterol: 184mg
- Sodium: 1309mg
- Potassium: 804mg
- Total Carbohydrates: 44.1g
- Fiber: 5.6g
- Sugar: 14.2g
- Protein: 42.4g

Recipe 4: Chicken Cacciatore

Tips to cook properly
- Don't forget to remove bay leaf before you add salt and pepper

Ingredients
- 2 tablespoons olive oil
- 900g boneless skinless chicken thighs
- 1 large onion
- 3 garlic cloves
- 1 teaspoon dried oregano
- 1/4 teaspoon red pepper flakes
- 1 bay leaf
- 800g diced tomatoes
- 1/4 cup low sodium chicken broth
- 2 green bell peppers cut into 1-inch squares
- Salt and pepper

Preparation Method
- Heat olive oil in the electric pressure cooker using brown option. Sprinkle chicken with salt and pepper. Working in batches cook chicken until golden brown, about 5 minutes total, adding more olive oil as necessary. Transfer chicken to plate.
- Add onion to the pressure cooker, select Sauté and cook onion until it is soft, scraping up browned bits, about 4 minutes. Add garlic, oregano, and red pepper flakes and cook until fragrant, about 1 minute.
- Add bay leaf, tomatoes and chicken broth, return chicken to pressure cooker and press into tomatoes until they are mostly covered.
- Close pressure cooker and set cooking time for 10 minutes. After that open and add green peppers and stir into mixture. Close once again, increase cooking time to 2 more minutes, use quick release.
- Remove bay leaf. Season to taste with salt and pepper. Serve over rice or pasta.

Nutritional Information
- Preparation Time: 30 minutes
- Total Servings: 6
- Calories: 321
- Calories from Fat: 112
- Total Fat: 12.4g
- Saturated Fat: 2.8g
- Cholesterol: 69mg
- Sodium: 269mg
- Potassium: 562mg
- Total Carbohydrates: 13.3g
- Fiber: 2.6g
- Sugar: 7.6g
- Protein: 22.2g

Recipe 5: Chicken Mushroom Masala

Tips to cook properly
- Wait for natural release for better tasty gravy

Ingredients
- 1/2 cup diced bacon
- 1350g skinless chicken thighs
- Salt and pepper
- 1 medium yellow onion
- 2 cloves garlic
- 1 cup red wine
- 1 cup chicken broth
- 1 tablespoon tomato paste
- 1 bay leaf
- 2 sprigs thyme
- 2 carrots
- 1 tablespoon vegetable oil
- 1 tablespoon butter
- 340g white mushrooms
- 2 tablespoon cornstarch
- 3 tablespoon cold water
- 2 tablespoons parsley

Preparation Method
- Select Browning and add diced bacon to pressure cooker pot. Brown the bacon until crisp, stirring frequently. Remove bacon to a plate, leaving the bacon fat in the pot.
- Season chicken with salt and pepper. Add the chicken to the pot and brown on both sides in the bacon fat. Remove the chicken to a platter, leaving the fat in the pan.
- Add the onions and cook, stirring frequently, until softened and lightly caramelized. Add the garlic and cook for 1 minute.
- Add the wine to deglaze the pot and let it almost completely evaporate to concentrate the flavor and remove most of the liquid.
- Stir in the chicken broth, tomato paste, bay leaf, thyme, and carrots.
- Add the browned chicken to the pot, along with any juices that have collected on the platter. Close cooker.
- Select cooking for 10 minutes. While the chicken is cooking, heat a large Sauté pan over medium-high heat until hot. Add oil and butter. When butter is melted, add the mushrooms and cook until golden. Season with salt and pepper.
- When the timer beeps, do a quick pressure release and remove the chicken from the pressure cooker pot to a serving dish.
- Combine the cornstarch and water, whisking until smooth. Add cornstarch mixture to the sauce to the pot stirring constantly. Select Simmer and bring to a boil, stirring constantly. After sauce thickens, add mushrooms and stir to coat with sauce.

- Taste, adjust seasoning if desired. Combine sauce with chicken in the serving bowl. Serve topped with crumbled bacon and chopped parsley.

Nutritional Information
- Preparation Time: 25 minutes
- Total Servings: 6
- Calories: 293
- Calories from Fat: 98
- Total Fat: 10.9g
- Saturated Fat: 3.7g
- Cholesterol: 80mg
- Sodium: 932mg
- Potassium: 418mg
- Total Carbohydrates: 17.2g
- Fiber: 2g
- Sugar: 1.9g
- Protein: 28.1g

Recipe 6: Mushroom Meat

Tips to cook properly
- Before serving add ground black pepper and ½ teaspoon purified butter

Ingredients
- 6 boneless goat meat pieces
- 1 teaspoon onion powder
- 1 teaspoon garlic powder
- Salt and pepper
- 2 tablespoon olive oil
- 1 medium onion
- 6 garlic cloves
- 2 cups low sodium chicken broth
- 2 tablespoon white balsamic vinegar
- 1 tablespoon tomato paste
- 1 teaspoon dried thyme
- 450g white button mushrooms
- 1/4 cup evaporated milk
- 1/2 cup grated Parmesan cheese
- 2 tablespoon cornstarch
- 3 tablespoon cold water
- 2 tablespoon fresh parsley
- Hot cooked rice or pasta

Preparation Method
- Season the chicken breasts on both sides with onion powder, garlic powder, salt and pepper to taste.
- Heat 1 tablespoon olive oil over brown setting in a pressure cooker. Add the chicken in batches and brown lightly on both sides. Remove browned chicken from the pressure cooker, place on a plate.
- Heat the remaining 1 tablespoon olive oil in the pressure cooker over brown settings. Add the onions and Sauté for 2 minutes or until translucent. Add the garlic, stir for 30 seconds.
- Stir in the chicken broth, vinegar, tomato paste, and thyme. Put the browned chicken on the rack. Add the sliced mushrooms. Close cooker and, set a timer and cook for 6 minutes.
- Remove chicken to a platter and keep warm. Stir the evaporated milk and Parmesan cheese into the sauce. Combine the cornstarch and water, whisking until smooth.
- Stir the cornstarch mixture into the sauce and stir in the chopped parsley. Pour the sauce over the chicken. Serve over rice or pasta.

Nutritional Information
- Preparation Time: 55 minute
- Total Servings: 6
- Calories: 445
- Calories from Fat: 210

- Total Fat: 20.4g
- Saturated Fat: 6.9g
- Cholesterol: 23mg
- Sodium: 493mg
- Potassium: 282mg
- Total Carbohydrates: 33.5g
- Fiber: 2.5g
- Sugar: 3.6g
- Protein: 17.9g

Recipe 7: Chicken Tortilla Soup

Tips to cook properly
- If desire, add extra cream over the soup before serving

Ingredients
- 4 tablespoons vegetable oil
- 2 boneless, skinless chicken breasts
- 4 anaheim peppers
- 1 jalapeno
- 2 cloves garlic
- 2 large onions
- 5 cups chopped tomatoes
- 900g chicken stock
- 1 1/2 cups heavy cream
- 1 cup chopped cilantro
- Garnish: tortilla chips, queso blanco, sour cream

Preparation Method
- Cook the chicken breasts in an electric pressure cooker for 20 minutes with 1/2 cup of chicken broth. Keep aside.
- Heat the vegetable oil in pressure cooker on browning setting, add chopped onions, cook and stir until onions start to soften, roast peppers, add the peppers and garlic to the onions and Sauté for a few more minutes, add salt and pepper then add tomatoes and stir until warm. Transfer to a food processor and blend until it looks smooth.
- Transfer back to pressure cooker, add chicken broth and then adjust cooking to 20 minutes. Let the pressure release naturally. Shred the chicken and add it to the soup.
- Stir in cream and cilantro. Serve with tortilla chips, queso blanco, and sour cream.

Nutritional Information
- Preparation Time: 30 minutes
- Total Servings: 4
- Calories: 377
- Calories from Fat: 172
- Total Fat: 19.1g
- Saturated Fat: 7.3g
- Cholesterol: 46mg
- Sodium: 943mg
- Potassium: 704mg
- Total Carbohydrates: 30.2g
- Fiber: 8.7g
- Sugar: 2.7g
- Protein: 23.1g

Recipe 8: Turkey Noodle Soup

Tips to cook properly
- You can replace egg noodles with normal noodles

Ingredients
- 1 tablespoon butter
- 1 large onion
- 4 carrots
- 1 celery rib
- 6 cups turkey stock
- 2 cups diced turkey
- 1 teaspoon salt
- Fresh ground pepper
- Cooked egg noodles

Preparation Method
- Select Sauté and add butter to the pressure cooker pot. When butter is melted, add the onion and cook, stirring occasionally until the onion starts to soften about 1 to 2 minutes. Add the carrots and celery and Sauté for about 5 minutes stirring occasionally.
- Add turkey stock and turkey. Close and set the timer for 5 minutes. When beepers sounds, wait 5 minutes and then use a quick pressure release to release pressure.
- Add salt and pepper to taste. Serve soup spooned over prepared egg noodles.

Nutritional Information
- Preparation Time: 15 minutes
- Total Servings: 3-4
- Calories: 311
- Calories from Fat: 75
- Total Fat: 8.4g
- Saturated Fat: 1.9g
- Cholesterol: 53mg
- Sodium: 1021mg
- Potassium: 551mg
- Total Carbohydrates: 29.1g
- Fiber: 3.8g
- Sugar: 4.6g
- Protein: 21.5g

Recipe 9: Green Pepper Casserole

Tips to cook properly
- Sprinkle ground cheese on the top of casserole and wait until it melts

Ingredients
- 450g lean ground beef
- 1/2 cup chopped onion
- 2 cloves garlic
- 2 large green peppers
- A handful of spinach leaves, coarsely
- 400g diced tomatoes with juices
- 220g tomato sauce
- 1/2 cup beef broth
- 1/2 cup long grain rice (uncooked)
- 1 tablespoon Worcestershire sauce
- 1/2 teaspoon salt
- 1/4 teaspoon pepper
- 1 cup shredded mozzarella cheese

Preparation Method
- Preheat the pressure cooking pot on the Browning/Sauté setting. Add the ground beef and onion and cook until beef is browned and crumbled. Add garlic and Sauté 1 minute more.
- Stir in green peppers, spinach, tomatoes, tomato sauce, beef broth, rice, Worcestershire sauce, salt, and pepper. Close and select High Pressure and 4 minutes cook time. When the timer beeps, do a natural release for 10 minutes.
- Turn off pressure cooker and pour casserole into an oven-safe baking dish. Sprinkle the cheese on top of casserole and broil until the cheese is melted and starting to brown.

Nutritional Information
- Preparation Time: 15 minutes
- Total Servings: 4
- Calories: 510
- Calories from Fat: 275
- Total Fat: 30.5g
- Saturated Fat: 11.1g
- Cholesterol: 105mg
- Sodium: 1052mg
- Potassium: 675mg
- Total Carbohydrates: 37.7g
- Fiber: 3.6g
- Sugar: 6.3g
- Protein: 21.3g

Recipe 10: Rice Beef Soup

Tips to cook properly
- No need to wait for natural release and add some freshly chopped parsley before serving

Ingredients
- 450g lean ground beef
- 1 tablespoon oil
- 1 large onion
- 1 rib celery
- 3 cloves garlic
- 800g beef broth
- 400g crushed tomatoes
- 340g spicy hot juice
- 1/2 cup long grain white rice
- 425g garbanzo beans
- 1 large potato
- 2 carrots
- 1/2 cup frozen peas
- salt and pepper

Preparation Method
- Preheat the pressure cooking pot using the browning or Sauté setting. Add ground beef to the pressure cooking pot and cook until browned. Remove to a plate lined with paper towels.
- Add oil to the pressure cooking pot. Add onion and celery and cook, stirring occasionally until the onion is tender, about 5 minutes. Add garlic and cook 1 minute more.
- Add beef broth, tomatoes, hot juice, rice, garbanzo beans, potatoes, carrots, and browned ground beef to the pot and stir to combine. Close and select 4 minutes cook time.
- When timer beeps, turn off pressure cooker and do a quick pressure release. Stir in peas and season with salt and pepper to taste.

Nutritional Information
- Preparation Time: 15 minutes
- Total Servings: 4
- Calories: 386
- Calories from Fat: 45
- Total Fat: 5g
- Saturated Fat: 1.6g
- Cholesterol: 22mg
- Sodium: 1403mg
- Potassium: 515mg
- Total Carbohydrates: 68.3g
- Fiber: 3.4g
- Sugar: 16.1g
- Protein: 13.3g

Recipe 11: French Sandwiches Dip

Tips to cook properly
- Try using a liner in your electric pressure cooker for easier cleanup

Ingredients
- 680g boneless beef top round roast, thinly sliced
- 400g beef broth
- 1 packet dried onion soup mix
- 1 teaspoon dried rosemary
- 1/2 teaspoon garlic powder
- 4 sub rolls, sliced lengthwise
- 8 slice provolone cheese

Preparation Method
- Place beef, broth, soup mix, rosemary and garlic powder in the pressure cooking pot. Close and select 10 minutes cook time. When timer beeps, turn off and use a natural pressure release for 10 minutes.
- Remove meat from broth. Strain broth and skim off any fat. Butter and toast sub rolls under a broiler. Top the rolls with meat and two slices of cheese. Broil again just until cheese is melted and starting to bubble. Serve with broth in small cups for dipping.

Nutritional Information
- Preparation Time: 15 minutes
- Total Servings: 4
- Calories: 372
- Calories from Fat: 129
- Total Fat: 14.4g
- Saturated Fat: 5.3g
- Cholesterol: 76mg
- Sodium. 1173mg
- Potassium: 326mg
- Total Carbohydrates: 29.6g
- Fiber: 1.5g
- Sugar: 1.6g
- Protein: 21.8g

Recipe 12: Shepherd's Pie

Tips to cook properly
- Use potato masher to smash the potatoes

Ingredients
- 1 tablespoon vegetable oil
- 1 cup onion
- 1 cup diced carrot
- 3 cloves garlic
- 900g ground lamb
- 1 cup beef stock
- 1 tablespoon tomato paste
- 1/2 teaspoon salt
- 1/2 teaspoon ground pepper
- 2 tablespoon cornstarch
- 3 tablespoon cold water
- 2 tablespoons parsley
- 1/2 cup frozen corn
- 1/2 cup frozen peas

Potato Topping:
- 900g potatoes
- 1/2 cup whole milk
- 1/4 cup unsalted butter
- 1/2 teaspoon salt
- 1/4 teaspoon pepper
- 2 cup Cheddar Cheese

Preparation Method
- Preheat oven to 375 F. Lightly greases a 2-quart casserole or 9-inch deep dish pie plate.
- Select Browning and add oil to pressure cooking pot. When hot, add the onion and carrots and Sauté until onion is translucent about 3 minutes. Add garlic and Sauté an additional minute. Add ground meat and brown, breaking the meat apart as it cooks. Drain grease from the meat.
- Add beef stock, tomato paste, salt, and pepper to beef mixture in pressure cooking pot. Close and select 3 minutes cook time. When timer beeps, turn off and use a quick pressure release.
- Combine the cornstarch and water, whisking until smooth. Add cornstarch mixture to the pressure cooking pot. Select Simmer and bring to a boil, stirring constantly. After sauce thickens, taste, adjust seasoning if necessary. Add the parsley, corn, and peas to the meat mixture. Pour meat mixture into the bottom of prepared baking dish or pie plate.
- Rinse out pressure cooking pot. Place potatoes into a steamer basket or on a metal trivet in the pressure cooking pot. Add 1 cup water. Close and select 5 minutes cook time. When timer beeps, turn off and use a quick pressure release.

- Drain potatoes. Put drained potatoes into a mixing bowl and mash with a potato masher. Stir in milk, butter, salt and pepper, and grated cheese.
- Spread mashed potatoes evenly over the meat mixture right to the edges. If desired, use a pastry bag with a large star tip to create a decorative topping with the mashed potatoes.
- Bake in preheated oven 30 to 35 minutes until golden brown. Serve hot.

Nutritional Information
- Preparation Time: 60 minutes
- Total Servings: 8
- Calories: 474
- Calories from Fat: 257
- Total Fat: 28.6g
- Saturated Fat: 12.3g
- Cholesterol: 93mg
- Sodium: 755mg
- Potassium: 632mg
- Total Carbohydrates: 29.1g
- Fiber: 4.1g
- Sugar: 6g
- Protein: 19.5g

Recipe 13: Orange Meatballs

Tips to cook properly
- You can add sriracha sauce for extra hot flavor

Ingredients
- 900g lean ground beef
- 1 cup uncooked white rice
- 4 tablespoons all-purpose flour
- 1 small white onion, chopped fine
- 2 teaspoons salt
- 1 teaspoon fresh ground pepper
- 4 cans condensed tomato soup
- 2 1/2 soup cans of water

Preparation Method
- Place ground beef into large mixing bowl. Add chopped onion, rice, flour, salt, and pepper. Using your hands, gently mix ingredients together taking care not to overwork the meat. Form meat mixture into walnut-size balls, again not packing the mixture too tightly.
- In a pressure cooker pot, add 4 cans of tomato soup and 2 1/2 soup cans of water and select soup settings. Use a wire whisk to stir soup and water together until no lumps remain. Carefully add meatballs to pot.
- Close and select 25 minutes cook time. Using a slotted spoon, remove meatballs to a large serving bowl and keep warm.
- Taste the orange gravy remaining in the pot and season to taste with additional salt and pepper. Stir in a bit of hot water if the gravy is too thick. Pour orange gravy into a separate serving bowl.

Nutritional Information
- Preparation Time: 45 minutes
- Total Servings: 8
- Calories: 265
- Calories from Fat: 79
- Total Fat: 8.8g
- Saturated Fat: 2.2g
- Cholesterol: 80mg
- Sodium: 615mg
- Potassium: 226mg
- Total Carbohydrates: 29.8g
- Fiber: 0.9g
- Sugar: 21.5g
- Protein: 14.5g

Recipe 14: Pork Stroganoff

Tips to cook properly
- If desire, add some grated cheese before you serve

Ingredients
- 900g pork sirloin tip roast
- 3 tablespoons vegetable oil
- 1 large onion
- 1/4 cup dry sherry
- 2 tablespoons chili sauce
- 1 teaspoon dry mustard
- 1 cup chicken broth
- 1 tablespoon butter
- 225g pound fresh mushrooms, sliced
- 2 tablespoons cornstarch
- 3 tablespoons cold water
- 1/2 cup sour cream
- Salt and pepper
- Noodles
- Poppy seed

Preparation Method
- Trim excess fat from pork and cut into thin strips ½-inch wide. Season pork generously with salt and pepper. Put 1 tablespoon oil in the pressure cooker pot and select browning.
- When oil begins to sizzle, brown meat in batches until all the meat is browned - do not crowd, add more oil as needed. Transfer meat to a plate when browned.
- Select Sauté, add the onions and cook, stirring frequently, until the onions soften and begin to brown, about 3 minutes.
- Add sherry to deglaze the pot, scrap up any brown bits on the bottom of the pot. Add chili sauce and mustard. Add chicken broth, browned pork and any accumulated juices. Set timer for 5 minutes.
- Again keep cooker in Sauté mode and add 1 tablespoon oil and butter. When butter is melted, add the mushrooms and cook until golden, season with salt and pepper.
- Combine the cornstarch and water, whisking until smooth. Add cornstarch mixture to the broth in the pot stirring constantly. Select Simmer and bring to a boil, stirring constantly until sauce thickens.
- Add 1/3 cup of gravy to the sour cream and mix until well combined. Add the sour cream mixture to the gravy and stir until well blended. Stir in the Sauté mushrooms. Add salt and pepper to taste.Your stroganoff ready.
- On other side cook noodles in salted water. Drain noodles and serve stroganoff over noodles sprinkled with poppy seed.

Nutritional Information
- Preparation Time: 45 minutes

- Total Servings: 8
- Calories: 299
- Calories from Fat: 171
- Total Fat: 19
- Saturated Fat: 6.6g
- Cholesterol: 82mg
- Sodium: 384mg
- Potassium: 182mg
- Total Carbohydrates: 4.8g
- Fiber: 0.8g
- Sugar: 1.7g
- Protein: 22.4g

Recipe 15: Cornbread

Tips to cook properly
- Be careful while placing in and out and for extra flavor add butter before serving

Ingredients
- 500g Corn Muffin Mix
- 1 cup milk
- 2 large eggs

Preparation Method
- In a large mixing bowl, stir together the corn muffin mix, milk and eggs just until blended. The batter will be lumpy.
- Spoon batter into half sized bundt pan sprayed with non-stick spray.
- Pour 1 cup of water into the pressure cooker and place the trivet in the bottom. Put the bundt pan on the trivet.
- Close and set the timer for 20 minutes. When beep sounds, turn off pressure cooker and use a natural pressure release.
- After 5 minutes, gently loosen edges, remove from pan and cool on a wire rack.

Nutritional Information
- Preparation Time: 25 minutes
- Total Servings: 5-6
- Calories: 131
- Calories from Fat: 23
- Total Fat: 2.5g
- Saturated Fat: 0.8g
- Cholesterol: 20mg
- Sodium: 165mg
- Potassium: 64mg
- Total Carbohydrates: 25.3g
- Fiber: 0.5g
- Sugar: 13.3g
- Protein: 2.5g

Recipe 16: Cauliflower Alfredo

Tips to cook properly
- If desire, add extra ground cheese on top with freshly chopped cilantro

Ingredients
- 2 tablespoons butter
- 2 cloves garlic
- 8 cups cauliflower florets
- 1 cup chicken or vegetable broth
- 2 teaspoons salt
- 2 cups spinach
- 2 green onions
- 450g fettuccine pasta
- Garnish
- Gorgonzola cheese
- Sun-dried tomatoes
- Thick balsamic vinegar

Preparation Method
- Select Sauté on the pressure cooker and add butter. When melted, add garlic cloves and Sauté until fragrant, about 2 minutes, stirring constantly so the garlic doesn't burn. Add cauliflower, broth, and salt. Select 6 minutes cook time.
- While the cauliflower is cooking, heat a pot of water to boiling on the stove top. Add pasta and cook until al dente. Reserve about 1 cup of water and then drain the pasta. Return pasta to the empty pot.
- When pressure cooking is complete, use a 10-minute natural release.
- Blend with an immersion blender right in the pot until very smooth and silky, or carefully transfer to a blender and puree until smooth. By hand, stir in the chopped spinach and green onions and allow the hot sauce to wilt the spinach.
- Pour sauce over the pasta and toss. Add a half cup or so of the reserved pasta water to the pasta if needed. The starchy water will help the sauce to stick to the pasta.
- Serve hot with a garnish of gorgonzola cheese, sun-dried tomatoes, and a drizzle of balsamic vinegar.
- The sauce heats back up very nicely so you could also make the sauce in advance and have it ready to pour over pasta for a quick, healthy, delicious meal any night of the week. Also amazing over rice, as a sauce on pizza, or a dip for bread and roasted veggies.

Nutritional Information
- Preparation Time: 35 minutes
- Total Servings: 4
- Calories: 660
- Calories from Fat: 208
- Total Fat: 23.1g

- Saturated Fat: 8.2g
- Cholesterol: 35mg
- Sodium: 413mg
- Potassium: 620mg
- Total Carbohydrates: 65.4g
- Fiber: 9.4g
- Sugar: 4.5g
- Protein: 21.7g

Recipe 17: Pork Sirloin Roast

Tips to cook properly
- Try using a liner in your electric pressure cooker for easier cleanup

Ingredients
- 1/2 teaspoon coarse black pepper
- 1/2 teaspoon salt
- 1/2 teaspoon onion powder
- 1/2 teaspoon garlic powder
- 1/4 teaspoon chili powder
- 1350g pork sirloin tip roast
- 1 tablespoon vegetable oil
- 1 cup water
- 1/2 cup apple juice

Preparation Method
- Mix together spices in a small bowl and rub spice mixture all over pork roast.
- Put oil in the cooking pot and select browning. When oil begins to sizzle, brown roast on both sides.
- Add the water and apple juice to the pressure cooking pot. Close and set timer for 25 minutes and press start. When beep sounds turn off pressure cooker and use a natural pressure release for 5 minutes and serve.

Nutritional Information
- Preparation Time: 30 minutes
- Total Servings: 6-8
- Calories: 406
- Calories from Fat: 171
- Total Fat: 19g
- Saturated Fat: 8g
- Cholesterol: 92mg
- Sodium: 506mg
- Potassium: 327mg
- Total Carbohydrates: 32.6g
- Fiber: 1.4g
- Sugar: 16.2g
- Protein: 23.2g

Recipe 18: Greek Tacos

Tips to cook properly
- Add extra lemon juice before serving for extra delicious flavor

Ingredients
- 1800g boneless picnic pork shoulder
- 1/2 teaspoons salt
- 1/4 teaspoon pepper
- 1 teaspoon marjoram
- 2 tablespoon olive oil
- 1/2 cup fresh lemon juice
- 1/4 cup water

Tzatziki Sauce:
- 1 small cucumber
- 1/4 teaspoon salt
- 1 cup plain Greek yogurt
- 1 tablespoon lemon juice
- 1 teaspoon dried dill weed
- 1 clove garlic
- 1/8 teaspoon pepper

Preparation Method
- Mix the marjoram, salt, and pepper with the olive oil and rub all over pork.
- Add lemon juice and water to the cooking pot. Place the pork in the pressure cooking pot.
- Set the timer for 25 minutes. When beep sounds, turn off the pressure cooker. After 10 minutes, release any remaining pressure. Using a slotted spoon, to remove meat from juices. Serve on a pita with diced tomatoes, shredded lettuce, and tzatziki sauce.

Tzatziki Sauce:
- In a fine mesh strainer toss the cucumber with the salt. Allow the cucumber to drain for 15 minutes over a bowl or the sink to remove excess water.
- In a medium size bowl, combine the drained cucumber, Greek yogurt, lemon juice, dill weed, garlic, and pepper.

Nutritional Information
- Preparation Time: 40 minutes
- Total Servings: 8-10
- Calories: 467
- Calories from Fat: 281
- Total Fat: 24.1g
- Saturated Fat: 9.3g
- Cholesterol: 299mg
- Sodium: 881mg
- Potassium: 356mg
- Total Carbohydrates: 30.2g
- Fiber: 4.1g

- Sugar: 2.4g
- Protein: 24.2g

Recipe 19: Spanish Masala Rice

Tips to cook properly
- If desire, before serving add freshly chopped herbs

Ingredients
- 1 tablespoon vegetable oil
- 1/4 cup onion
- 1 cup long grain white rice
- 1 1/4 cup chicken broth
- 1/2 cup mild salsa

Preparation Method
- Select Sauté and add oil to the cooking pot. When hot, add the onions. Cook, stirring occasionally until onion is tender, about 3 to 5 minutes.
- Stir in rice and cook, stirring frequently, until rice becomes opaque, about 1 to 2 minutes. Add broth and salsa. Cover and set timer for 4 minutes.
- When beep sounds wait 5 minutes and then use a Quick Pressure Release to release pressure. Fluff rice with a fork and serve immediately.

Nutritional Information
- Preparation Time: 20 minutes
- Total Servings: 4
- Calories: 286
- Calories from Fat: 56
- Total Fat: 6.3g
- Saturated Fat: 1g
- Cholesterol: 2mg
- Sodium: 697mg
- Potassium: 218mg
- Total Carbohydrates: 48.3g
- Fiber: 1.6g
- Sugar: 2.3g
- Protein: 4.7g

Recipe 20: Herbed Polenta

Tips to cook properly
- After cooking, immediately remove the bay leave

Ingredients
- 2 tablespoons olive oil
- 1/2 cup finely chopped onion
- 2 teaspoons minced garlic
- 4 cups vegetable stock or water
- 1/3 cup finely diced sun-dried tomatoes
- 1 teaspoon salt
- 1 bay leaf
- 2 teaspoons chopped fresh oregano
- 1 teaspoon chopped fresh rosemary
- 3 tablespoons chopped fresh basil
- 2 tablespoons chopped fresh parsley
- 1 cup coarse polenta

Preparation Method
- Set an electric cooker to Sauté, add the oil. Add the onion and Sauté for 1 minute. Add the garlic and cook for another minute.
- Add the water, sun-dried tomatoes, salt, bay leaf, oregano, and rosemary, along with half of both the basil and parsley, stir. Sprinkle the polenta over the water, do not stir.
- Close and set 5 minutes cooking time. Remove and discard the bay leaf. Whisk the polenta to smooth out any lumps. If the polenta seems too thin, stir and close the cooker and let sit for 5 minutes. Stir in remaining basil and parsley.

Nutritional Information
- Preparation Time: 10 minutes
- Total Servings: 4
- Calories: 199
- Calories from Fat: 77
- Total Fat: 5.8g
- Saturated Fat: 2.5g
- Cholesterol: 38mg
- Sodium: 749mg
- Potassium: 207mg
- Total Carbohydrates: 22.2g
- Fiber: 2.2g
- Sugar: 1.3g
- Protein: 6g

Recipe 21: Green Chile Salsa Rice

Tips to cook properly
- If desire, add sriracha sauce for extra hot flavor

Ingredients
- 2 teaspoons olive oil
- 1 medium-sized onion
- 200g diced green chilies with juice (not Jalapenos)
- 1/4 teaspoon ground cumin
- 1/2 cup salsa
- 1 1/4 cup chicken or vegetable broth
- 2 tablespoons lime juice
- 1 cup long-grain rice
- 1/2 cup cilantro
- Green Tabasco Sauce

Preparation Method
- Select Sauté and add olive oil to pressure cooking pot. When the oil is hot, add the chopped onions. Cook, stirring occasionally until onion is tender, about 5 minutes.
- Add the cumin and diced green chilies with juice and cook 2-3 minutes more. Add the salsa, chicken or vegetable stock, and 1 tablespoon lime juice and bring to a boil, then stir in the rice.
- Set timer for 3 minutes. When beep sounds turn pressure cooker off, wait 5 minutes and then use a Quick Pressure Release.
- Open and stir in one tablespoon lime juice and the chopped cilantro. Cover the rice and let it steam for two minutes before serving.

Nutritional Information
- Preparation Time: 20 minutes
- Total Servings: 4
- Calories: 231
- Calories from Fat: 126
- Total Fat: 14g
- Saturated Fat: 1.8g
- Cholesterol: 0mg
- Sodium: 943mg
- Potassium: 1297mg
- Total Carbohydrates: 9.4g
- Fiber: 6.3g
- Sugar: 2.5g
- Protein: 6g

Recipe 22: Israeli Couscous

Tips to cook properly
- Add grated cheddar cheese before you serve

Ingredients
- 2 tablespoons butter
- 2 1/2 cups chicken broth
- 450g Harvest Grains Blend
- Salt and pepper

Preparation Method
- Set pressure cooker in Sauté mode and melt the butter. Add broth and Harvest Grains Blend. Stir to combine.
- Close and set cooker timer for 5 minutes. When timer beeps, turn pressure cooker off and do a quick pressure release. Fluff with a fork and add salt and pepper to taste.

Nutritional Information
- Preparation Time: 15 minutes
- Total Servings: 4-6
- Calories: 258
- Calories from Fat: 121
- Total Fat: 14.3g
- Saturated Fat: 4.2g
- Cholesterol: 71mg
- Sodium: 540mg
- Potassium: 100mg
- Total Carbohydrates: 30.1g
- Fiber: 2.1g
- Sugar: 1g
- Protein: 8.3g

Recipe 23: Mexican Green Rice

Tips to cook properly
- To decrease calories, you can substitute water for chicken broth

Ingredients
- 1 1/4 cups chicken or vegetable broth
- 1 cup uncooked long-grain rice
- 1/ 2 large ripe avocado
- 1/ 2 cup fresh cilantro
- 1/ 4 cup green salsa or green hot sauce
- Salt and freshly ground pepper

Preparation Method
- Add the broth and rice to the pressure cooker pot and set 3 minutes cooking time. When the timer beeps after 10 minutes do a quick pressure release.
- Fluff rice with a fork and let cool to warm. Blend in a blender the avocado, cilantro, and salsa, adding a little water as needed to blend smoothly, to the consistency of sour cream. Stir into rice. Season with salt and pepper.

Nutritional Information
- Preparation Time: 15 minutes
- Total Servings: 5
- Calories: 191
- Calories from Fat: 34
- Total Fat: 21.5g
- Saturated Fat: 1.1g
- Cholesterol: 5mg
- Sodium: 23mg
- Potassium: 95mg
- Total Carbohydrates: 24.7g
- Fiber: 1.4g
- Sugar: 1.7g
- Protein: 2.1g

Recipe 24: Thai Quinoa Salad

Tips to cook properly
- This salad tastes great right away, and even better the next day when you add freshly chopped herbs over it

Ingredients
- 1 cup quinoa
- 1 1/2 cups water
- 1/2 teaspoon salt
- 1 carrot
- 1 cucumber
- 1 cup frozen edamame
- 6 green onions
- 2 cups shredded red cabbage

Dressing:
- 1 tablespoon soy sauce
- 1/4 cup lime juice
- 2 tablespoons sugar
- 1 tablespoon vegetable oil
- 1 tablespoon freshly grated ginger
- 1 tablespoon sesame oil
- pinch of red pepper flakes
- 1/2 cup peanuts
- 1/4 cup freshly cilantro
- 2 tablespoons basil

Preparation Method
- Add quinoa, water, and salt to the pressure cooking pot. Select 1 minute cook time. When beep sounds turn pressure cooker off, wait 10 minutes.
- Add the cooled quinoa and vegetables to a large bowl. In a small bowl, whisk together the soy sauce, lime juice, sugar, vegetable oil, sesame oil and red pepper flakes until the sugar has dissolved.
- Taste for sweetness and for heat and add more sugar or red pepper flakes to taste. Pour the dressing over the quinoa and vegetables and stir to combine. Sprinkle the cilantro, basil, and peanuts over the salad and stir lightly. Serve or refrigerate for up to a day.

Nutritional Information
- Preparation Time: 30 minutes
- Total Servings: 4
- Calories: 270
- Calories from Fat: 104
- Total Fat: 11.5g
- Saturated Fat: 1.4g
- Cholesterol: 0g
- Sodium: 675mg
- Potassium: 404mg

- Total Carbohydrates: 33.8g
- Fiber: 7.8g
- Sugar: 1.7g
- Protein:8.9g

Recipe 25: Wild Herb Rice

Tips to cook properly
- Before serving, garnish with freshly chopped herbs

Ingredients
- 1 teaspoon olive oil
- 1/2 a small red onion
- 1 teaspoon garlic
- 3/4 cup wild rice
- 1 1/2 cups whole grain farro
- 6 cups broth/stock
- 1 tablespoon fresh herbs (parsley, sage, rosemary, thyme)
- 1 teaspoon sea salt
- Fresh ground black pepper
- 3/4 cup dried cherries
- 1/2 cup hazelnuts and coarsely chopped
- Fresh herbs to garnish (chives, thyme, parsley)

Preparation Method
- Sauté the onion and garlic in a drizzle of olive oil in the pressure cooker. Add the wild rice and farro. Continue cooking until they are fragrant.
- Add the broth/stock, herbs, salt, and pepper. Close and set 25 minutes cooking time on high pressure.
- Meanwhile, cover the dried cherries with boiling water for 10 minutes. Drain.
- Toast the hazelnuts, and coarsely chop.
- After 25 minutes, allow the pressure cooker to de-pressurize 5 minutes, then release pressure fully.
- Drain the liquid from the pot. Add the rehydrated cherries and toasted hazelnuts. Toss to combine. Garnish with fresh herbs such as chopped chives and thyme leaves.

Nutritional Information
- Preparation Time: 25 minutes
- Total Servings: 4
- Calories: 253
- Calories from Fat: 103
- Total Fat: 11.4g
- Saturated Fat: 1.8g
- Cholesterol: 0g
- Sodium: 323mg
- Potassium: 348mg
- Total Carbohydrates: 32.6g
- Fiber: 5.6g
- Sugar: 5.6g
- Protein: 6.7g

Conclusion

The information provided in this book will help you in the right way toward your successful dream to become expert chef in cooking and making electric pressure cooker recipes and maintain good health throughout your life. Once again thank you for downloading our book and we hope you will enjoy while reading and practicing each and every recipe.

About the Author

Hello! I'm Rachael Martin, a passionate person to share electric pressure cooker recipes to all. I live in USA. I have been teaching self-cooking for people, since 24 years old. Electric pressure cooker recipes is not a rocket science, it is an easy lifestyle which makes us more comfortable to cook in less time with single button press. I feel, due to busy work tensions, people are not able put 100% interest and effort to cook healthy recipes, so I want to help and share my own experience for the people who are seeking for a right and healthy guide for cooking in electric pressure cooker. When you start making your own food, without knowing you are going to improve your health and beauty with dramatic control of your life. I sincerely recommend you to follow the book and explore benefits yourself.

-- [Rachael Martin]

Made in the USA
San Bernardino, CA
26 February 2017